DOWNFALL

DOWNFALL

The destruction of Charles Mackay

PAUL DIAMOND

MASSEY UNIVERSITY PRESS

CONTENTS

FOREWORD

harles Mackay, the man who defined what it meant to be homosexual for New Zealand's newspaper readers during the 1920s, has been an underappreciated figure in our history until now. Paul Diamond's *Downfall* drags him out of the shadows and puts him firmly under the spotlight.

In multi-layered and intricate detail, *Downfall* recounts the high drama of a shooting, revelations of blackmail, and debates about forbidden sexuality. Diamond reveals Mackay, one time mayor of Whanganui, to be a complex character whose life was profoundly shaped by local politics and rivalries, familial dissolution and disgrace.

In 1914 he sought a cure for his homosexuality and quietly consulted a taxi-driver-turned-metaphysician, who offered his patients autosuggestive therapies and a bit of hypnotism. In prison, after his conviction for shooting the returned soldier D'Arcy Cresswell, Mackay taught Esperanto to his fellow inmates and helped them with their writing — but he was an imperfect prisoner with a pugilistic streak. He hid contraband in the library where he worked, threatened a warden, and fought with another prisoner in the yard during parade.

Mackay left the country after his release and followed in the footsteps of others who escaped the confines of their homeland. Europe was a far cry from provincial New Zealand. Mackay slowly

recovered his equilibrium among London's social occasions, galleries and ballets, and he knew all about the men cruising in St James's Park and Trafalgar Square. He even found a Buckingham Palace guardsman of his own — a 'bit of scarlet', in the argot of the time.

The bustling queer world of Berlin, a city with an active homosexual rights movement, must have seemed astonishing to Mackay. He lived in the homosexual district, where rent boys hung out in the cabarets and bars, cadged cigarettes and arranged assignations. Even though his life in Berlin came to a sudden, shocking end, Mackay's move to the city had allowed him to stretch his wings.

Charles Mackay's story speaks to the present as well as the past. He steps out of the public record like an Oscar Wilde figure of the 1920s, persecuted by polite society, exposed by the press and locked away in jail. But when he sought out a cure for his 'homo-sexual obsessions', he took part in an early version of the conversion therapies banned in New Zealand as recently as 2022.

And Mackay's determination to build a new life for himself, travelling and seeking out fresh opportunities, is a path yet trodden by a great many queer people. Charles Mackay lived his life in a very different time to our own, but his odyssey has considerable significance in the twenty-first century.

Chris Brickell
University of Otago

INTRODUCTION

In German, a 'Spurensuche' is a search for traces, usually of forensic evidence at a crime scene, but also for traces in history. This book is my story of the search for signs of what, in 1920, was dubbed the 'Wanganui Sensation' — when Charles Mackay, the mayor of Whanganui, shot soldier-poet Walter D'Arcy Cresswell.

I first read about the shooting in a 1997 anthology of gay writing,[1] and in 2004 started work with a colleague on a radio documentary that became this book. I retraced the steps of Mackay and Cresswell, starting in 'Pretty, Prosperous, Progressive' Whanganui, the elegant river town where the two men met. I followed Mackay to New Plymouth, site of a prison then set aside for homosexual men. I also travelled to London, where both Cresswell and Mackay lived, and visited the sites where they met other men.

Finally, I went to Berlin, to the street corner where Mackay was fatally shot in the infamous Blutmai (Bloody May) fighting in 1929. Along with newspapers and books about the 1920s, I have pored over the archival traces of both men and their families — papers, letters, photos and newspapers — in libraries and archives. I have met people whose memories stretched back to the 1920s and listened to oral history interviews.

Along the way I have found evidence left behind by Mackay and Cresswell, what Peter Wells described as the 'dropped hairpins' in between the cracks.[2] Just as the 'Spuren' or forensic samples found

in a German crime scene are used to solve a crime, these fragments of homosexual lives, which escaped self-censorship and purges by others, tell us about same-sex love at a time when it was outlawed.

AUTHOR'S NOTE

Whanganui is used for contemporary references but in 1920 the town was known as Wanganui, and this form features in quoted historical sources.

Terms describing homosexuality have also changed. 'Homosexual' was in the 1920s used only by the medical profession. In the years before decriminalisation, the word had a different meaning from today, and was sometimes conflated with 'pervert' or 'pederast'. 'Gay' did not mean homosexual until later in the twentieth century and is used only when referring to this period. 'Queer', employed to describe homosexuals and homosexuality in the 1920s, has been reclaimed by gay people, and also appears in this book.

PROLOGUE:
DEATH IN BERLIN

About 20 minutes before midnight, a taxi makes its way down Neukölln's long main street, Hermannstraße, heading into a section of Berlin cordoned off because of fighting between police and communist protesters. Except for a few permitted people, no traffic, not even bicycles, is allowed on the normally busy street, which is eerily quiet, apart from the recurring sound of gunshots. The streetlights have been shot out during the fighting, so unless a police searchlight illuminates a building it is also darker than usual. Barricades made up of cobblestones, broken concrete, wood and other debris mark the battle lines between police and protesters.

When it can go no further along Hermannstraße because of the barricades, the taxi turns into a side street, Herrfurthstraße, stopping just before a set of police barricades. A man gets out. He is tall, in his early fifties, with greying hair and a prominent nose. He is wearing spectacles with dark horn rims, a soft grey hat and a small angular wristwatch with a narrow strap. He carries a large-format foreign newspaper. The man doffs his hat and introduces himself to the police, who tell him to go away. When the taxi driver gets out of the car to demand payment, he, too, is ordered to leave.

After his requests to go beyond the barricades are rebuffed, the man continues along Herrfurthstraße and walks around the block, re-

recovered his equilibrium among London's social occasions, galleries and ballets, and he knew all about the men cruising in St James's Park and Trafalgar Square. He even found a Buckingham Palace guardsman of his own — a 'bit of scarlet', in the argot of the time.

The bustling queer world of Berlin, a city with an active homosexual rights movement, must have seemed astonishing to Mackay. He lived in the homosexual district, where rent boys hung out in the cabarets and bars, cadged cigarettes and arranged assignations. Even though his life in Berlin came to a sudden, shocking end, Mackay's move to the city had allowed him to stretch his wings.

Charles Mackay's story speaks to the present as well as the past. He steps out of the public record like an Oscar Wilde figure of the 1920s, persecuted by polite society, exposed by the press and locked away in jail. But when he sought out a cure for his 'homo-sexual obsessions', he took part in an early version of the conversion therapies banned in New Zealand as recently as 2022.

And Mackay's determination to build a new life for himself, travelling and seeking out fresh opportunities, is a path yet trodden by a great many queer people. Charles Mackay lived his life in a very different time to our own, but his odyssey has considerable significance in the twenty-first century.

Chris Brickell
University of Otago

INTRODUCTION

In German, a 'Spurensuche' is a search for traces, usually of forensic evidence at a crime scene, but also for traces in history. This book is my story of the search for signs of what, in 1920, was dubbed the 'Wanganui Sensation' — when Charles Mackay, the mayor of Whanganui, shot soldier-poet Walter D'Arcy Cresswell.

I first read about the shooting in a 1997 anthology of gay writing,[1] and in 2004 started work with a colleague on a radio documentary that became this book. I retraced the steps of Mackay and Cresswell, starting in 'Pretty, Prosperous, Progressive' Whanganui, the elegant river town where the two men met. I followed Mackay to New Plymouth, site of a prison then set aside for homosexual men. I also travelled to London, where both Cresswell and Mackay lived, and visited the sites where they met other men.

Finally, I went to Berlin, to the street corner where Mackay was fatally shot in the infamous Blutmai (Bloody May) fighting in 1929. Along with newspapers and books about the 1920s, I have pored over the archival traces of both men and their families — papers, letters, photos and newspapers — in libraries and archives. I have met people whose memories stretched back to the 1920s and listened to oral history interviews.

Along the way I have found evidence left behind by Mackay and Cresswell, what Peter Wells described as the 'dropped hairpins' in between the cracks.[2] Just as the 'Spuren' or forensic samples found

recovered his equilibrium among London's social occasions, galleries and ballets, and he knew all about the men cruising in St James's Park and Trafalgar Square. He even found a Buckingham Palace guardsman of his own — a 'bit of scarlet', in the argot of the time.

The bustling queer world of Berlin, a city with an active homosexual rights movement, must have seemed astonishing to Mackay. He lived in the homosexual district, where rent boys hung out in the cabarets and bars, cadged cigarettes and arranged assignations. Even though his life in Berlin came to a sudden, shocking end, Mackay's move to the city had allowed him to stretch his wings.

Charles Mackay's story speaks to the present as well as the past. He steps out of the public record like an Oscar Wilde figure of the 1920s, persecuted by polite society, exposed by the press and locked away in jail. But when he sought out a cure for his 'homo-sexual obsessions', he took part in an early version of the conversion therapies banned in New Zealand as recently as 2022.

And Mackay's determination to build a new life for himself, travelling and seeking out fresh opportunities, is a path yet trodden by a great many queer people. Charles Mackay lived his life in a very different time to our own, but his odyssey has considerable significance in the twenty-first century.

Chris Brickell
University of Otago

INTRODUCTION

n German, a 'Spurensuche' is a search for traces, usually of forensic evidence at a crime scene, but also for traces in history. This book is my story of the search for signs of what, in 1920, was dubbed the 'Wanganui Sensation' — when Charles Mackay, the mayor of Whanganui, shot soldier-poet Walter D'Arcy Cresswell.

I first read about the shooting in a 1997 anthology of gay writing,[1] and in 2004 started work with a colleague on a radio documentary that became this book. I retraced the steps of Mackay and Cresswell, starting in 'Pretty, Prosperous, Progressive' Whanganui, the elegant river town where the two men met. I followed Mackay to New Plymouth, site of a prison then set aside for homosexual men. I also travelled to London, where both Cresswell and Mackay lived, and visited the sites where they met other men.

Finally, I went to Berlin, to the street corner where Mackay was fatally shot in the infamous Blutmai (Bloody May) fighting in 1929. Along with newspapers and books about the 1920s, I have pored over the archival traces of both men and their families — papers, letters, photos and newspapers — in libraries and archives. I have met people whose memories stretched back to the 1920s and listened to oral history interviews.

Along the way I have found evidence left behind by Mackay and Cresswell, what Peter Wells described as the 'dropped hairpins' in between the cracks.[2] Just as the 'Spuren' or forensic samples found

emerging on Hermannstraße. By now he has been joined by several other people. Suddenly, police posted in doorways start yelling: 'Clear the streets! Go into the houses! Go around the corner!' Others surrounding the man move into a doorway, but he stands in front of the windows of the Hirschowitz clothing shop on the corner, just before the barricade.

Even as shooting starts in the street, the man remains immobile. A shot goes into the glass behind him, followed by several others that hit other windows. He continues to stand there. A shot from a police sniper on the opposite corner, about 110 metres away, hits him. He lurches forward, then convulses and falls back.[1]

After a few minutes the shooting ends and a police medical officer rushes to the man, who is lying on his back, his head towards Hermannstraße. At first no external wounds are obvious, but when the officer turns him onto his stomach and draws his coat and waistcoat over his head, he sees a large patch of blood on the man's back. His pupils are glassy and there is no pulse. He is dead.

Other police summon a taxi driver, who has also seen what happened. With difficulty, they put the man into the car, but as it is about to drive off an ambulance arrives and the body is put on a stretcher and taken to the mortuary at Buckow Hospital.

At this stage, all the police know is that the man is a journalist and that his name is Charles Mackay. They do not know that he is the former mayor of a town in New Zealand called Whanganui, and a distinguished lawyer, and that he lost his family, his career and his reputation because of another shooting nearly a decade before.

Ridgway Street, Whanganui, looking south towards Cooks Gardens, photographed around 1915. Charles Mackay's legal office was in Norfolk Chambers (the building in the middle of the block on left). He shot D'Arcy Cresswell in a different office, on the same side of the street but behind where the photographer would have stood to take this shot. *Auckland Libraries Heritage Collection, 35-R1684*

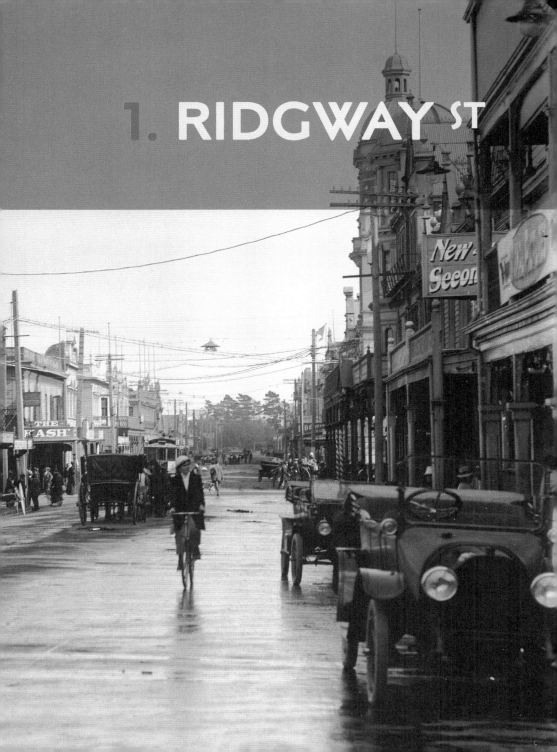

1. RIDGWAY ST

t is five minutes to one on a Saturday afternoon in May 1920 in the town centre of Whanganui.[1] Engineer Colin Cameron is standing on the back of a lorry when he hears shots being fired from the first floor of a two-storey wooden building on Ridgway Street, the town's main commercial thoroughfare, which runs parallel to the Whanganui River.

A chair then crashes through a window and lands on the pavement, scattering glass. Cameron looks up at the window, where a man appears. This is Walter D'Arcy Cresswell, a 24-year-old returned soldier who lives in the South Island town of Tīmaru but is in Whanganui visiting relatives. Cameron and his father George, standing nearby, hear Cresswell shout, 'Help! I have been shot!', and see him struggling with an older man. This is 44-year-old barrister Charles Mackay, the mayor of Whanganui. The pair disappear from view and a further four or five shots are heard.

Colin Cameron enters the building and runs up the stairs with Sydney Sykes, a labourer. The stairs open onto a landing. To the right is an open corridor with a wooden balustrade. There is a door near the landing and another off the corridor, from which Cresswell emerges, holding a revolver. Sykes takes it from him.

'Mr Mackay has shot me,' Cresswell tells Cameron and Sykes. 'Get a car and take me to a doctor.'

Mackay appears behind Cresswell. 'I accidentally shot him while I was demonstrating an automatic revolver,' he says.

With Mackay and Sykes following, Colin Cameron helps Cresswell halfway down the stairs. He and his father then get Cresswell to the bottom of the stairs, which open directly onto the street. There they lay him down on the footpath, Sykes and Colin Cameron supporting his head. George Cameron, who has a notebook, is trying to copy down what Cresswell is saying. Mackay remains on the stairs about a yard away, between Sykes and George Cameron.

'I am dying,' Cresswell tells Cameron. 'I feel I am going. Give my love to my mother.'

'If you think you are dying you had better tell us all you know,' says Sykes.

'I discovered a scandal and Mr Mackay shot me,' Cresswell replies.

'I accidentally shot him while showing him the revolver,' says Mackay.

'It was not an accident. I was shot,' Cresswell replies, and then lapses into unconsciousness.

When police constables John McMullin and David Wilson arrive, Mackay tells them the shooting was an accident and gives himself up. After handing the gun to McMullin, Wilson goes upstairs to Mackay's office to phone for a doctor. An ambulance arrives and takes Cresswell away. Sykes also heads upstairs to Mackay's office, where he finds the mayor putting papers into a safe and turning the key. Sykes leaves the office and McMullin goes upstairs, where he meets Mackay on the landing.

The pair go back into the office, which is in a state of disarray. Mackay's high-backed chair is lying on the floor, the window behind his table, which faces onto the street, is broken, and there is shattered glass on the floor. Mackay explains that he was showing Cresswell his revolver when it went off by mistake. The young man then fell against the window and broke the glass, he says. When McMullin asks, 'How did the chair get outside?', Mackay replies, 'What chair?'

McMullin instructs Mackay to lock up his office, then hands him, and the revolver, over to another police officer, Sergeant James Reid, who takes Mackay to the police station, around the corner from Ridgway Street.

At the station, Mackay again insists, this time to Senior Sergeant Thomas Bourke, that the shooting was an accident, and says he fears for Cresswell's life: 'Sergeant, I shot a young man through the chest. I believe he will die.' Bourke tells him the Camerons reported hearing the disturbance in the office before the shots were fired, and then seeing the chair falling from the window onto the street.

Soon after this, Bourke goes to Mackay's office, where he finds five photographs of naked women in a locked drawer of the office table. He searches unsuccessfully for the resignation letter Mackay told him he had written. He finds four revolver bullets: two in Mackay's chair, one at the back of some books and a bookcase on a wall and one at the back of the roll-top desk. One bullet has gone through the wall into the next room and the other into some books.

Back at the station Bourke charges Mackay with the attempted murder of Walter D'Arcy Cresswell.

'I understand, Sergeant,' is Mackay's reply.

n Whanganui, the first report of the shooting appeared two days afterwards:

A PAINFUL SENSATION.
YOUNG MAN SERIOUSLY WOUNDED.
MR C. E. MACKAY UNDER ARREST.

A painful sensation was caused on Saturday afternoon when it became known that a returned soldier, Walter D'Arcy Cresswell, aged 24 years, had been admitted to Wanganui Hospital suffering from a bullet in the right breast and Mackay, the Mayor, was implicated in the affair.[2]

The brief *Wanganui Chronicle* article summarised the eyewitness accounts of the shooting and Mackay's arrest and remand in custody. It also noted that Cresswell's parents had arrived from Tīmaru the previous day, and that their son was progressing satisfactorily in Wanganui Hospital. The bullet, believed to be in his lung, had not been located and an operation would probably be necessary. Updates about Cresswell's condition — steadily improving — were the only

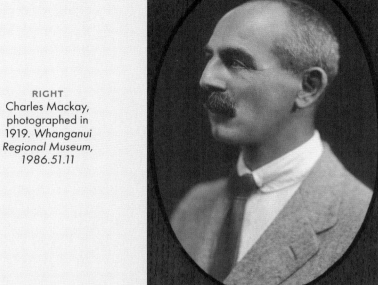

news reported about the case, as both Whanganui newspapers were observing a suppression request from Mackay's lawyers.

Newspapers elsewhere, such as the *Te Puke Times*, were more forthcoming:

> A WANGANUI SENSATION
> MAYOR OF TOWN ARRESTED
> RETURNED SOLDIER WOUNDED
> Wanganui, May 15
>
> The greatest and most painful sensation Wanganui has experienced for some considerable time, was the shooting affray in Ridgway Street this afternoon, when Mr C. E. Mackay, solicitor and Mayor of the borough, shot and badly wounded a returned soldier named Darcy Cresswell who hails from Timaru. The police are very reticent over the affair, but it is stated that an altercation took place in Mr Mackay's office, and the crashing of a chair through a window preceded the report of a gun.[3]

Although the facts of the case were 'shrouded in mystery', reported the tabloid *N.Z. Truth*, it was 'known that Mackay entertained the wounded man at dinner at a local hotel' the week before the shooting, and that the pair had had a big fight before the shot was fired.[4] The paper also mentioned Mackay's row with the Returned Soldiers' Association (RSA) over the visit of the Prince of Wales, the future Edward VIII, 12 days earlier, on 3 May, and noted that the mayor had been in poor health since an accident the previous year.

Cresswell had arrived at Wanganui Hospital with a small bullet wound in the right side of his chest, about level with his heart. Although his condition was pronounced serious, he improved rapidly, according to Medical Superintendent Dr Herbert Hutson.[5] Cresswell was unable to appear in court to give evidence, but was well enough to give the police a statement.[6]

Exhibit B in the eventual case Police v. C. E. Mackay is a three-page typed document, recording Cresswell's account of events from when he arrived in Whanganui on Monday 10 May until the shooting a few days later. Cresswell apparently dictated the statement from his hospital bed but did not, as was normal police practice when there was a risk of a witness not surviving, sign or date it. Had he been physically unable to do so, there would normally have been a signed note from an inspector or a 'professional' person explaining the absence of a signature. Cresswell was also able to draw a sketch plan of Mackay's office.

On 26 May, the day before the trial, Mackay asked to see Whanganui police inspector Charles William Hendry, who, arriving at the gaol, found Mackay with his lawyer, William Treadwell, the Whanganui borough solicitor.[7] Hendry handed Treadwell Cresswell's statement for Mackay to read. After speaking with Treadwell in private, Mackay returned 20 minutes later, having, at the inspector's suggestion, initialled each page and added this endorsement: 'I have read the above statement and as far as it relates to my own acts & deeds I admit the statement to be substantially true.'[8]

The next day — 12 days after the shooting — Inspector Hendry read Cresswell's statement at Mackay's trial for attempted murder.

The Rutland Hotel, on the corner of Victoria Avenue and Ridgway Street, where Charles Mackay, D'Arcy Cresswell and Cresswell's cousin had dinner two days before the shooting. *Alexander Turnbull Library, 1/1-07742-G*

2 BLACKMAIL

When Whanganui celebrates its heritage, it often refers to Victorian times and the arrival of Pākehā. Traces of these days have survived, and even fewer from the pre-European period, but Whanganui prospered and grew in the Edwardian era, and it is the buildings from that period that still stand and make its architecture so distinctive. These were boom years for the city. From the 1910s to the 1920s the port, the freezing works, the woollen mills and the phosphate works were busy, the farms and sawmills of the hinterland were prosperous, and local merchants were confident enough that many new buildings were erected.[1] The town's embrace of the Arts and Crafts movement influenced the design of many of its houses and other buildings. The movement was so popular that in 1905 a local storeowner became the first agent in the country to stock goods from the famous London department store Liberty & Co., including William Morris fabrics and Tudric pewterware.[2]

Whanganui had moved well beyond its rural origins, becoming 'a centre for law and order, rail and river transport, postal and telephone services, education and arts, and the maritime bridge between the Lower North Island and the wider world.'[3]

The prosperity was not to last. The Depression of the 1930s had a severe effect on the town, and many high-profile businesses collapsed.[4] The shift of freight from the river port to the railway exacerbated the economic decline. This helps to explain why so many Edwardian buildings remain: it was cheaper to leave them and there was no demand for the land on which they sat. Many are still in use, sometimes for their original purposes — grand edifices like the Sarjeant Gallery and the Wanganui Club, for example — as is the building that contained Mackay's office and the Rutland Hotel.

That economic decline was still well in the future the evening that the town's progressive, dynamic and at times controversial mayor met D'Arcy Cresswell. The two men had first met the day Cresswell arrived in Whanganui. Mackay invited the younger man and his cousin (who has never been identified) to dinner that night at the Chavannes Hotel, which stood on the site of what is now the National Bank building on Victoria Avenue, close to the Sarjeant Gallery. It is not known why Cresswell, who had come to visit family, had dinner on his first night in town with the mayor, whom he had never met before. Did Mackay know about him? Or did the cousin bring them together? Cresswell's statement to the police gave no insight into their connection.

'Nothing abnormal happened while at dinner,' Cresswell noted in his statement to the police. 'I spoke to Mr MacKay between the time I had dinner with him on Monday night and entering his office on Saturday morning last the 15th instant. My cousin and myself went to Hawera races [89 kilometres north of Whanganui] Tuesday the 11th instant and returned to Wanganui the following evening.'[5]

On Thursday, the day after his return from Taranaki, Cresswell invited Mackay to dinner, again with his cousin. This time the trio dined at the Rutland Hotel, on the corner of the Avenue — as Whanganui locals call Victoria Avenue — and Ridgway Street. There has been a succession of hotels on this site since 1849; two of them burned down. The building the men visited still stands, although it was extensively renovated after being gutted in a 1983 fire.

This meal led to a further invitation from Mackay to visit the Sarjeant Gallery, which had opened the year before — Mackay had been a driving force in its construction — the following afternoon. He and Cresswell met in the Ridgway Street office before walking to the Wanganui Club in St Hill Street for a cup of tea and then going on to the gallery. Mackay, who had the keys, unlocked the door, then they looked through the building.

Ridgway Street is now part of the city's heritage precinct, full of old buildings in various states of repair. Today, a park opposite the Rutland marks where a group of buildings burned down in the 1990s; one of them contained what had been Mackay's legal premises. For some reason, he met Cresswell in a different office, on the same side of the street but further along, in the next block. It is not clear why Mackay was using two offices in addition to his mayoral office in the council building. He was apparently having trouble paying his bills around this time, and this may have prompted the shift to an office further from the Avenue,[6] in a wooden two-storey building owned by estate agent, sharebroker and valuer Charles Duigan, who was keenly interested in the Sarjeant Gallery, and who later served as an honorary curator. Perhaps Duigan let Mackay use the office for a reduced rent. He had two rooms on the first floor: his faced the street and a smaller room, connected by a door, was occupied by his secretary.

These days, what was then known as Duigan's Building is one of three owned by Meteor Print, which has been there since the 1940s. The original building had sets of offices on the ground floor; upstairs was a space intended to be used as an auction room and offices designed for solicitors, complete with a strongroom. Mackay's office, used for many years as the Meteor staff tearoom, is remarkably well preserved; only the door between the former office and an anteroom is missing. On the opposite, Queens Park, side of the street is a concrete-block substation which, in 1920, was occupied by a carrier/taxi stand. The office was also diagonally opposite the former public library,[7] now used by the Whanganui Repertory Theatre.

The Wanganui Club is a large, two-storey neo-Georgian brick building in St Hill Street, one street over from the Avenue and about 10 minutes' walk from Mackay's office. Designed, like others of its ilk throughout the country, to emulate an English gentlemen's club, it originally opened as a farmers' club in the Avenue. In 1915 it had

ABOVE
The Wanganui Club, on St Hill Street. *Whanganui Regional Museum Photographic Collection, photograph by Allen Russ, c. 1915–1920s, 2020.32.64*

BELOW
The underground urinals in Maria Place, Whanganui, photographed some time after 1919. The Sarjeant Gallery is in the distance at right. *Whanganui Regional Museum Photographic Collection, 1800.1227*

moved to this much grander building, which had a lounge, a billiard room with four tables, sitting rooms, a dining room, committee rooms, card rooms, a secretary's room and a 'strangers' room', where women, who were not allowed in the club, would wait for their husbands.[8] Upstairs were bedrooms to accommodate members from out of town. The staff and kitchen quarters were at the back of the building, which had its own electricity plant.

To get to the gallery after leaving the club, Mackay and Cresswell turned left and then left again into Maria Place, at which point the gallery would have loomed up in front of them. They then crossed the Avenue. On their way, they passed the town's underground urinals, which still exist but were closed around the time of the Second World War, following complaints that they were 'detrimental to the best interests of the business premises in the neighbourhood'.[9]

As in other urban areas in the 1920s, the urinals were a meeting place for men seeking sex with other men. Case files for indecency cases in the town testify to the existence of what British historian Matt Houlbook has termed a network of sexual opportunity.[10] Men would meet in bars or on the street but, unable to go back to boarding houses where they might be seen by nosy landladies, they would go to a public place like the urinals or, in Whanganui's case, Queens Park.

The Sarjeant Gallery, which dominates Queens Park, has been called 'the mausoleum on the hill'. The nickname is apt: the squat, white, domed stone structure does look like a tomb. It sits on the highest point in the town centre — a hill known to Māori as Pukenamu before it was renamed Queens Park by European settlers — and is visible from all over the city. Even more impressive, as visitors approach, is the building's alignment with Maria Place on a north-south axis that connects Cooks Gardens/Patupuhou, the other high point in the city, with Queens Park/Pukenamu, in what has been described as one of the most important planned streetscapes in the country.[11]

It was not surprising that Mackay had a key to the gallery; he had been a driving force in its construction. The gallery was funded by a bequest from Henry Sarjeant, a wealthy local farmer who died in 1912, and was opened by Prime Minister William Massey on 6 September 1919. Building a gallery during the late stages of the Great War, when labour and materials were scarce, was a considerable achievement. In 1915 the gallery committee had recommended that the council appoint Christchurch architect Samuel Hurst Seager to judge a national competition for a suitable design. By June 1916, four of the 33 entrants had been selected to develop their ideas.[12]

In October, an entry from Dunedin architect Edmund Anscombe was named the winner. It was, in fact, the work of Anscombe's articled pupil, 21-year-old Donald Hosie, who, because he was not yet registered, could not take on the commission.[13] Hosie was called up for military service in November 1916, but he kept working on the drawings over the summer before going into camp. As mayor, Mackay wrote to the Featherston Military Camp, arguing it was absolutely essential that Hosie be allowed to continue with the drawings.[14] He then met with the commandant of the New Zealand Defence Forces, Major General Alfred Robin, who granted Hosie 12 days' leave to do so. In March 1917 Hosie embarked with the Otago Infantry Regiment. He had been in Europe for only three months when he was killed at Passchendaele on 12 October 1917. His body was never found.

And so the gallery, which Seager had specified in his competition conditions was to be a memorial,[15] did end up being a poignant monument to the losses in the Great War; at the opening, Mackay noted Hosie's death.[16] Seager had also instructed that particular attention be paid to the interior lighting to provide a soft indirect light. The system used has been the prototype for lighting in similar buildings in many parts of New Zealand.[17]

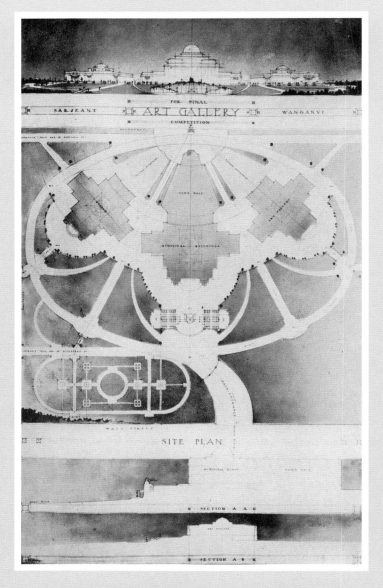

This site plan from the winning design for the Sarjeant Gallery — showing the gallery alongside the municipal buildings, the town hall and the museum — was printed in a competition booklet found in a time capsule in a gallery wall during strengthening work of the Sarjeant Gallery in 2021.
Collection of the Sarjeant Gallery Te Whare o Rehua Whanganui

Mackay remained closely involved in running the gallery and sourcing material for exhibitions from New Zealand and overseas, including an important collection of several hundred Great War cartoons and posters.[18]

By May 1920, when Mackay was showing the gallery to D'Arcy Cresswell, the Sarjeant Gallery had been open for only eight months and did not have much of a collection; the initial exhibitions were of borrowed items. On permanent display already, though, was a marble, three-quarter-sized copy of Raffaello Romanelli's *The Wrestlers*, the original of which resides in Florence's Uffizi Gallery.

Ellen Neame, the much younger widow of Henry Sarjeant, and her second husband John Neame, the art master at Wanganui Collegiate, whom she married less than a year after her first husband died, had bought the sculpture in 1914 while in Florence.[19] At that time buying copies, either reproductions or plaster casts, was commonplace and respectable, a way of allowing visitors to see famous works. *The Wrestlers*, itself a Roman marble copy of a lost third-century Greek bronze, has been extensively reproduced. The one other copy in New Zealand is in the Dunedin Public Art Gallery, which was presented to the gallery in 1928 by wealthy Dunedin businessman and philanthropist David Theomin.[20] Whanganui could not compete with the size and wealth of Dunedin, but the Neames clearly had similar aspirations for the Sarjeant. John Neame considered *The Wrestlers* as perhaps one of the six most famous works of Greek art in the world.[21]

The Wrestlers is also famous among homosexual men, who have admired the entwined naked male bodies for their homoerotic beauty and association with what the Romans called 'the way of the Greeks'. As Robert Aldrich has explained, 'Greek love' was the most clearly articulated and influential homosexual subculture before the words 'homosexual' or 'subculture' were invented.[22] Homosexual men experienced it both by travelling to southern Europe and through the art and literature of the period. This was important at a time when

Prime Minister William Massey speaking at the opening of the Sarjeant Gallery on 6 September 1919. *Collection of the Sarjeant Gallery Te Whare o Rehua Whanganui. Gift of Johanna Spittal and Henry Newrick, 2022*

homosexuality was condemned. During the twentieth century, this classical focus was overtaken by the development of new subcultures in places such as Berlin, New York and San Francisco, but in 1920 cultured men like Mackay and Cresswell would have recognised the coded significance of *The Wrestlers*.

According to Cresswell's statement to the police, after the gallery visit, things turned nasty:

> When we left the Art Gallery we went to Mr MacKay's office in Ridgway Street and while there I discovered a certain disgusting feature in Mr MacKay's character, I purposely encouraged him to display his qualities in his nature which I expected, he also showed me several photographs of nude women. On making that discovery I told him that I had led him on, on purpose to make sure of his dirty intentions, and I told him also amongst a lot of other candid things that he must resign the Mayorality [sic] at once.

How did Cresswell encourage Mackay? Did he make some sort of pass at the older man? Did the men have sex?[23]

Mackay showing Cresswell photos of naked women is a strange segue from viewing a statue of naked men wrestling, but this was not an untypical way of discovering if someone was gay in an era when men were having sex with each other before any modern notion of a gay identity had emerged. If mistaken, the man with the photos could say, 'Ah well, I fuck them all.'[24] The photos could also be used to arouse the other man, which would fit a scenario of offering sex for money. The photos also suggest that Mackay might have thought he had a chance of seducing Cresswell.[25] If so, it was to be a terrible miscalculation.

The Sarjeant Gallery's marble, three-quarter-sized copy of Raffaello Romanelli's *The Wrestlers*, acquired by Henry Sarjeant's widow Ellen in Florence in 1914. It was one of the first items of the collection to go on public display. *Collection of the Sarjeant Gallery Te Whare o Rehua Whanganui. Gift of Mr and Mrs Neame, 1915*

Cresswell's statement to the police was that Mackay 'then pleaded for mercy and asked me to think over it for the night, and come and see him next morning and let him know my decision. I stayed at the Rutland Hotel on Friday night as I was going to a dance in the Druid's Hall that evening. During the night I decided that he should resign the Mayorality in a weeks [sic] time.'

By the time of the third meeting in his office, Mackay had become increasingly desperate about his indiscretion with Cresswell, but the younger man remained resolved.

> As arranged I called on him at 9-30am at his Office in Ridgway Street on the Saturday morning, and the whole morning was spent by him in pleading with me on account of his wife and family and not to force him to resign. I, however, was quite determined that he should resign, even though he threatened to commit suicide, I did not believe that he had the courage. At my suggestion and partly at my dictation MacKay wrote a letter to my cousin and I saw it posted on Saturday morning. I did not believe him when he said that his wife was dependent on the £200 he got from being Mayor. I was very anxious to be just and do nothing cruel to his family.

Two hundred pounds was a lot of money in 1920, roughly the annual salary for a skilled council worker. Mackay's in-laws, the Duncan family, were wealthy landowners whose assets included property in Whanganui and Christchurch. Perhaps Mackay was unwilling to humiliate himself by asking them for support. Problems with Mackay's own legal business might also have been a factor; after his conviction, his affairs were described as being in a mess.

The letter Cresswell forced Mackay to write has never emerged and the police do not appear to have pursued it as part of their investigation, even though it was supposedly sent to Cresswell's cousin and would not have been difficult to find. (This relative managed to stay out of the case entirely; given that the police asked Cresswell about the period when the cousin was present, it is odd that he was not asked to give a statement.)

Unable to reach any resolution, the two men left Mackay's office: 'After useless talking and long silence he asked me to come round to the Club and try and reconsider my decision over a cup of tea. As I could not stand being in his office much longer, and was very knocked up I consented . . .'

But if Mackay hoped Cresswell would back off, it did not work. According to Cresswell, he then 'became very earnest about his decision to commit suicide, and the absolute impossibility of resigning' and offered a medical explanation for his actions.

> He told me that he was suffering from a complaint which made it impossible for him to control his passions and said that his Doctor could satisfy me in that respect. He rang up his Doctor on two or three occasions but each time the Doctor was out. Nothing more happened here than had happened in his office and he then pleaded with me to come back to his office, I think I was very foolish not to have left him, but I was anxious to be quite just to him. I should say here that I had promised to say nothing about what I discovered if he would resign at the end of the week, I did not want to judge him but I was determined he had no business to be Mayor.

Cresswell's resolve undiminished, the men walked back to the office for a fourth and final time.

> I being very tired took a more determined stand about it and threatened that if he didn't immediately give me a letter promising to resign at the end of the week I would at once wire

to my Dad in Timaru to come up as I felt that it was getting too much of a strain on me alone. He seemed so terribly upset that I then extended the time to a fortnight. Then he implored me for a months [sic] time and spoke a lot about his wife and family, I was quite firm about the fortnight and he then asked me for a few minutes alone to clear his head or something of the sort, and went into the Anti [sic] room where the girl worked.

Mackay returned after a few moments and said, '[G]ive me a month and I will sign a letter straight away.' Once Cresswell agreed to this, Mackay 'came over to his table and wrote a letter promising to resign the Mayoralty a month from that date and put it into a large envelope. We then arranged that it should be addressed to me at the General Post Office, and registered and I promised to let it lie at the Post Office until the month was up so he put it in his pocket.' This second resignation letter has also never been found, although the police did try to locate it.

Then, as they approached the door, Mackay turned and pointed a revolver at Cresswell's chest: 'We were only about a foot or two apart, I think that he said this is for you but I am not positive, then he fired almost immediately before I could recover from my amazement and I felt the bullet enter my right breast and I fell down.' Mackay stood over the prone Cresswell and 'thrust' the revolver into his right hand in an effort to make it look as if Cresswell had killed himself.

But Mackay's bullet had missed his blackmailer's heart and had instead hit him in his right lung. Cresswell managed to stand up and brandished the revolver at Mackay, holding him at bay. Mackay, who 'looked very surprised and wild', then ran out of the room. Cresswell followed but when he reached the door into the other office he could not open it: either Mackay had locked it or he was holding onto the handle on the other side.

addressed to me at the General Post Office , and registered and I
promised to let it lie at the Post Office until the month was up so he
put it in his pocket and we walked towards the door marked (a) Mr MacKay
leading the way, before reaching the door Mr MacKay suddenly turned round
and I found that he had a revolver pointing at my chest, we were only ab-
ut a foot or two apart, I think that he said this is for you but I,am not
positive , then he fired almost immediately before I could recover from
my amazement and I felt the bullet enter my right breast and I fell down.
He stood where he was and looked at me and then came over and thrust the
revolver into my right hand. Immed'ntley I got the revolver I rose to
my feet and kept him covered, he looked very surprised and wild and then
ran out through the door marked.(b) , I followed him and when I reached th
door I found that it was either locked or else he was holding on to the
handle. I did not wait to see but ran back into Mr MacKay's Office to
the window facing Ridgway Street and threw a chair through it to bring
assistance, and when I had smashed the window I called out to some chaps
on the street to come up . Then eveidently Mr MacKay hearing my calls
for help and thinking he could not escape, came back and asked me to
shoot him, and then he rushed me and I kept the revolver pointed clear
and pulled all the shots off, the next thing I can remember I was
running down the stairs and telli g someone that MacKay had shot me,
and I heard MacKay say over the stairs that he had shot me by accident,
I dont remember much more . I was wearing the clothes produced when shot.

*I have read the above statement and as
far as it relates to my own acts & deeds I admit
the statement to be substantially true.*

C L Mackay

26 5 20

The final page of D'Arcy Cresswell's statement to the police, taken at his hospital
bedside and later signed by Charles Mackay. *Archives New Zealand, Rex v.
Charles Evan Mackay: Attempted Murder, W3559/314 11/1920, R20558725*

Cresswell then ran back into the office and hurled the chair through the window to attract attention and assistance:

> . . . when I had smashed the window I called out to some chaps on the street to come up. Then eveidently [sic] Mr MacKay hearing my calls for help and thinking he could not escape, came back and asked me to shoot him, and then he rushed me and I kept the revolver pointed clear and pulled all the shots off, the next thing I can remember I was running down the stairs and telling someone that MacKay had shot me, and I heard MacKay say over the stairs that he had shot me by accident, I dont [sic] remember much more. I was wearing the clothes produced when shot.

Whanganui's main retail street, Victoria Avenue, in the early 1920s. *Alexander Turnbull Library, 1/2-046210-G*

3. THE TRIAL

Following the dramatic scenes in Mackay's office, police and court procedure took over. With the mayor in custody and Cresswell in hospital, the waiting began. If Cresswell did not recover, the attempted murder charge could be revised to murder. Mackay was refused bail and held over the weekend to appear at the Magistrate's Court on Monday morning, 17 May. Wyvern Wilson was the stipendiary magistrate, Colin Campbell Hutton appeared for the Crown and Tread-well, assisted by Donald McBeth, a friend of the accused, for Mackay.

At the hearing, Hutton asked for a seven-day remand period because Cresswell was not well enough to give evidence and it was uncertain whether he would survive. Treadwell passed on his client's thanks for the courtesy and kindness extended by police staff 'in discharging what must be a painful duty' and made a request of the town's two daily newspapers, the morning *Wanganui Chronicle* and the *Wanganui Herald*, published in the afternoon:[1] out of fairness to Mackay, who had been placed in a very serious position, he asked that they not publish 'statements obtained from outside individuals' as these might be prejudicial to the case. The prosecution opposed a request for bail, since the charge of attempted murder might develop into a more serious one and bail might not be in Mackay's interest 'as he was naturally in a high state of nervous tension'.[2] The magistrate agreed and remanded Mackay in custody for a week.

Mackay was an experienced defence lawyer, but his claim, repeated six times, that the gun went off by accident was a dubious strategy, undermined by Cresswell's throwing the chair out of the office window in a bid for help. Perhaps Mackay, stressed and desperate, thought the defence might stick should Cresswell die.

When Mackay appeared at the police court on Monday 24 May, Hutton stated that doctors would be able to say whether Cresswell could give evidence by Wednesday of that week, and asked for a further adjournment. His request was granted and the trial began on Thursday 27 May, by which time it was clear that Cresswell would live.

On the day of the trial an expectant crowd gathered outside the Magistrate's Court an hour before the hearing was due to start. There were so many people that police had to clear the steps to allow the witnesses to enter. Only a third of those waiting had managed to get in when the trial began at three o'clock.[3] Cresswell's statement, reprinted verbatim in newspapers across New Zealand and Australia, was read by Inspector Hendry, after which Hutton produced Cresswell's sketch plan along with photos of the office taken after the shooting.[4]

The prosecution then presented the rest of its evidence. The eyewitnesses and police officers read their statements to the court. Only one witness, Senior Sergeant Bourke, who had spoken to Mackay at the police station after the shooting, was cross-examined by Treadwell, who asked, 'Did [Mackay] say how long he carried the revolver?' Bourke replied that 'he carried it during the Prince's visit'.[5]

There was no evidence for the defence.

Mackay was then asked to plead. Standing with his arms folded, he said quietly and distinctly: 'I plead guilty.' He was then committed by the magistrate to a sitting of the Wanganui Supreme Court the following day for sentencing. Before he was taken away, Mackay shook hands with several friends and thanked the police for their fairness.

If the trial was about the blackmail and what happened in Mackay's office, then the sentencing hearing the next morning, before Chief Justice Sir Robert Stout, was about why it happened and the consequences. Once again Mackay, who 'had a haggard appearance, and seemed to feel his position keenly', let others speak on his behalf.[6]

Treadwell began by outlining why the shooting happened. Mackay, he explained, had no choice but to plead guilty and was also keen to completely excuse Cresswell. He revealed that there was a reason for Mackay's actions: his homosexuality. In statements attesting that Mackay had sought treatment six years before the shooting, his doctor and a specialist described this as a medical condition he had tried to overcome. The 'condition', aggravated by his stressed state, had caused him to become 'unhinged' and 'not in his right mind' when he shot Cresswell.

It is hard to see how pleading not guilty could have been a possibility, unless Treadwell had been able to make something of Cresswell's role as a blackmailer, and he was not going to do that: 'I have first of all to exonerate the young man Cresswell — and I do this with the full concurrence and approval of accused — from any blame whatsoever,' he told the court. 'I fully acknowledge the fact that no blame can be attached to Cresswell, and say that no one can, with justification, reflect in any way upon his character. The action he took must meet with the commendation of all right-thinking men.'[7] In praising Cresswell, Treadwell was perhaps seeking to deflect attention from Mackay's sexual activities. If the young man were forced to provide more detail about exactly what happened in the office, it could make things worse for Mackay.

Treadwell then set about trying to reduce his client's sentence, in the process providing a rare glimpse of how homosexuality was regarded in 1920. This approach ensured that the case, ostensibly about attempted murder, would also be linked with same-sex attraction. 'The circumstances,' Treadwell pointed out, were 'most distressing. [The] accused is a man of considerable scholastic attainments, a member of an honorable profession, and until recently, he has occupied the highest position his fellow citizens can bestow.' The reason he had 'thrown away' all these things 'will be found to be a subject of regret and deep concern'; it was given only 'in justification of the accused, and in hope of somewhat mitigating the sentence'.

It seemed that, 'for a number of years', Mackay had been 'suffering from homo-sexual monomania. We have gone considerably into the matter with him and I think I am justified in saying that it is

William James Treadwell (right) and his son Charlie Treadwell,
around 1922. *Courtesy Richard Austin, Treadwell Gordon*

heartrending to think of the efforts that accused made to cure himself of the trouble with which he was afflicted.' Mackay had consulted 'doctors and metaphysicians', who had supplied reports, but Treadwell was not going to read these out in court: 'There is no reason that those who attend a court out of curiosity to see a man placed in the position of accused should have their evil or prurient desires acceded to.'[8] Mackay's 'affliction' had made it difficult for him to control himself and that had led to the shooting, Treadwell contended.

The diagnosis of monomania, meaning partial insanity, is now obsolete, though the word retains its meaning of an unhealthy, singular obsession. Treadwell was suggesting that this was the problem, rather than an attraction to younger men. It was unusual for monomania to be used in association with homosexuality.

Treadwell's strategy relied on what was later known as the 'medical model' of homosexuality, which emerged in the late nineteenth century and replaced moral and religious explanations. In order 'to understand a social phenomenon which was appearing before their eyes: before them as patients, before the courts, in front of them as public scandals, on the streets in a still small but growing network of meeting places',[9] sexologists such as Karl Heinrich Ulrichs, Richard von Krafft-Ebing and Havelock Ellis had redefined the homosexual as a distinctive and aberrant person. Although this model was well established by 1920, homosexuality was not widely discussed and the term was rarely used in New Zealand newspapers. The term 'sodomy' was sometimes seen from about 1850, but apart from reports in the early 1900s on a German scandal known as the Eulenburg Affair, 'homosexual' had appeared in very few news stories before 1920.[10]

The medical reports referred to by Treadwell, but not made public in 1920, contain more information about Mackay's homosexuality and how this was 'treated'. Both statements show that it was seen as a nervous condition, in a period when such mental states were regarded as somatic — based in the body as opposed to psychological, as they would later be understood.

The first statement was from Mackay's GP, Dr Maurice M. Earle, whose rooms were in Wicksteed Street, the Harley Street of Whanganui. On 27 May Earle wrote: 'This is to certify that some six years ago Charles Evan Mackay of Wanganui, solicitor, consulted me with reference to Homosexual Monomania. I advised him to obtain suggested treatment & I believe that he acted on my advice.'[11] The second statement came from Albert Godfrey Mackay, apparently no relation, who described himself as a metaphysician:

> This is to certify that Mr C. E. Mackay, in August 1914, acting on the advice of his medical adviser, came to see me about treating him for Obsessions of 'Homo-Sexual' nature. He was in a very worried & depressed frame of mind, & said if I could not help him, life would be <u>impossible</u>.
>
> He had treatments (intermittently) until the end of November 1914. He then stopped the treatments because he said the Homo-sexual ideas were gone, & he felt quite alright again.
>
> In my opinion, intermittent treatments should have been kept up for twelve to eighteen months, then the cure would have been permanent.
>
> I have treated other cases of Homo-sexual desire with success.
>
> The two chief causes of relapse are alcoholism & neurasthenia. For the last few months we know Mr C. E. Mackay has had great mental strain, & worry & I'm sure if this had not been so, this trouble would have never come to pass.[12]

The term neurasthenia — literally nervous exhaustion, or lack of nerve strength — became popular in the late nineteenth century and was used to describe a disorder covering a range of physical and mental symptoms, including headache, muscle pain and subjective sensory disturbances. Neurasthenia was widely employed during and after the Great War to describe what was also called shell shock. As one writer has suggested, 'Neurasthenic symptoms were thought to be caused by a lack of nerve force, which in its turn was supposed to stem from excessive demands on the brain, the digestive organs and the reproductive system, while these excess demands were attributed to the fast pace of modern life.'[13] Ellis, Krafft-Ebing and others identified neurasthenia or some other form of nervous illness as part of the supposed background of homosexuals or inverts, as they were also known.[14]

Mackay could have, and might have, sought help from a priest or other spiritual adviser, but chose to go to his doctor, who referred him to a specialist. It is intriguing that this was an option in a New Zealand town in 1914. Mackay had perhaps sought treatment out of fear that he would be punished if he was caught, or perhaps his wife had instigated it. Although the precise nature of the treatment is unknown, it took place from August to November 1914, during the two years when Mackay was not mayor of Whanganui and was perhaps less in the spotlight.

Earle, remarkably, had referred Mackay to a man with no medical qualifications. Albert ('Bertie') Mackay was a taxi driver who wanted to become a doctor but, according to his granddaughter, could not afford the training. In 1916, Albert Mackay started calling himself a metaphysician — a slippery term referring to anyone using non-physical means to treat physical illness — and relocated to Wicksteed Street, near Dr Earle's rooms. Despite his lack of medical

A. **G. MACKAY.**

PROFESSOR OF HYPNOTISM AND SUGGESTIVE THERAPEUTICS.
Functional and Nervous Disorders Successfully Treated.
Beyond all question, what is commonly called SUGGESTION is one of the Greatest Curative Forces available to suffering humanity.

CONSULTATION FREE.
Patients attended and Treated in their own Homes.

Address :—
BIGNELL ST.,
GONVILLE,   'Phone 633.

training, his granddaughter remembers 'all the doctors' being his friends.[15] During the 1918 influenza epidemic he stopped practising so he could take charge of aid in one of the Whanganui suburbs. All the conditions he claimed he could cure, including homosexuality, were then considered to have a physical origin and to be curable using suggestive therapeutics.[16] Albert Mackay was known as a skilled hypnotist and gave public demonstrations.[17] Some doctors in Germany and other countries used hypnotism to treat homosexuality,[18] but it appears that Albert Mackay relied more on suggestive therapeutics.

As well as using regular classified advertisements, he publicised his services in what would now be known as advertorials. In one of these, in May 1919, he reassured prospective clients: 'There is a great misunderstanding on the part of the general public as to how Suggestion is applied, the popular idea being that the patient must submit to Hypnosis. In my treatment by Suggestion, I find it rarely necessary to resort to Hypnotism, and then ONLY with the full understanding and consent of the patient . . . otherwise, only simple Suggestion is used.'[19]

The French psychologist and pharmacist Émile Coué developed the technique of autosuggestion, a talk therapy still used to treat functional and nervous disorders, which has two main aspects: first, every idea that exclusively occupies the mind is transformed into an actual physical or mental state; second, the efforts we make to conquer an idea by exerting the will serve only to make that idea more powerful. The therapy sought to harness the power of thought and influence the subconscious to accept ideas, using a process called 'spontaneous autosuggestion.' As C. Harry Brooks explained in a book about Coué's method: 'If we fill our minds with the thought of the desired end, provided that end is possible, the Unconscious will lead us to it by the easiest, most direct path. And so, various conditions (asthma, epileptic fits, depression and so on), could be cured through the power of thought, rather than the will, which it was argued, cannot be more than the servant of thought.'[20]

n court, Treadwell argued that it was 'a matter of common knowledge in Wanganui' that, for the last few months, Mackay had been suffering from 'considerable mental strain, which I am convinced has to a considerable extent unhinged his mind. Only as late as the Friday before this unfortunate occurrence took place, accused was in my office in a state of terrible agitation, and broke down on account of something which had appeared in one of the local newspapers.'[21]

The offending article may have concerned Mackay's bitter row with the RSA over the visit of the Prince of Wales to Whanganui on 3 and 4 May. On that Friday, 14 May, the *Wanganui Herald* had reprinted letters and telegrams from the Prince's staff congratulating Mackay on the visit,[22] but this did not redeem an event that had not been a success and exposed Whanganui to mockery on both sides of the Tasman (see Chapter 4).

The paper also published an editorial expressing regret at having published an RSA allegation of 'disloyal utterances and . . . contemptible conduct' on Mackay's part, and stating that 'the whole wretched business should now be relegated to the past':

> We trust all those nearly affected will view the matter in the same light. We have not written this article with any idea of continuing, or encouraging the continuance of a further discussion on the matter. The whole thing should stop, be buried, forgotten. May we ask the late president, the Mayor, the Returned Soldiers' Association, and everyone else concerned, for the good of the town, for the good of the community, for the good of themselves, to let the matter drop. There has been a great deal too much recrimination, bad feeling, hot air, appearing in the local newspapers lately. What is the good of it? As far as our columns are concerned we intend to take our own advice. We are absolutely done with the matter.[23]

Rather than bring the row to an end, however, this piece, which appeared the same afternoon that Cresswell threatened to reveal the mayor's homosexuality unless he resigned, may have pushed an already stressed Mackay over the edge. As Treadwell observed, it was not difficult to imagine Mackay's mental state. 'On the Friday he was threatened with exposure, and on the Saturday exposure still threatened him. One can only say, sir, that at the time the shooting took place ... the man was for the time being absolutely unhinged and did not realise the seriousness of what he was doing.'[24]

Treadwell suggested this state was revealed in the behaviour described in Cresswell's statement: the agreement to his requests on Friday and Saturday, then the writing of the resignation letter, followed by the sudden presentation of the gun. 'Cresswell stated that accused's manner was wild. Mackay at that moment was bereft of reason. He endeavoured to take the life of a human being to cover up the exposure that would follow, and yet the whole of that exposure could have been avoided by accused following the course that Cresswell had suggested and which he also had already followed. He had already written the letter resigning his position as Mayor. At the moment he shot Cresswell one could only conclude that accused was not in his right mind.'[25]

Treadwell's argument is reminiscent of the temporary insanity defence still used in murder trials. During his legal career, Mackay himself had used it in at least two cases where he had appeared for the accused; on neither occasion had it worked.[26] The argument also has echoes of the provocation approach that became known as the 'gay panic defence' after it was used in cases from the 1960s. A man charged with murdering a gay man would argue that some sort of sexual provocation had made him temporarily disturbed and therefore not responsible for his actions; his lawyers would then argue down his sentence from murder to manslaughter. The defence was controversial because the victims were unable to defend themselves. The controversy and changes in the attitudes to homosexuality led to its elimination from New Zealand law in 2009. In 1920, Treadwell was using this defence, but with a strange twist, arguing that it was Mackay's *own* homosexuality that made him temporarily insane and led to the murder attempt.

Treadwell tried to reinforce his line of reasoning by arguing that there was 'no truth in the suggestion that Mackay coldly and deliberately procured the pistol from another room and shot Cresswell in cold blood'. In fact, Mackay had 'for some considerable time [been] in dread of violence'. Since someone had rung him at home and threatened his life, he had been carrying the gun — Treadwell referred to it as a pistol[27] — for the last four or five weeks. When he used it, he did so 'suddenly and impulsively'.[28]

It was not a convincing argument. Bourke had already testified that Mackay was carrying a gun during the royal visit but the information about the death threat was new, and interesting. Treadwell concluded, 'I can only, in the name of that compassion for the faults and frailties of others, ask your Honor to temper justice with mercy.'[29]

His Honour, Sir Robert Stout, Liberal Party grandee, former attorney-general, former premier (twice) and now chief justice, and 30 years older than Mackay, knew him well, as he noted in his summing up:

> I knew you first as a lad only 16 years of age, when you attained a university scholarship. You took a degree of Arts when you were only nineteen years of age — a rare acquirement in New Zealand, and your future seemed bright. You afterwards devoted your attentions to law, and as a member of the board that looked over your papers, I can say that you attained the highest marks in equity of your year and that altogether you were one of the brightest students at that time.

He had watched his career flourish since, and observed how Mackay had been honoured by his fellow citizens 'and placed in the highest position they can bestow for a number of years, and now you stand in this place'.[30]

Stout, a brilliant lawyer and an intellectual, was an unusual figure in New Zealand politics.[31] By 1920 he had had a significant influence on the country's public life for several decades, and was a progressive thinker, well informed on contemporary social and political theories. These included eugenics, which aimed to improve a population by controlling breeding. Stout and his wife, Anna, were both enthusiastic advocates of what he praised as 'the science of noble birth, or that which relates to the development and improvement of the human race'.[32] As a pamphlet in Stout's collection put it, 'The mentally better stock in the nation is not reproducing itself at the same rate as it did of old; the less able, and the less energetic are more fertile than the better stocks.' Improved education would not 'bring up, in the scale of intelligence, hereditary weakness to the level of hereditary strength. The only remedy, if one be possible at all, is to alter the relative fertility of the good and the bad stocks in the community.'[33]

Homosexuality, framed in such terms as 'sexual deviancy', was part of the 'bad stocks' or degenerates Stout and other eugenicists wanted to eliminate from their ideal society. While living in Britain in 1910, when she supported the British suffragettes campaigning for the vote, Anna Stout told a newspaper interviewer that New Zealand had 'no class of men who are effeminate in dress or intellect or degenerate in morals, as in old countries'.[34]

Her husband accepted homosexuality was a sickness, which could be improved with the right environment, but this was not enough to absolve Mackay: 'I am not going to refer to the circumstances in which you were placed, or what you did, further than to say that it was not an impulsive act, as the placing of the revolver in Cresswell's hands shows.'

Chief Justice Robert Stout, former premier and attorney general in the Liberal government, presided over Mackay's trial. *Alexander Turnbull Library, 1/2-098550-F*

At the time there was some confusion about this statement because the two Whanganui newspapers each reported in differently. Stout later confirmed he meant to say it was *not* an impulsive act,[35] and that this was the reason for his imposition of an unusually harsh sentence for attempted murder: 15 years' hard labour.

> I have to remember that this is an attack upon human life and I have to remember that the ideal of justice is that human life must be kept sacred. Such a community is damned where there is any slackening of that ideal. I must not do anything to make people think that human life is not always held sacred in the temple of justice. At the same time I believe you were laboring under a sad affliction, but I will have to impose a heavy sentence.

Stout did, however, note that the sentence would be revised by the Prisons Board, of which he was the founding president — a role he still held — and the Executive Council: 'It does not mean you will spend all that time in gaol.' He thought it possible that Mackay could redeem himself and 'yet become a moral citizen. You have taken the first step in that direction by pleading guilty and not trying to brazen it out as some would have done. I believe that, however wrong and wicked a man may be, there is always some good left in him and that there is yet hope for him.' In inflicting such a heavy sentence, he hoped, 'you will try yet to redeem yourself and in the years to come you may be found clothed in your right mind'.

Mackay, who had listened to the proceedings with folded arms and bowed head, said nothing and left the dock, looking stunned.

There had been an air of haste about the court case, as if the town was trying to dispatch the scandal as soon as possible. Cresswell was a remote presence, represented by his hospital-bed statement and eyewitness accounts. Mackay had said nothing and there was little evidence besides the eyewitness accounts. What could be reported was printed in local and metropolitan newspapers across the country and also in many Australian papers — an indication of the case's high profile.

Many unanswered questions remained, including who the Cresswell cousin was, how Cresswell knew that Mackay was homosexual and why the younger man had an interest in Mackay resigning as mayor. References to speculation in the town, banned from the papers, suggests there was more going on. But the citizens of Whanganui were denied the chance to find out what really happened in Mackay's office that Saturday, and the resulting vacuum was quickly filled with stories and speculation.

The Sarjeant Gallery, photographed in 1926. Collection of the Sarjeant Gallery Te Whare o Rehua Whanganui. Gift of Mary Powell, Marjorie Marshall and Harold Denton, 1965

4. MACKAY

C harles Evan Mackay's sensational fall from grace overshadowed a remarkable career in local politics.[1] Aged just 31 when he was first elected mayor in 1906, he was seen as a challenger to the cliques who ran Whanganui. 'One of those earnest, pushing chaps,' said the *Free Lance* that year, 'with a lot of vivacity and personal charm. He wears, besides, a thoughtful look, a close-cropped moustache . . . and his face is classical in its contour.'[2] He held his ground against fierce criticism to champion electric trams, which transformed the town — the first outside the main centres to boast this innovation.

After being re-elected as mayor every year from 1907 to 1911, he had resigned in February 1912 following a row with the borough engineer, but stood again in the elections later that year. His 'retirement' in 1913 was short-lived and he was re-elected in 1915, 1917 and 1919. Felicity Campbell, one of the few Whanganui historians to have written about Mackay, describes 'his long history of "mackayevellian" machinations in local politics, when for 16 years he spun most of the very busy wheels in Whanganui in the direction that he wanted to go'.[3] His bold, energetic mayoral style also revealed his character, and explained why he accumulated so many enemies who tried so hard to unseat him.

During Mackay's nearly 12 years as mayor, the groundwork was laid for major cultural amenities in Whanganui. Only the Sarjeant Art Gallery opened before he went to prison in 1920, but this became the foundation of a cultural precinct in Queens Park, followed by the Whanganui Museum (1928), the Alexander Library (1933) and the War Memorial Hall (1960). The 'Greater Wanganui' vision to incorporate the satellite suburbs into the borough was around before Mackay became mayor, but he adopted and drove it. Although the plan was not fully realised until after 1920, he played a key role. When Gonville and Castlecliff, the two last separate suburbs, were included in 1924, the borough of Whanganui became a city.

Mackay had arrived in Whanganui in 1901 after qualifying as a

Waata Wiremu Hīpango (standing, eighth from left), rangatira of Ngāti Tuamango hapū, who lived at Putiki Pā, near Whanganui, presenting the deeds to Hīpango Park to Charles Mackay, mayor of Whanganui, in 1913. *Alexander Turnbull Library, 1/1-017475-G*

lawyer in Taranaki, home to his family since his father had retired as headmaster of Wellington College in 1891. In 1865, Joseph Mackay, originally from the north-east of Scotland, came to New Zealand via Geelong Grammar in the Australian state of Victoria, to be mathematical and resident master at Nelson College. Remembered as 'scholarly, gruff but kindly', Joseph (Joe) Mackay had a large beard and the same high forehead as his son, and was an ardent Scot who retained his Aberdonian Doric accent.

Photos show a man with a piercing gaze who was remembered as having a formidable presence. His rough and ready methods, and his belief that everyone should be mathematically inclined, had an adverse affect on boys who were afflicted with a sensitive and nervous temperament.[4] Descriptions of Joseph Mackay's teaching — 'He worked at high pressure himself, and expected everyone else to do the same'[5] — and his sudden resignation from Wellington College because of financial pressure on the school are both reflected in his son's style and career.

I n 1872 Joseph Mackay married Jessie Wilkie, the daughter of a Nelson settler who had become a successful shopkeeper. After the family moved to the capital, Charles, the couple's second son, born in 1875, thrived at the academic Wellington College. He was dux in 1891 and won a university scholarship. After completing an arts degree at Canterbury in 1894, he taught at Kings College in Auckland from 1896 to 1898, then moved to Taranaki to complete his training as a lawyer. He qualified while working at the firm run by William Malone, later famous for leading the New Zealand assault on Chunuk Bair at Gallipoli in 1915. He graduated with an LLB in 1900 and was admitted as a barrister and solicitor of the Supreme Court in 1901.[6]

When Mackay came to Whanganui at the turn of the century, it was growing rapidly, the busy heart of a pastoral and agricultural district

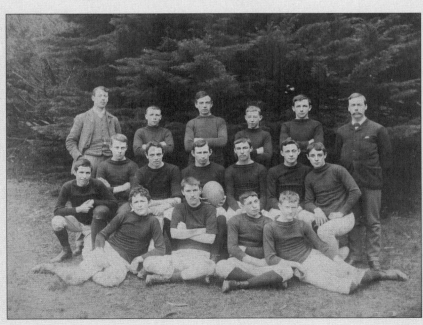

that was also becoming known for manufacturing. In the words of one historian, 'The town was enveloped in an air of prosperity and its optimistic outlook was well known throughout the colony. This optimism tended to attract other industries to the town encouraging expansion . . .'[7] This expansion attracted ambitious young men on the make, like Mackay who, as a later profile noted, had

> migrated to a larger sphere for his activities to find scope. He made the astounding discovery that there are more six and eightpences to be transferred from one pocket to another in a large than in a small town; Mr. Mackay has a shrewd notion on which side his bread is buttered. He rapidly established himself as a favourite with the criminal classes; he is ready to tackle the most apparently hopeless cases, replying upon the eccentricity of Judges and Magistrates and the stupidity of juries to obtain verdicts against the weight of evidence. However black a case may be [he] may be relied upon to paint it whiter than snow.[8]

Mackay set up his own practice in January 1902 but joined the firm of Borlase & Barnicoat in April of that year.[9] Alongside his legal work, he threw himself into local life, joining the Cosmopolitan Club and the newly formed parliamentary union and debating society, and becoming commodore of the Wanganui Sailing Club. The well-known and popular solicitor came within the orbit of Isobel Duncan, the daughter of Andrew Duncan, an early Scottish settler and major landowner. The couple married in January 1904 and moved into Totarapuka, the family homestead, with Isobel's widowed mother.[10] The 24-room house with steeply pitched gables had stables, a tennis court and cottages for a coachman, gardener and servants. Named after the original Māori name for the area, it stood at the centre of some 89 acres of land on the opposite side of the river to the town centre.

Now a suburb known as Whanganui East, this area was then

separate from the Wanganui Borough and called Eastown, after the Eastown Railway Workshops, which opened in 1880. The railway presence increased demand for housing on that side of the river, and the large estates owned by European settler families were being subdivided for housing. After Andrew Duncan's death in 1893, his family, like others, began to sell off their land.

Several months after his marriage, Mackay announced that he was standing for the Mataongaonga Road Board, one of six under the Wanganui County Council, responsible for roads and bridges in the rural land surrounding the town. The subdivided acres in Eastown owned by the Duncans and others lay within the Mataongaonga board area. Mackay was duly elected in May 1904 and re-established his own legal practice the following year.[11]

The board was pushing for the eastern side of the river to become a borough, which would give it access to the services enjoyed by the town, and would benefit the Duncans and other landowners. Initially named Eastbrook, but shortly afterwards called Wanganui East, the new borough combining Eastown and the Sedgebrook estate was approved and held its first mayoral elections in December 1907. During the election campaign, Mackay deployed the kind of techniques described by Felicity Campbell. Robert Nielson, the long-time Mataongaonga Road Board chair, who had led the push for a borough, was standing with two other candidates. In order to discredit him, in the week before the election Mackay released a letter from the Audit Department criticising the board's accounting. The ploy worked: Nielson lost, and the Eastbrook Borough appointed Mackay as its solicitor.

As well as helping his in-laws, who rewarded him by naming a street after him on their subdivided land, Mackay used his road board membership to become politically known. He was elected a Whanganui borough councillor in 1905 and the following year caused an upset by successfully contesting the mayoralty, ousting local builder, Arthur Bignell.

Totarapuka, the Duncan family homestead, was located across the river from the town centre in what is now Whanganui East. This photograph was taken in 1911. *Whanganui Regional Museum Photographic Collection, Josephine Duncan collection, 2008.60.345*

Isobel and Charles Mackay's son Duncan Mackay, photographed not long before he died of diphtheria, aged two years and eight months. *Whanganui Regional Museum Photographic Collection, Josephine Duncan collection, 2008.60.309*

The bridesmaids at Isobel Duncan and Charles Mackay's wedding on 20 January 1904, wearing bonnets decorated with ostrich feathers. From left, cousins Muriel Addenbrook, Winifred Montgomerie and Beryl Addenbrook. Photograph by F. J. Denton, 1904. *Whanganui Regional Museum Photographic Collection, 2011.52*

Isobel Duncan, photographed in 1903, a year before her marriage to Charles Mackay. *Whanganui Regional Museum Photographic Collection, Josephine Duncan collection, 2008.60.310*

I n 1907 Mackay featured in *Familiar Faces*, a collection of satirical portraits of Whanganui personalities. The sketch suggested that he had transformed the mayoralty into something grander, in keeping with the town's lofty aspirations. With his distinctive Roman nose and walrus moustache, Mackay was depicted chained to a throne-like mayoral chair. A tiny crown perched on his head, he held the town gas works as a sceptre in one hand and a vegetable or fruit (a tomato?) in the other. As the accompanying text indicated, the tumult that would mark his civic career was already evident.

> The most desperate job he has yet tackled was his contest for the Mayoralty. The odds against him were heavy, but by dint of pluck and good riding, he romped in with plenty to spare. His career as Mayor has been somewhat strenuous — 'Riding the whirlwind and controlling the storm,' as the poet has it. During his term of office he has had to contend with strong opposition, but by firmness and tact he has so far held his own against all comers.[12]

By 1906 Whanganui's public transport, which used horse-drawn buses and cabs, had become inadequate. Industrial and population growth had led to the development of the Aramoho, Gonville and Castlecliff housing areas, which urgently needed better links with the town.[13] These three suburbs were also the location of significant industries, including the freezing works and the port. After investigating the best options, the borough council opted for steam trams, a decision subsequently approved by ratepayers, together with the loan necessary to build the network. Planning was under way to lay the rails, buy rolling stock and erect buildings, when Mackay forced a dramatic change in direction.

During the mayoral election campaign he did not criticise the proposed trams, instead questioning Bignell's record as a member of the harbour board. Bignell offered to pay a hefty donation to the

ABOVE
Members of the Wanganui Borough Council in 1906. The mayor, Charles Mackay, is front row centre. *Alexander Turnbull Library, G-16003-1/1*

LEFT
Tram tracks being laid in Victoria Avenue, Whanganui, connecting the town centre to the fast-growing suburbs. The first tram began service in 1908, making Whanganui the first town outside the four main centres to have an electric tramway. *Whanganui Regional Museum Photographic Collection, 1967.113.57*

hospital board if Mackay could prove his allegations. The local papers swung in behind Bignell, but Mackay won by 116 votes. As soon as he was mayor he 'had the proposal scrapped' and began negotiating with the General Electric Company to supply electric rather than steam trams.[14] This success cemented Mackay's reputation as mayor, but also laid the groundwork for resentment from powerful forces in the town. These included another former mayor, Alexander Hatrick, who had held the office from 1897 to 1904. A successful merchant, ship-owner and tourism entrepreneur, he was a large presence in Whanganui public life, and a major advocate of steam trams, which he had seen while visiting Europe. But Mackay overcame stout opposition from Hatrick and the majority of the councillors, and when a vote was taken in 1908, support for the loan for electric trams, 18 votes to one, was one of the most clear-cut council mandates on record.[15]

On 10 December 1908, the electrical current was switched on and Isobel Mackay drove the first tram out of the tramway barn.[16] The tram system was spectacularly successful and there was pressure for it to expand in line with the Greater Wanganui vision. By the time the trams were running, the town had a population of 10,000. More tram routes would be required in the future — in Wanganui East, Upper Aramoho and St John's Hill, as well as Gonville and Castlecliff — if the system was going to pay its way.[17]

Mackay's political style — discredit your opponents and create a popular following — has a modern ring. Unlike his opponents, he was comfortable speaking in public, thanks to his court experience. As one newspaper noted just after he became mayor, Mackay had 'a persistent way that wears down opposition. As a lawyer, he is not, perhaps, a brilliant pleader, but he gets there by "keeping on, keeping on".'[18]

Until 1915, throughout New Zealand mayors were elected

Isobel Mackay turns the first sod for the Whanganui electric tram system instigated by her husband, in 1908. *Alexander Turnbull Library, G-17440-1/1*

annually.[19] This meant that when Mackay was re-elected unopposed in May 1911, it was his sixth term. As he pointed out in a speech, when he first became mayor there were only 80 borough staff. Now there were about 200, and when work began on the new bridge — a second road crossing over the Whanganui River at Dublin Street, linking the town with Whanganui East — there would be more like 250.[20] The bridge was another decision that would benefit his Duncan in-laws and other landowners, but Mackay was not the mayor when it eventually opened in November 1914. The interruption to his mayoral career was sparked by a row with the borough engineer, William T. Mansfield.

Relations between the two men had deteriorated to the point where Mackay, citing 'incompatibility of temper', persuaded the councillors to ask for the engineer's resignation. When it came to the vote, however, three councillors changed their minds, and Mackay resigned in protest in February 1912. Another councillor, Edward Liffiton, took over as mayor for the few months remaining in the term, and Mackay was understood not to be seeking re-election in April.[21]

He did, however, decide to stand again, this time against another builder, Nicholas Meuli, who was pressured into his candidacy by a group led by Arthur Bignell. Meuli's campaign focused on Mackay's alleged financial mismanagement, which had resulted in a rise in the council overdraft and an increase in rates. Meuli produced a pamphlet, distributed with the local newspapers, which listed 20 reasons why Mackay should not be re-elected, and referred to his political aspirations beyond Whanganui. Mackay had stood as a Liberal candidate for Parliament in 1908 and 1911 but had failed to get elected. His local popularity did not translate to national politics.[22]

Mackay responded vigorously to his critics, arguing that Meuli was the nominee of a clique, that council expenditure was warranted, and rates rises justified.[23] He ran a presidential-style campaign, addressing crowds at meetings, unlike Meuli, who gave no speeches and was reluctant to solicit votes.

WHY A CHANGE OF MAYOR IS NECESSARY.

BECAUSE
The rates have been seriously increased without just reason.

BECAUSE
The Valuations have also increased by over 33 per cent.

BECAUSE
We are paying an increased valuation and increased rates combined, fully 75 per cent. more than a few years ago.

BECAUSE
The Overdraft on Ordinary Account has gone up from Hundreds to Thousands of pounds sterling: now about £17,000.

BECAUSE
As Valuations increase, so should rates decrease, but under Mr. Mackay's regime both have increased.

BECAUSE
During Mr. Mackay's administration nearly £100,000 has been spent out of ordinary revenue with nothing of a substantial or permanent nature to show for it.

BECAUSE
£174,000 has been raised by borrowing and, in the opinion of authorities, has not all been spent to best advantage.

BECAUSE
The Council is a Bear Garden, and the re-election of Mr. MACKAY will mean a continuance of wrangle.

BECAUSE
Mr. Mackay in his original manifesto, six years ago, promised filter beds and settling tanks for the Okehu water, and we are still without them.

BECAUSE
He promised Field's Scheme, and we are still without it.

BECAUSE
He stated that the present scheme of the Harbour Works was a mere waste of

sobel Mackay's vocation, according to her daughter Josephine, was 'organising people'.[24] Praised for her work as mayoress, she had until 1912 taken an active role in her husband's political career, forming ladies' committees to help with each campaign, but in 1912 she had no time to do this because the election was called at such short notice. Nonetheless, as she explained in a letter to the *Herald*, 'Already a large number of my friends in all parts of the town are working quietly to secure Mr Mackay's return. I shall be pleased to assist if any others who would like to assist would either call and see me at home, or ring me up on the telephone.'[25]

Both Whanganui papers backed Meuli and criticised Mackay for running a personality-based campaign. They predicted that his re-election would mean a continuation of the row over the engineer and conflict around the council table. Despite this prognostication Mackay won by a landslide: 1955 votes to just 700 for Meuli.

In July 1912, a letter from 'Beaten Before and Beaten Again' appeared in the *Wanganui Herald*, arguing that people were tired of the council and how it ran things. In particular, the letter writer alleged the borough council planned to increase the mayoral honorarium by £100 to £250, and argued that the engineer's job was not properly advertised: 'Rumour hath said applications are not wanted, as the man is ready, and only waiting the council meeting.'[26] Mackay sued the paper for libel. When the case was heard in September 1912, the judge maintained the statements were not libellous, and were directed at the whole council. The jury agreed and found against Mackay.

Mackay did not stand for the mayoralty at the 1913 election partly, perhaps, because he and Isobel had lost their two-year-old son, Duncan Charles, to diphtheria and heart failure the previous July. A local auctioneer named Tom Boswall Williams won the mayoral contest, and in June 1913 he presented Charles and Isobel Mackay with an illuminated address and gold jewellery paid for by a number of citizens in recognition of Mackay's service as mayor.[27] In October

Charles Mackay, photographed around 1912, after winning
the mayoralty for the seventh time. *Alexander Turnbull Library,
Who's Who in Wanganui, 1915, B-K-1442-39_detail*

of that year, Isobel Mackay gave birth to a second daughter, Josephine Ruth; Isobel Jessie Elizabeth, known as Elizabeth or Beth, had been born in 1905. A third daughter, Sheila (also known as Sheillah), was born in 1917. By the end of April 1915 Mackay was back in the mayoral chair.

The war, declared at the beginning of August 1914, had not ended by Christmas, as everyone hoped and expected, and the appalling casualties of the Gallipoli campaign in April 1915 drove home the ghastly reality of the conflict. On 7 May that year, the British ocean liner *Lusitania* was attacked and sunk by a German U-boat off the Irish coast; nearly 1200 passengers, mostly civilians, were drowned and the news triggered anti-German violence in Britain, South Africa and New Zealand. In New Zealand, there was also anger in some quarters at a perceived leniency in the treatment of Germans and Austrians.[28] On Saturday 15 May, evidently taking matters into their own hands, some Whanganui locals attacked German-owned businesses on Victoria Avenue.

That day, recruitment for the National Reserve was in full swing and the garrison band was playing on the balcony of the drill hall in Queens Park. There had been persistent rumours that violence was imminent and a crowd had gathered. Numbers swelled when the hotels closed and around 8 p.m. people started throwing stones. The first shop to be targeted was a pork butchery owned by Conrad Heinold, a naturalised German. He had closed up early, after receiving 50–60 anonymous letters and several telegrams threatening an attack.[29]

After the plate-glass windows of Heinold's shop were smashed, Mackay arrived and tried to address the crowd of several thousand, but he was howled down. An adjoining business was attacked, and by 11 p.m. Heinold's stock was looted and the shop completely wrecked. According to a journalist eyewitness, 'the culminating scene was witnessed when a Territorial in uniform climbed on to the verandah above the street and hoisted the Union Jack, amidst great excitement, the crowd singing the National Anthem and patriotic songs'.

During the rioting, Mackay was hit under the eye by a stone and a cracker bomb exploded in his face. His face bleeding, he tried again to address the crowd, urging them not to descend to the level of the Germans. Further up the avenue, the renaming in January of German-Jewish David Theomin's Dunedin-based Dresden Piano Company as the Bristol Piano Company could not protect the local branch from the angry crowd, who broke its showroom windows.[30]

The centennial history of Whanganui, published in 1939, referred to the 1915 riot as a discreditable incident that had lent the town some notoriety for a time; Mackay's attempt to intervene, though not his name, got a mention. Apart from this incident, the book argued, 'the town went through the same [wartime] experiences as other centres. Patriotic meetings and speeches were the first order of the day to stimulate recruiting. Then followed the raising of money for war purposes, and finally the settling of soldiers on their return.'[31] The reality was not, however, as straightforward as this summary suggests.

In October 1915, Mackay argued the council should not pay the wages of married men who had joined up, and contended that 'so long as single men of military age are available, married men should not be encouraged to enlist'.[32] Some letter writers disagreed — 'No Shirker, Though Married' was 'quite shocked' and asked if Mackay thought family men had 'no interest in whether our nation goes under'[33] — and the mayor came under pressure to sign up himself. Around this time there was a national recruiting crisis, and the government, reluctant to introduce conscription, had extended the maximum age for military service from 40 to 45.

The problems with voluntary recruitment persisted, and in March 1916 the government introduced a bill that would enable it to introduce conscription: the Military Service Act became law on

A NEW ZEALAND ECHO OF THE ANTI-GERMAN RIOTS IN ENGLAND:
THE SHOP OF A NATURALISED GERMAN, NAMED C. HEINOLD, PORK
BUTCHER, OF WANGANUI, DAMAGED BY AN EXCITED AND UNRULY
CROWD AT WANGANUI ON SATURDAY NIGHT, MAY 15.

A. E. Watkinson, Photo

The Heinold butcher's shop after the riot in 1915. *Auckland
Weekly News Supplement, 27 May 1915.* Auckland Libraries
Heritage Collections, AWNS-19150527-48-3

1 August that year. From November that year, and until the war ended, first single men, then married men without children and, finally, family men would be called up each month. Because there was now a real possibility that married men could be conscripted, many were anxious to avoid that disgrace and chose to volunteer.[34]

Mackay, aged 40, enlisted in February 1916,[35] and not in a low-key manner: newspapers across the country reported his decision and Prime Minister William Massey sent his congratulations.[36] But despite being called up in July to train as part of the Nineteenth Reinforcements,[37] Mackay did not go to camp, citing as an excuse difficulty in finding a replacement to run his legal business. When challenged again about his decision during the 1917 local body elections — the closest New Zealand came to a vote on conscription — Mackay again stood firm: 'After I volunteered, circumstances in connection with my business, and family reasons, arose which rendered it impossible for me to get away . . . I do not suppose you wish me to go into my private affairs, but my friends know the reasons which have kept me here, and those reasons do me as much credit as going to the front would have done.'[38] The family reasons to which Mackay alludes are unclear, although his third daughter, Sheila, had been born in February 1917 and his mother-in-law had died in March. His involvement with the Sarjeant Gallery may have been another factor.

Mackay's excuses for not serving did not wash with Tom Williams, who had lost the mayoralty to Mackay in 1915 and who chaired the campaigns of the two unsuccessful challengers in 1917 and 1919. 'Rather thin, quick of gait, white of hair, with appropriate moustache', Williams was a partner in the auctioneering firm Williams and Harper.[39] During the war, too old to enlist, he chaired the Wanganui Patriotic Committee. After the war had ended, in 1919, on the day of the mayoral elections, he wrote a letter to the editor of the *Chronicle* headed 'Mr Mackay and the Limelight'. 'I am opposed to shams,' he

Charles Mackay (centre) and other Whanganui businessmen, 1915. Alexander Turnbull Library, G-15993-1/1

wrote. 'Having enlisted, . . . he should not have allowed any private reasons to hold him back from where his example had induced other mothers' sons to go.'[40]

Mackay leapt to his own defence, pointing out that the mayor of a town like Whanganui 'must needs be in the limelight . . . But let me remind Mr Williams that not everyone can stand that pitiless and searching beam. It quickly exposes the weakling, the feeble and the incapable. Bustling folly and garrulous ineptitude soon shrink beneath its penetrating glare. I shall give an instance? There was a Mayor of Wanganui a few short years ago — but why pursue a painful subject further?'[41]

Williams' attack, and other critical letters, suggest that Mackay was seen as a shirker, 'perceived as withholding duty and ignoring obligation. The archetype was a caricature of the ideal male citizen, possessing poor physical, mental and moral stature.'[42] With its link to moral laxity and suspect masculinity, the 'shirker' label connects the homosexual and wartime retellings of Mackay's story. Even if his enemies did not know about his homosexuality, having sought treatment in 1914 he would have been fearful of exposure.

By the end of the war Whanganui's rapid growth was putting pressure on the council. On the surface, the town's prospects seemed rosy. A 1918 profile in a Wellington paper, proudly reprinted in the *Wanganui Chronicle* and headlined 'As Others See Us', painted a picture of seemingly unstoppable progress: 'A stranger entering Wanganui must be immediately impressed with its vigorous vitality. It is a town which throbs with life and industry . . . [It] is fast approaching the city stage, and it may be safely stated that it is one of the Dominion's prettiest and most prosperous centres . . .' Few people who really knew the place would 'predict any hesitation in the onward march'.[43]

The population had grown from 6800 in 1899, to nearly 22,000 in 1919, putting Whanganui ahead of Invercargill and making it the biggest town outside the four main cities. But by 1920, 'municipal services, such as trams, lighting, and water have been proved to be totally inadequate to meet present requirements. Loans have had to be secured to keep the town progressing, whilst rates have increased. Hostile criticism concerning municipal management developed.'[44]

The opposition to Mackay's mayoralty had begun to build much earlier, after his return to office in 1915. Some of the resentment stemmed from his ambitious and expensive projects, the tram network (and the associated power supply), the water works, the Dublin Street bridge and the Sarjeant Art Gallery; despite Sarjeant's original bequest, much more investment was required. Then there was Mackay's refusal to train for military service. He defended himself and batted away criticism, but the situation remained uncomfortable. Families were mourning lost family members and welcoming home damaged survivors, many of whom were angry about not receiving the financial support they expected during a period of economic downturn. The visit of the Prince of Wales on 3 and 4 May 1920 brought Whanganui's various simmering grievances to the surface.

When Whanganui was confirmed on the Prince's itinerary, the organising committee, headed by Mackay, proposed a programme including a civic concert and a supper party for the town's young people at the newly completed art gallery. Securing the only New Zealand concert for the Prince should have been a coup for Mackay, but things quickly unravelled. After he engaged out-of-town musical soloists, a storm of angry letters to the papers asked why local performers were not good enough for royalty. Another row erupted when temperance groups objected to a claret cup being served at the supper. But these upsets paled alongside the argument between Mackay and the soldiers.

Unhappy with its role in planning the visit, the RSA asked to be allowed to mount its own concert in the Opera House. This was

Charles Mackay (centre at rear, seated in mayoral chair) in the Wanganui
Borough Council Chamber with councillors and staff, around 1915.
Whanganui Regional Museum Photographic Collection, GG.MG.28

agreed to, but the quarrel flared up again when Mackay refused to apologise to RSA president Nelson Gordon Woods for remarks made at a council meeting held 'in committee'. The RSA banned Mackay from its concert and Mackay then withdrew permission for the RSA to use the Opera House, prompting the association to meet with the government ministers organising the royal visit. Mackay wrote to the *Wanganui Chronicle* defending his actions,[45] and the RSA's subsequent reply contained a threat:

> Mr Mackay has disqualified himself from taking the lead among returned soldiers when the Prince is present. We had hoped that it would not be necessary to refer to this, and we do not wish to publicly discuss this aspect of the question before the Prince comes to Wanganui or while he is in New Zealand ... Mr Mackay knows very well what we refer to, and if we are made to publicly explain further at this juncture, on his head will be it.[46]

The association was 'quite prepared to make an affidavit regarding certain matters which in our opinion unfit him from attending our entertainment' and, after depositing it with the court, to 'hand copies to the local papers, to be published after the Prince's departure from New Zealand, in order that the people of the town may judge whether or not we acted with due cause'.

The affidavit has never surfaced, but apparently contained 'the faithful record of a Mayoral utterance made in our presence and hearing concerning the Prince and a motor-car, supplemented by an extract from the local Press reporting a somewhat similar reference concerning His Majesty the King'.[47] Were these patriotic reasons genuine, or was the RSA also alluding to Mackay's homosexuality? Or would it have been enough for Mackay to think that they were?

Originally the Prince was to arrive in Whanganui on Friday 30 April and leave the following day, but because of a rail strike the visit was cancelled, and then reinstated, but for Monday 3 May, and leaving the next day.

There was a power cut during the civic concert, and the Prince spent barely any time at the Sarjeant Gallery supper before going to drink with the soldiers. When 1600 people rushed for the food, there was chaos. Thieves stole the food and looted the silverware belonging to the mayoress, and the royal visitor was not impressed. Writing later that night to his mistress, Freda Dudley Ward, the Prince described Whanganui's Imperial Hotel as 'a miserable hole' and the '2 ghastly concerts and a civic supper party in a marquee where there were 3,000 people!!' Then 'the hotel boilers elected to burst before dinner so no baths & a vewy nasty dinner!! But we are all pretty peeved tonight as we've really had a desperately twying day.'[48]

The problematic visit exposed Whanganui to ridicule in New Zealand and Australian newspapers. One account, published in papers in Perth, Tasmania and Melbourne under the headline 'Blunder of Party Jealousy', read: 'The concert given by the returned soldiers at the Opera House drew a crowded house but was not an artistic success. A scene was set resembling an oasis in the desert. Several performers dressed as Arabs sang old ballads such as the "Bedouin Love Song," introduced personalities and made jokes about beer. There was also some poor dancing. The concert was not an "oasis"; it resembled rather the desert itself.'[49]

Getting offside with the soldiers over the visit of the popular 'Digger' Prince was a serious misjudgement on Mackay's part. As the Prince himself noted, 'of course the most important item of this trip are the returned men & all would be over if I got wrong with them!!'[50] Mackay was also under fire from a fellow borough councillor for requesting invitations to events to welcome the Prince in Dunedin and Christchurch.

Visit of His Royal Highness the Prince of Wales to Wanganui

The Wanganui Borough Council invite

M_____

to a Supper Party to be held in the Sarjeant Gallery at 9.30 p.m. on Friday, April 30th, 1920, to meet His Royal Highness the Prince of Wales and his Staff.

C. E. MACKAY, Mayor
GEORGE MURCH.
Town Clerk

This card of invitation is not transferable, and must be shewn at the entrance.

ABOVE
The invitation to the supper party held at the Sarjeant Gallery in honour of the Prince of Wales in 1920. The date is for 30 April, the date originally scheduled for the Prince's visit to Whanganui.
Whanganui Regional Museum, 1968.89.10

LEFT
The Imperial Hotel (formerly the Newmarket Hotel) on Victoria Avenue, whose accommodation so displeased the Prince of Wales.
Whanganui Regional Museum Photographic Collection, B-H-059

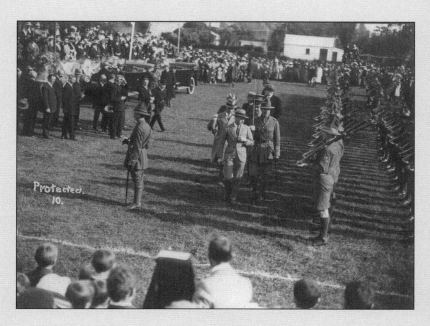

ABOVE
The Prince of Wales inspects troops during his official welcome at Cooks Gardens on 3 May 1920. Afterwards the Prince presented medals to Great War servicemen. *Whanganui Regional Museum Photographic Collection, 1970.23.2*

BELOW
Charles Mackay welcomes the Prince of Wales at Cooks Gardens. *New Zealand Free Lance, 12 May 1920, p.15*

Mackay's row with the soldiers did not end with the Whanganui visit. The day before Mackay had dinner with Cresswell and his cousin, the RSA's annual meeting heard how its president, Woods, had confronted Mackay after learning that the cars for the royal visit were to be obtained 'from a firm of alleged foreign extraction' and had asked the mayor to 'make representations to the returned soldiers'. Woods told the members that the row started when Mackay did not respond to the association's complaints about the alleged neglect of soldiers' graves in the cemetery; the mayor had also said that Woods was not a suitable person to be on the entertainment committee for the royal visit. Mackay had failed, too, to send Woods tickets to the concert. There were allegations that Mackay had 'uttered disloyal statements regarding the Prince and the King'. And Woods claimed that Mackay had published resolutions that had not been put before the council.[51]

On their own, the RSA grievances seem petty, and it is hard to understand why they might have upset Mackay so much. The criticisms make more sense when viewed in the context of a letter to the *Wanganui Herald* published in late April, just as the Prince arrived in New Zealand, which made a link between the soldiers and Mackay's enemies: 'When the whole business is analysed there is very little in it, but I guess the Returned Soldiers' Association is being used as a tool to assist in the lowering of Mr Mackay in the eyes of the ratepayers for political purposes. There are certain people in this town who have a personal grudge against Mr Mackay, and never fail to ventilate some imaginary grievance in order to "show him up".'[52]

The most prominent member of this group was mayoral aspirant Tom Williams, who epitomised the 'sound business brains' that Mackay's critics believed were required in the man occupying the mayoral chair.[53] Unlike Williams, Mackay was energetic and driven, an

Nelson Gordon Woods (centre) and his fellow members of the Wanganui RSA committee, photographed around 1920. *Alexander Turnbull Library, G-016558-1/1*

ambitious advocate for himself, his in-laws and Whanganui. He was also younger than many of the other city fathers — 44 in 1920, compared with Williams, who was 67 — and not shy about self-promotion, or being in the limelight. But Mackay's electoral dominance over his opponents had been steadily declining. In 1915 he won more votes than his two opponents combined; in 1917 he had beaten Whanganui's MP, William Andrew (Bill) Veitch, by 909 votes. In 1919, up against fellow councillor Leslie Sigley, he won by only 324 votes.

The successive controversies, culminating in the compromised and ridiculed royal visit, placed Mackay under extraordinary pressure at a time when he was trying to maintain his legal business and his roles as mayor, and as husband and father. He was also still recovering from an accident; in July 1919 his legs were injured when he was run over by a milk cart while walking along the riverbank from his home to a council meeting. The wording of his claim for £100 in damages from the driver, John Woodham, was published in Whanganui's morning paper in September; on 26 November, Mackay sued the man and won his case, though he was awarded only £50.[54] Two days later, the *Herald* published a letter from Mackay to Woodham, explaining that it was only because the *Chronicle* had published 'a mutilated form of a confidential letter dealing with a purely business matter between yourself and me' that he had felt compelled to go to court.

He did not consider that Woodham had leaked the letter. This apparent reasonableness, however, did not prevent him from asking for 'my bare out-of-pocket expenses for medical treatment and fees of Court, amounting in all to £17 18s 6d'. This claim was regarded as unfair and unreasonable. Woodham could pay the fine only by selling his horse, cart and furniture; his lawyer, Louis Cohen, urged Mackay to use his influence 'to secure footpaths for main highways, so that men . . . carrying on their business and having to drive on this or similar highways should not be in a position of incurring expense if an accident befall'.[55]

Criticism of Mackay's failure to serve his country and his poor organisation of the Prince's visit came together in an April 1920 letter to the *Chronicle* from someone signing herself 'The Mother of Digger Sons': 'What riles me is that hardly any of these naice people had sons or husbands up at the front until they were called up. Yet these are the ones who talk loudest now . . . By the way, the town seems begging about a knighthood to be given. Perhaps its [sic] to the President of the R.S.A. He fought in the Great War. I don't think any other high official did Sir.'[56]

O n 22 May, a week after the shooting, Mackay resigned as mayor. The rules allowed councillors to elect one of their own, or a resident who was not a councillor, and editorials in both Whanganui newspapers urged them to select Tom Williams, who was duly elected. James Donaldson, the councillor who nominated Williams, paid Mackay the backhanded compliment of saying that although he 'had sometimes found it necessary to oppose some of the methods of the late mayor, he would like to acknowledge the natural ability with which the latter filled his position'.[57]

Charles Mackay's political enemy Tom Williams (front row, second from right) sat next to the mayor at the Cosmopolitan Club when Prime Minister William Massey (front, centre) visited Whanganui in September 1919 to open the Sarjeant Gallery. *Alexander Turnbull Library, 1/1-016931-G*

5. MOTIVE

Was Charles Mackay framed? To answer that question it is necessary to investigate whether D'Arcy Cresswell acted alone.

In the statement dictated from his hospital bed in May 1920, D'Arcy Cresswell had described himself as a returned soldier who lived with his parents in Tīmaru. His ancestors had come to New Zealand from England in December 1850 on one of the first four ships of immigrants brought out by the Canterbury Association, which aspired to create an Anglican-based settlement that spanned all social classes, from those who could afford to buy land to agricultural labourers, domestic servants and tradespeople.

The Cresswells were firmly in the last group. Thomas Richard Marshall Cresswell, a carpenter, and his wife Jemima arrived on the *Sir George Seymour* with the first four of their 14 children, who included D'Arcy's grandfather, Robert Marshall Cresswell, who married Elizabeth Pattrick in 1862. Their son, Walter Joseph, married Hannah Reese in 1891; their third child, Walter D'Arcy, known as D'Arcy, was born in 1896.

Walter Cresswell became a successful lawyer in Christchurch and grew wealthy by speculating in property. He later farmed in Tīmaru and the family spent extended periods of time in England. When D'Arcy was 10 he was sent to board at the remote Robin Hood Bay Public School in the Marlborough Sounds, established for the sons of people who travelled 'Home'.[1] He then spent three undistinguished years, 1910–12, at Christ's College before beginning work at a Christchurch architecture firm. In mid-1914 he travelled to London to study at the Architectural Association; the following year he enlisted as a signaller with the Middlesex Regiment.

In early 1916, while serving in France, he was wounded by shrapnel and diagnosed with shell shock.[2] After convalescing in hospital, he was discharged in August 1916 from the British Expeditionary Force on the grounds of a nervous breakdown. In February 1917, 'having picked up strength and lost all nervous symptoms', Cresswell enlisted with the New Zealand Engineers.[3]

Although assessed as fit for service, he remained at the engineers' camp at Boscombe, near Christchurch in Dorset, until July 1918, when he was sent to London to work in the war records section of the New Zealand Expeditionary Force headquarters. He returned to New Zealand late in 1918, was discharged the following March and began pursuing a career as a writer. By the time he visited Whanganui, as part of a recuperative North Island tour, he had contributed pieces to English magazines and was working on a historical romance for an English publisher.[4]

The shadowy cousin who introduced Cresswell to Mackay may have been a son of D'Arcy's uncle, Charles Marshall Cresswell, and his wife, Eleanor Mary, who lived in Whanganui. They had been drawn to the town by the meat industry, a major contributor to the booming local economy. In 1891 D'Arcy's grandfather, Robert Cresswell, became the manager of the newly established Wanganui Freezing Works at Castlecliff, near the mouth of the Whanganui River. He left after three years, but in 1893 his son Charles returned from Australia and he then managed the works for over 30 years.

Charles Cresswell, like Mackay, was active in public life. He chaired the Castlecliff Town Board from its formation in 1911 until 1918, and was involved with both the Castlecliff and Wanganui Tramway boards. The two men also had a shared interest in racehorse breeding and freemasonry.

The lives of Charles and Eleanor Cresswell and their family were utterly changed by the Great War and they were still deeply traumatised in May 1920. Their second son, Jack Tennison, was killed on 12 October 1917 in the attack on Bellevue Spur at Passchendaele, as was another Cresswell cousin, Gordon Hallam Cresswell, and Sarjeant Gallery designer Donald Hosie.[5] In her scrapbook, Eleanor recorded her inconsolable grief over the loss of her favourite son: 'A great piece

ABOVE
Montage of photographs of Wanganui Borough Council
councillors, officers and the town wharves. Charles
Mackay is centre front. *New Zealand Graphic, 9 February
1910, Auckland Libraries Heritage Collections*

BELOW
The freezing works at Castlecliff, Whanganui, photographed
by Alfred Martin around 1892. *Whanganui Regional
Museum Photographic Collection, 1802.3889*

of my life seems to have gone.' Charles Mackay was the Cresswell's family lawyer: he had prepared Jack Cresswell's will and so would have known D'Arcy's relations.

Jack was last seen by a family friend with blood pouring from his mouth; his body was never found. From 1918 until days before she died in 1946, Eleanor wrote to him on every anniversary of his death and on his birthday. On 18 March 1939, she wrote: 'I have often been asked "Why do you always wear black?" I just say I have not worn colours since 1917. The colour went out then.'[6] Charles and Eleanor's youngest son, William Free, known as Free, had signed up to serve in the army but was too young to be sent overseas.

Eleanor's love for her sons did not extend to one of her daughters, Nella, whom she described in 1944 as 'her father's daughter a Cresswell. Free is my loved son . . . Jack was my loved boy too, very much like Free. True kind gentle, has sympathy and understanding. Not so much for the £sd as the Cresswells, which was first with them. The very name I dislike. How I have been hurt by more than one Cresswell.'[7]

This bitter, spiteful tone is a striking contrast to the tenor of the rest of her writing in the scrapbook. Was her scorn for 'the Cresswells' directed at her husband or at D'Arcy?[8] Or at whichever son introduced D'Arcy to Charles Mackay in May 1920? There are only two possibilities: Free, who would have been 21 in 1920, and his older brother, Roland Marshall Cresswell, who was also known as Ronald.[9] Eleanor's praise for Free makes him an unlikely candidate, especially as he was three years younger than D'Arcy. That leaves Roland, who was 30 in 1920.

Roland volunteered in 1915 and was wounded in France. Of his three and a half years' service overseas, he spent a total of six months at the front and 198 days in hospital.[10] An appeal in 1918 by Charles Cresswell to the Military Service Board for Roland to be returned from his second term of service was unsuccessful,[11] and he came home in 1919 and was discharged from the army as medically unfit.

LEFT
D'Arcy Cresswell's uncle, freezing works manager and Castlecliff politician Charles Marshall Cresswell. *Alexander Turnbull Library, Who's Who in Wanganui, 1915. B-K-1440-18_detail*

LEFT
Jack Tennison Cresswell, Charles Marshall and Eleanor Cresswell's son and D'Arcy Cresswell's cousin, who was killed in action at Bellevue Spur, Passchendaele, in 1917. *Auckland Weekly News, 29 November 1917, Auckland Libraries Heritage Collections*

He ended up running the farm his father had intended as a wedding present for Jack. Like so many veterans, Roland did not talk to his family about the war, but one of his sons remembers overhearing him describing a grisly reconnaissance mission on the battlefield. After hearing German voices, Roland dived into a water-filled shell hole where he slid over rotting corpses; he still stank days later. Stories like this help to explain family memories of the happy-go-lucky man who was never the same when he returned.[12]

D'Arcy and his Cresswell cousins exemplified the 'other mothers' sons' who Tom Williams said were induced to go to war by Mackay's 'sham' example of enlisting. It is plausible that Mackay's enemies, if they knew about his homosexuality, saw an opportunity to recruit members of a family seriously damaged by the war.

There are a number of different ways this could have happened, perhaps even simultaneously. As historian Bill Mitchell has speculated (see Chapter 12), D'Arcy Cresswell might have been used by Mackay's enemies, via Roland who, as a returned soldier, was possibly an RSA member. Famous for being short of money later in his life, Cresswell could have blackmailed Mackay on behalf of, and paid by, the mayor's enemies.

Another possibility is that Cresswell took it upon himself to blackmail Mackay as part of a moral crusade. Perhaps he had heard about Mackay's homosexuality from his family in Whanganui and decided to act. The presence of his cousin at the initial meetings with Mackay suggests his local relations were involved in some way. It is not impossible, either, that Cresswell was trying, out of self-loathing, to deny his own homosexuality by punishing another homosexual; he would not be the first to lash out in such a way. Perhaps Cresswell was being blackmailed by people who threatened to reveal *his* homosexuality unless he agreed to blackmail the mayor.

The other interesting possibility was that Cresswell was trying to save a young man mentioned in a 1965 letter to Helen Shaw, who was editing a collection of Cresswell's correspondence. The writer was Charles Carrington, a Christ's College classmate who kept in touch with Cresswell throughout his life.

> I first heard of the Wanganui adventure in a letter from my mother, some time in 1920 . . . I was interested in the physical adventure, which, no doubt, you can reconstruct from the newspapers. All I recall of the motive is that Darcy had a young friend ('Ronnie'?) who had fallen into the clutches of the Mayor who 'had a bad influence on him.' Darcy threatened the Mayor. If he would not break his association with 'Ronnie'(?), Darcy would expose him. The Mayor then asked Darcy to his private office for a discussion, shot him with a revolver, and tried to frame it as a suicide. I'm extremely vague about this, and I expect that Darcy was deliberately vague with me, perhaps deceptive.[13]

It seems unlikely that this was Roland/Ronald Cresswell, who was too old to fit Carrington's description. Shaw may have thought that the young friend was Ronald Alexander Cuthbert, who had also been at Christ's College with Cresswell and had remained in Christchurch, becoming a solicitor in 1919. In his memoir, *The Poet's Progress*, Cresswell described Cuthbert as 'Ronald, my greatest friend'.[14] As part of her research, Shaw contacted Cuthbert, who wrote to her in 1966:

> Could you send me a copy of the newspaper account — best of all a newspaper cutting — [telling?] about the Wanganui [murder?] as narrated before [I think] Robert Stout. D [D'Arcy] on one occasion did tell me at some length of that incident but before writing about what D [told?] me, I would like to read at least the 'Press Association' account of what happened. Failing

that, perhaps you can mention what you yourself have already learnt and its source and give me particulars of the press [accounts] of the trial.[15]

It seems significant that Cresswell chose to recount the story of the shooting to a friend 'at some length'. Perhaps Cuthbert was checking what Shaw knew, especially given that, in 1966, the details he mentioned were not well known. There is no evidence that Cuthbert, who was 28 in 1920, was ever based in Whanganui, but Mackay may have known him from visits to Christchurch.[16] It is not clear whether Shaw heard back from Cuthbert, who died in 1967.

No one knows exactly how Cresswell became aware of Mackay's homosexuality, and why he had an interest in the mayor resigning. Perhaps Cresswell was fearful of the consequences of accepting his own sexuality. His statement has led many to assume that Mackay's homosexuality was revealed because of something that occurred between the two men. But information that emerged in 1926, not long after Mackay had been released from prison, suggests something quite different.

A dolescent males were having sex with adult men, sometimes for money, in New Zealand cities and rural areas as far back as the early twentieth century.[17] These lads tended to be labourers and shop assistants or, as in a scandalous 1889 British case known as the Cleveland Street affair, messenger boys.[18] Evidence has emerged that Mackay was involved in this subculture.

When Mackay was released from Mount Eden Prison in 1926, after serving only six years of his 15-year sentence, the accompanying storm of controversy led the justice minister to demand that the Prisons Board justify its decision. The board's report, published in newspapers across the country, included a summary of Mackay's case that mentioned allegations of homosexual behaviour in a much more explicit manner than Cresswell's 1920 statement: 'It appeared . . . that Cresswell had discovered that Mackay had been guilty of indecent practices with young men, that he had interviewed Mackay on the subject on several occasions, and that he had insisted upon Mackay resigning from his position as Mayor or otherwise he would expose him.'[19]

This suggested that Mackay's homosexual activities allegedly involved young men, and not 24-year-old Cresswell. In 1920 Cresswell did not refer directly to Mackay's alleged immoral activities but instead wrote of 'dirty intentions', 'qualities' and 'a certain disgusting feature in Mr Mackay's character', which were framed in his statement, and by Mackay's lawyer, as a medical complaint that meant Mackay was unable to control his urges.

Not long after the report appeared, an unrelated court case in Auckland may have shed some light on the 'indecent practices with young men' mentioned by the Prisons Board. In 1927 Gordon William McNamara was charged with indecent assault after a farmer to whom he spoke in an Auckland urinal reported him to the police. McNamara, a 21-year-old draper's assistant, had come to Auckland in 1922, having also lived in Whanganui.[20] He was questioned by a detective, who said the farmer had described McNamara as a 'queen'. When the detective asked if he had been accosted before, McNamara said several suggestions had been made to him and 'Charlie Mackie was the man that was mentioned at the time'. It is not possible to be definitive, but Mackay's surname was pronounced 'Mackie' and he was sometimes known as 'Charlie'.[21] If McNamara *was* referring to Mackay, did he perhaps feel it was safe to use his name because he was already in prison?

The other man McNamara mentioned to the police in connection with homosexuality was Theodore Trezise, whom he had known in Whanganui. 'I was in the Operatic Society there. I told the police that.

Nothing happened in the dressing room in Wanganui. I asked him [Trezise] about some joke that was going on in the dressing room. It was through that that I first had any idea that anything like this handling [of] men went on.'[22]

Trezise was born in England in 1883 but grew up in Wellington. A talented entertainer, from 1910 he worked in theatrical productions in England, later performing in such major venues as Covent Garden and the Hippodrome. When war broke out, Trezise served as a sapper until he was wounded at Gallipoli. He was then transferred to the Divisional Entertainers, where he excelled as a director and performer. After returning to New Zealand in 1918, Trezise became well known as a dancing teacher and cabaret owner. He was one of the earliest 'evangelists for jazz dancing', which brought him to Whanganui.[23]

If McNamara's testimony can be believed — and it needs to be remembered that he was trying to fend off a charge of indecent conduct — Trezise was also introducing younger men around the country to same-sex pleasures.[24] If 'Charlie Mackie' was indeed Charles Mackay, and if he did meet him, the boy would not have been much older than 14.

It is important to emphasise that before decriminalisation in 1986, 'homosexual' referred to all males who preferred their own sex, whether adults or adolescents. As social historian Chris Brickell has argued, 'The twenty-first-century category of male homosexuality is not timeless. Indeed, the "pervert" of the 1920s and the "homosexual" of the mid-1940s, as they were understood by those involved in the legal process, are quite different people from the gay man of today. The relative ages of the sexual partners are an important part of that variation.'[25]

If Mackay and other men in Whanganui were having sex with adolescents, this would have been regarded as completely unfit for public discussion. It is possible that this is why both Whanganui papers obeyed the request from Mackay's lawyer not to publish 'statements obtained from outside individuals'. This did not stop the press from outside the town, however. In an editorial published shortly after Mackay was sentenced, the *Patea & Waverley Press*, which covered the area north of Whanganui, suggested that 'the public should not overlook . . . the service rendered to the community by the young man Cresswell who courageously took it upon himself to remove a deadly cancerous growth that had unhappily taken root, in the neighbouring town'. The article confirmed that there was a determined effort to get rid of Mackay.

> There were probably others that knew of the existence of the evil in their midst and the part played by the chief actor who is now paying the penalty, but not having the proofs that young Cresswell apparently had, had to be content with a vigorous and unrelenting campaign of hostility towards the culprit in the hope that he would take a hint and retire from public life. Instead of doing so he brazened things out until the crash came and the campaign of righteous hostility was for a long time regarded by many as a persecution. They are wiser now. Everything, somehow, comes to those who wait and those who fight in a good cause.[26]

The *New Zealand Times*, too, hinted at homosexual activity in the town, not only involving Mackay. In a short article published on 6 July 1920, and reprinted in many other papers, the newspaper's special correspondent reported that 'additional information was secured by Cresswell consequent on his discoveries in connection with the first case, and though no information under this detail has been published, it is understood that certain people have shaken the dust of Wanganui off their feet'.[27]

Writing to a friend from prison in 1920, Mackay described himself as having been 'pinched', slang for being caught or arrested.[28] A retired lawyer who worked with a colleague of Donald McBeth was told that Mackay was set up as a fall guy and carried the can for 'a little coven of gays'.[29] This chimes with his daughter Josephine Duncan's belief that her father was part of a group of men involved in molesting boys at a Whanganui secondary school, and this was why he was arrested.[30]

Although there is no sure evidence that sex took place between younger and older men in Whanganui, there were strong suggestions that it was happening, which may explain Mackay's odd and irregular endorsement of Cresswell's unsigned statement: 'as far as it relates to my own acts & deeds I admit the statement to be substantially true'. This left open the possibility that Cresswell was not telling the whole truth, and that other people may have been involved in homosexual practices. By adding his endorsement, Mackay avoided any further questioning on this subject, and may have protected others.

When the Prisons Board said Cresswell had discovered that Mackay had been guilty of indecent practices with young men, it was relying on a second statement, written by Cresswell 'some two years after he was wounded'.[31] By then Cresswell was living in Europe, and it is interesting to consider why he was asked, or offered, to write this statement, which has never come to light, and whether it was a factor in the board's decision to release Mackay from prison early. Remorse may also have been a factor: according to the poet Kevin Ireland, Cresswell later told the writer Frank Sargeson that he felt terrible about what had happened in Whanganui.[32]

Mackay's inmate file contains a possible clue about how the statement came to be written. About 19 February 1922, he wrote to a family friend, Jean Frame, who had just left on a trip to London and Europe: 'Jeannie [Mackay's sister] told me of your kind reference to me in your letter & how you had seen Archie Blair & meant to see

Cresswell. I can't tell you how grateful I am to you for all your kindness.'

Archibald Blair was a leading defence lawyer who had been at Wellington College with Mackay. If Frame, after talking with Blair, met Cresswell in London, this was perhaps how the additional statement was obtained. That would fit with a reference in Mackay's inmate file to a letter he received from D'Arcy Cresswell on 27 April 1922.[33] Blair is also mentioned in an earlier letter from Mackay in February of that year to his sister Jean: 'I had a very nice letter from [brother] Frank, & was pleased with what he said about Blair. I quite understand that I shall have to wait patiently, & am fully prepared to do so.'[34]

Whether the second Cresswell statement included an account of what was happening in Whanganui at the time of the shooting remains unclear, but it must have differed from the first. Perhaps it included more detail. The board was silent on whether it referred to men having sex with youths, but it did mention another aspect of the statement: when the two men had their final meeting in Whanganui, Mackay was in a state of 'anguish and hysteria' and 'his mind was unbalanced'. That description may explain this conclusion from the Prisons Board report: 'It seems clear, from a perusal of the evidence, that the crime was not premeditated, but was, as stated by the Chief Justice in passing sentence, "an impulsive act".'[35] This is the opposite to what Stout, who was at the Prisons Board meeting that considered Mackay's case, had said in 1920.[36]

Author, novelist and biographer Hector Bolitho, who as a boy was mentored by Mackay, wrote about his friend in a book of recollections, published in 1935:

It was strange that he should have chosen the pomp of being mayor of his town, for he was a scholar and more at home with his books and his pen than among by-laws and foundation stones. There was one dark streak in his character which brought him to law-breaking in the end and then to imprisonment. He was dragged from his mayoral chair and from the cultivated air of his library and desk, to be flung into gaol.[37]

It initially seems odd that Bolitho, who left New Zealand because of his own homosexuality, should write of a 'dark streak' in Mackay's character. But if he was alluding to Mackay having sex with youths, the words make more sense. Bolitho may have been differentiating his own sexual preferences from Mackay's.

At the same time, it is important to remember that Mackay was charged with the attempted murder of a man, not a youth. The 'dark streak' could also have been the violence in his personality that caused him to draw a gun on Cresswell and shoot him. No evidence has emerged of any charges or cases related to his homosexuality, but the allegations of relations with 'young men' suggests a subtext that was clearly in people's minds at the time — including his wife's, who initially included sodomy as a ground for divorce (see Chapter 13). The references to Mackay and younger men could also explain the enforced silence and erasures in Whanganui after he was found guilty.

Auckland's Mount Eden Prison, viewed from the foot of Boston Road. *Auckland Libraries Heritage Collections, 7-A17670*

6. PRISON

On Thursday 3 June 1920, exactly one month after welcoming the Prince of Wales to Whanganui, Charles Mackay arrived at Mount Eden Prison in Auckland. The photograph taken the next day shows him wearing an undershirt and a worn jacket. His formerly well-kept walrus moustache has been shaved off, his face is covered in stubble and his once close-cropped hair is longer and unkempt.[1] At first glance, the image may seem to show a broken man, as in many ways he was, but in his gaze it is possible to read other emotions. There is determination there — he is not defeated by his change in fortune — and there is also, surely, some relief.

He was coming to a very tough place. As a controller-general of prisons wrote in 1926, 'The smell, Godstrewth, I can remember it to this day! Of human bodies, it was dreadful. Stink of unwashed sweat and all that sort of damn thing … you go into a cell, find a little window looking up to the sky and a concrete floor. You'd just think you were in your tomb. It was dreadful.'[2]

For any inmate in a New Zealand prison in these years, letters were a lifeline. Mackay, with his educated background and family support, used them to reach people, and bring the world — in the form of magazines, books and newspapers — to his cell. In 1920, a hard labour prisoner could receive and send two letters within one week from the date of their conviction, and then one letter every eight weeks — provided their conduct and industry had been good in the preceding month.[3] Shortly after he arrived at Mount Eden, the restriction on the number of letters Mackay could send and receive via his mother and siblings was removed. This let him get letters to others he was not allowed to correspond with: his family (mostly his main correspondent, his sister Jean) would pass these on and act on his requests. Once the rules were changed in 1925, Mackay was permitted five letters a month.

Prison regulations also governed the content of letters, all of which went through the hands of the gaoler or controlling officer. Prisoners

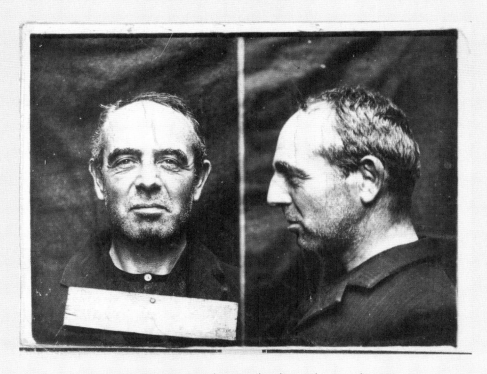

Charles Mackay's prison photograph, taken on his arrival at Mount
Eden and showing how far he had fallen, from mayor to convict.
Archives New Zealand, J, Acc W2636, 1920/31121

were not allowed to communicate with their friends concerning 'any matter happening within the prison or . . . connected with the discipline of the prison or the treatment of prisoners'.[4] Fourteen of Mackay's letters that did not comply — presumably because they contained descriptive detail about daily prison life — were not sent but retained in his inmate file. The prison's correspondence registers list around a thousand letters written and received over the time he was imprisoned.

Peppered with Mackay's sharp wit and wry observations, his letters are entertaining and personable. This one, written in December 1920 to a friend, Sir Graeme Sinclair-Lockhart, who inherited a British baronetcy from his father in 1918 and was known as a man about town, is typical of the tone:

> This is the biggest jail in N.Z., & it is mainly for longtimers like myself, & 'dogacters' (habitual criminals). We are a pretty rough lot, but you know I always had a great capacity for making friends . . . we are made fairly comfortable in here, each having a decent cell & plenty of blankets. The food is fair tho' pretty monotonous, & of course a man misses milk & butter. We get a weekly ration of tobacco, but it is so strong that I can't smoke it, & in self-defence have had to learn to chew.
>
> We get up at 6.30, work from 8 to 5, when we are locked up, lights out . . . Altogether, we don't do bad, altho' we don't exactly encourage each other with merry shouts as we bend over our tasks.[5]

Empathy and concern for others is a recurring theme; it is easy to see how Mackay was repeatedly returned as mayor, and had a reputation as a defence lawyer who would take on apparently hopeless cases. He writes about the books, magazines and newspapers he was able to receive in prison and which, for someone so literate, and with such an active and energetic mind, must have been sustaining. The range and breadth of his interests is evident, too.

What is most remarkable about the letters is their optimistic and positive tone. Very rarely does Mackay express sadness or self-pity. 'The great thing,' he told Sinclair-Lockhart, 'is always to fix your mind on the coming Saturday, when you get your weekly shave & hot bath, your weekly set of clean clothes, & your mail. The Saturday shave out in the big yard is quite the social event of the week.'[6]

On Sundays prisoners had to go to chapel for divine service, taken by clergy who were not always very tactful. 'We get different ones nearly every Sunday. A few weeks ago one of them gave out the hymn "For those in peril <u>on the sea</u>." I heard one old chap near me mutter, "<u>I</u>'d chance it, Hallelujah!" Another read us the parable about the man that <u>fell among thieves</u>. That <u>did</u> hurt. However, the weekly service is a great & enjoyable break, & does a lot of good.'[7]

Sometimes, though, his tone was plaintive, especially regarding his wife and daughters, who do not appear to have written or visited during the entire time he was in prison. As he told his sister Jean in December 1920, 'I cannot tell you how it cheers a man up when people stick to him. I am sleeping a good deal better now, but I cannot tell you how I am worrying over not seeing the children.' A letter in February 1922 revealed how little he knew about his family's lives — 'I was terribly pleased to get all that news about the children, & specially pleased that Beth is going back to Woodford House.'

But in April that year he wrote to his friend and fellow lawyer, Donald McBeth, whom he called Mac, 'I don't want to trouble you, but if you could write again & let me have some news of my children, I can't tell you how pleased I should be, or even about Belle God knows I tried to be a good father. I haven't even had a photo of them.'[8]

Mackay wrote to his siblings to request items of all kinds — 'I hope you will send me the dental floss I spoke of. My teeth, as a matter of

Dear Jeannie, Your letter arrived yesterday, & I was very glad to hear from you, and to know that it was pressure of business that had prevented your writing earlier. I was afraid it might have been ill health. Many thanks for the newspaper cuttings, which were most interesting to me. A large bundle of Century Magazines also came to hand, & I look forward with great pleasure to going through them. "Java Head" is one of the best novels I have read for a long time, & the other prisoners like it very much. As far as the Budgets are concerned, they have arrived all right, but there was some delay over censoring them. Just at present the staff is a little shorthanded, & the jail is exceptionally full. Your letters to Cunningham & Charlie Holt reached them all right, & I had a very kind letter from Cunningham & a long letter from Charlie, accompanied by two photos of himself, one in character. Did I tell you that Archdeacon Hawkins called to see me on Sunday last, & spent quite a time with me? He is a very fine man, & has charge of the district north of Auckland. That prayerbook you sent me is just the thing for church. To-day, Sunday, is a lovely day, & I couldn't help thinking of what it would be like down the harbour. By the way, would you please drop a line to Mrs Oliver, Marton, & say I was pleased to hear the case had gone so well. All last week they have been very busy with the Prisons Board here. It sits once a year, & interviews all habitual criminals & reformative men, and decides which are to be liberated. Both Mr Edmanson & Alastair Campbell are coming up in Xmas week, & I am looking forward to seeing them. I cannot tell you how it cheers a man up when people stick to him. I am sleeping a good deal better now, but I cannot tell you how I am worrying over not seeing the children. I feel sure Lizzie did all she could. Now that the interest is going up, I am pleased that you & Frank have been getting in Father's mortgages, as no doubt you will be getting a higher rate. With regard to Esperanto, on the other side of this I am writing a postscript, which please forward to Mr. A. A. Grace, Nelson. I think the idea is a good one, & hope you do too. Much love to all at home, & best wishes for Xmas. I mustn't forget to tell you that Jea. Cook was terribly pleased with your letter.

Your affectionate brother,
C. R. Mackay

A page from a letter from Charles Mackay to his sister Jeannie (Margaret Jean Mackay), around 19 December 1920. Unsent, it was retained in his inmate file. *Archives New Zealand, ACGS 17313 2194* fact, keep very well. Prisoners have a mania for getting false teeth & they are always asking me what dentist made mine & what he charged for them.'[9] Reading matter was always central: 'You ask me how I am off for books,' he wrote to his sister in January 1922. 'Very well, thank you, but if you could get me <u>paper-covered</u> copies of Huckleberry Finn & the memoirs of Constantine Dix (Barry Payn) [Pain] I should be grateful; but mind, <u>paperbacks only</u> however, there is one book I should very much like to have. It is the Fourth Dimension Simply Explained; you will see it in the enclosed advt.'[10]

'I have just finished reading the Inferno and the Purgatory in Carey's translation,' he told McBeth in April 1922, '& enjoyed it very much there is a calm hopeful beauty about the Purgatory that I don't know anything similar to. The Inferno suffered from the fact that I had just been rereading the Paradise Lost, which makes Dante's hell very cheap, except in a few passages, like Farinata's appearance.'[11]

By that time, Mackay had so many books that he successfully requested additional shelving in his cell. He bound magazines into volumes, and was given permission to receive the *Times* in intact form, without any paragraphs or portions cut or blotted out; normally, newspapers could only be supplied to prisoners minus the racing and court reports. 'I do enjoy that paper immensely,' he told Jean. 'There is a man in here whose father is an MP & he is anxiously waiting for the next one to see if his name is in the honours list. He is a great friend of mine & I am glad to say he goes out in a month or so … I cannot tell you how much I appreciate the London Times.'[12]

Given the restrictions on any newspapers, it is remarkable that Mackay was permitted to have a British paper. Perhaps this was a sign of his assertiveness and class. It was an improvement on the previous year: in April 1921 he was disciplined for being part of a group caught trying to hide a copy of the *New Zealand Herald*.[13]

n October 1920 Mackay began corresponding with Blanche Baughan, an acclaimed poet and prose writer who had turned her attention to prison reform. In March 1921 she was appointed as an official prison visitor at Addington Reformatory for Women in Christchurch, and allowed to write to prisoners at other institutions. '[A]bout five feet, two inches in height, with keen brown eyes, a very straight back and a resolute and searching presence',[14] Baughan was an effective advocate, who used newspapers skilfully to raise awareness of prison conditions.

An interview with Baughan in the *Auckland Star* early in 1922 prompted Thomas Vincent, the Mount Eden superintendent, to write to the head of the prison service, concerned that the interview gave the impression 'that the individual prisoner does not receive any benefit at the hands of the Prison Officers during his period of confinement, and that any benefit derived is solely at the hands of "Interested Parties" outside'. He clearly, however, respected her abilities: 'Miss Baughan is the only Woman I have dealt with who appears to have the necessary penetrating power for character building.'[15]

When Baughan met Mackay at Mount Eden in February 1922 the encounter went well, as Mackay wrote to Jean Frame: 'Miss Baughan was here last week, & I had an interview with her. She is a splendid woman, & it cheered me up a lot. The government now allows her to see prisoners in private, which of course is much pleasanter.'[16]

It is not surprising that the pair got on. Both were highly educated, articulate and forceful advocates. Baughan had a genuine concern for underdogs, 'life's flotsam' — the same people Mackay had defended as a lawyer. Both had written for the *Sydney Bulletin*, Mackay before he moved to Whanganui. He was still in prison when Baughan and others founded a New Zealand branch of the Howard League for Penal Reform in 1924. As well as visiting prisoners, Baughan would write letters on their behalf and she also did this for Mackay.

Prison reform campaigner and writer Blanche Baughan and her dog, around 1940. *Alexander Turnbull Library, PAColl-6289-1*

An unsent letter from Charles Mackay to Blanche Baughan, dated around 3 December 1925. The underlined text perhaps explains why this letter was censored and not sent: matters concerning the discipline or treatment of prisoners were not allowed to be mentioned in letters. *Archives New Zealand, ACGS 17313 R21948783*

Baughan wrote about Mackay in her 1936 book, *People in Prison*. Despite her use of pseudonyms for people and places — for example, Dominia is New Zealand — it is possible to spot Mackay, whom Baughan called Eteocles, the son of the Greek hero Oedipus. She quoted another prisoner, 'Cratinus', who pointed out that prisoners were 'deprived of all that is best in life . . . If we could realise that our sentences were just, we would willingly bear our punishment, but in very many cases of our kind no thought is taken by our Judges of the good — great good in many cases — we have done in our lives in other ways . . .' This, she continued,

> was especially true of the hapless *Eteocles*, who had fought for years against his passions, enlisting all the medical help available, and had been kind to every fellow-creature he met, because of the real pleasure he took in giving help. He had filled various useful posts with conspicuous success but, through 'inversion,' he had finally to meet exposure, disgrace and prison. 'Ubi lapsus? Quid feci?' [Where have I erred? What have I done?] he wrote, in bewilderment and despair. 'I ask myself these questions night and day, and can find no answer to them.'[17]

Just as Treadwell had done in court, Baughan used the medical model to argue that Mackay's homosexuality was the reason he had shot D'Arcy Cresswell.

In September 1920, after a hearing presided over by Sir Robert Stout, Mackay was struck off the roll of barristers and solicitors.[18] He also declared himself bankrupt. His estate was complicated, requiring considerable investigation, and a meeting of creditors was told that 'things were more or less in a state of chaos'.[19] Writing from Mount Eden to the deputy official assignee, E. M. Silk, Mackay reported that the public trustee had said his trust account was not in order: 'This came to a great surprise and shock to me.'[20] It was difficult for the official assignee, who handled bankruptcies and insolvencies, to work out how much Mackay's business was worth without his help.

Rather than transferring the case to Auckland, the Justice Department officials decided to bring Mackay back to Whanganui, but Silk worried that the town lacked the expertise to handle the case. He also explained that he was not the only one who did not want Mackay back:

> Yesterday I had occasion to visit Mrs. Mackay, (who has now assumed her maiden name of Duncan) and she requested me to endeavour to so arrange matters that it would not be necessary to bring the bankrupt to Wanganui.
>
> She expressed herself very strongly on the subject, and appeared to be very distressed at the prospect of Mr. Mackay being brought to Wanganui.
>
> It is impossible to wind up the estate satisfactorily without the assistance of bankrupt, but suggest that in view of the position of Mrs. Duncan, it might be advisable to have the bankruptcy transferred to Auckland.[21]

Silk and Isobel Mackay did not prevail, and Mackay spent about a fortnight in Whanganui, helping to clear up his business affairs. This enabled the process of winding up his estate to continue and he was eventually discharged from his bankruptcy in 1923. Blanche Baughan described his feelings about this experience: 'Once he was taken, on transfer, not in prison garb, I am glad to say, through the very district that once he had faithfully served; many prisoners would have welcomed the journey as a "change," but to one of his sensitiveness it was the worst of possible tortures. I often had occasion to fear for Eteocles' brain.'[22]

Baughan's accounts of Mackay in prison are vivid and moving. In her vignettes, a different picture emerges — of a man hurt and suffering, but resilient. She recounts the experience he described to her of meeting an organ-grinder, in Whanganui, who was an American Civil War veteran and did not know how to draw his pension in New Zealand. Mackay 'did what was necessary for him and he went his way'. The two men had another encounter, which Mackay described in a letter to Baughan:

> I had been (in prison) at Quidquid [Mount Eden] about six months when I got a letter from him to say that he was again in Dominia, that he hadn't forgotten me, and that the first fine evening he would be on the street outside the gaol to serenade me. Sure enough, a few nights later, I heard an old barrel-organ breaking into the opening bars of the 'Blue Danube,' and realised that my old friend was doing the Blondel act outside my cell. I can assure you I felt more at peace than I had for long enough, both with myself and human nature.[23]

Mackay was perhaps fortunate to arrive at Mount Eden during a period of penal reform and a more enlightened approach to incarceration. This was led by Charles Matthews, who became Inspector of Prisons in 1913 and later headed the Prisons Department until his death in 1924, and had introduced radical changes and improvements to the prison system, not all of which were popular with staff.

Matthews was an idealist who championed the 'new method' introduced by justice minister Sir John Findlay in 1910. This was a radical departure from the 1880–1909 regime led by Captain Arthur

Charles Matthews, the reforming head of the Prisons Department from 1917 until his death in 1924. When his title became 'Controller-General of Prisons', staff dubbed Matthews the 'Armchair General'. *Alexander Turnbull Library, 1/2-065372-F*

Hume, who believed that prisons should be 'places to be dreaded'.[24] In a 1923 speech, Matthews contrasted his philosophy with Hume's punitive approach: 'In more recent times we have quite a different definition of the purpose of imprisonment: it is that men "are punished by being sent to prison; they are not punished while in prison".' For Matthews, plenty of hard work, provided it was interesting and productive, was the 'very best reformative agent'.

Alongside this, he encouraged study, 'mental pabulum', particularly for more educated prisoners. Matthews also improved prison libraries, extended the time for lighting cells from 8 to 9 p.m., and introduced other measures designed to help a man 'retain his full mental and moral vigour through a long term of imprisonment'.[25] These changes were a boon for Mackay, who was probably one of Mount Eden's best-educated prisoners during his years there. He was given a job in the prison library, which he found 'fairly congenial & not so monotonous as most jail work'.[26]

Thanks to Matthews, prisons also provided educational and recreational facilities and 'concerts, classes, lectures and films'.[27] Mount Eden was the first to start a debating society and ran a class in the so-called universal language, Esperanto, which had been created in 1887. Promoted to increase international understanding after the Great War, it was used in more than 100 countries in the 1920s, including New Zealand. Esperanto clubs were dotted throughout the nation, and the language was taught in schools and approved for use in telegrams.

When Mackay arrived at Mount Eden, the Esperanto class was run by Arthur Roberts, the protagonist in a sensational murder trial in 1909. When he was 21, Roberts was tried for the murder of Alice Newman, a waitress at a Christchurch restaurant. Roberts had been in a relationship with Newman and grew angry when she became involved with other men. When delivering its guilty verdict, the jury 'added its grave doubts as to whether at the time of committing the crime Roberts was capable of understanding the nature and quality of his act and made a strong recommendation for mercy'.[28]

Despite this, he was sentenced to death, triggering a public outcry, and petitions and prayers calling for clemency. Prime Minister Joseph Ward said Roberts was not possessed of normal mental and physical faculties. Medical evidence, in the eugenic language of the day, suggested Roberts 'was physically, morally, and mentally what was generally described as a degenerate to proofs of inherited tendencies'. The Governor, Lord Plunket, reprieved Roberts' death sentence on 29 November 1909.

This case had been avidly followed by newspaper readers across the country, including Mackay, who described Roberts in a letter as 'my greatest pal here'.[29] Perhaps as a result of this friendship Mackay became an Esperanto enthusiast, urging his friends outside prison to take up the language as a hobby: '[Y]ou can learn it easily in 3 months, & it has a big literature, all sorts of curious Russian, Polish, Czech & other mid-European works being translated into it . . . I have set myself to translate a series of the purple patches of English prose — Burke's Marie Antoinette etc, — which I believe would take well on the Continent, & which I hope to publish later on.'[30]

Mackay was also keen to do some more local translation, as he told his sister:

> I well remember Mr Grace's stories of Maori Life & Legend [Alfred Grace's *Folktales of the Maori*], as they appeared in the Press, & believe that if translated into Esperanto they would meet with a ready sale. The war has focused attention on the Maori race, & Esperanto numbers millions of adherents in France, Germany, Switzerland & Poland, who belong to the educated classes & would be attracted by a little book giving an authentic account of their life & traditions . . . I should be willing to do the necessary translation, if Mr Grace would care to make the venture, & if it were a success, would be content

with a nominal fee for translation. Possibly, the government might be induced, in view of the wide public to be appealed to, to subsidise the book with an advertisement.[31]

After Roberts was released in March 1921, Mackay took over the teaching of the Esperanto class at Mount Eden. Matthews must have been impressed; in May he granted Mackay's request to continue this role and wrote to the prison superintendent: 'In view of the fact that Mackay is of superior education I shall be glad if you will see whether or not it is possible for him to teach the Esperanto students some other language or subject as well, so that the scope of his work may be enlarged.'[32] Mackay, who had studied French at Wellington College, was allowed to write to a French master in Whanganui, with one letter out of three sent to Wellington for translation, 'in order to have some sort of check on the correspondence'.[33]

Matthews seemed to hold Mackay in higher regard than did Vincent and the other Mount Eden officers. When forwarding Mackay's application to teach the Esperanto class, Vincent wrote that although he was only too pleased to do what was good for this prisoner, he was 'rather suspicious' of his request, 'for he appears to have lost a great deal of his self respect, and under the circumstances, I prefer many old time prisoners' sense of honour to that of Mackay's'.[34] The superintendent gave no further detail, but the withering comment suggested Mackay was having a rough time.

In July 1921 Vincent baulked at a suggestion that Mackay, who had been struck off, be allowed to provide a legal opinion for W. L. Edmanson, 'the father of Esperanto in Wellington': 'if I were to grant permission for a reply I would practically be making a precedent for this prisoner to act as a consulting solicitor.'[35] Matthews, however, approved the request: 'From the psychological view point I think it as well that Mackay's "legal" brain should be given some chance to "function" while he is in prison.'[36]

But Mackay was not always an exemplary inmate. In April 1921, he was fined for having a penknife and a book of cigarette papers concealed in his spectacles case. At the same time, a search of the prison library revealed a stash of contraband: a grill or toaster, cheese, sugar, tea, playing cards, matches, a handkerchief, a penknife and a newspaper clipping.[37]

And there were more serious incidents. In January 1921, Mackay criticised the wardens for being 'too lazy to even open a gate',[38] and in July he was being marched to labour at Mount Eden when he fell out of the group and said to Warder Lauder, 'My God, I only wish I can meet you outside when I'm out of here and I'll fix you.' Mackay accused Lauder of continually nagging him and said that he was 'worse than a damn old woman'.[39] Charged with threatening behaviour, Mackay was fined and sentenced to three days of bread and water.

In early 1922 he complained to the superintendent about his treatment by another warder: 'I feel sure that a word from you is all that is required to put the matter in order for the future.' Vincent, however, found that Mackay was in the wrong and had not taken up the opportunity to have the complaint investigated by a visiting justice.[40] In March 1922, Mackay was reported for fighting with another prisoner in the penal yard at the 1 p.m. parade.

The register of prison offences also includes a reference to Mackay being found guilty of 'indecent conduct' towards the end of his first stretch in Mount Eden. There is no further information about this in the file, but it contributes to a sense of mounting problems.

Perhaps these incidents of physical violence link back to Mackay's desperate outburst in 1920. They certainly contribute to a picture of a wired and angry man. He continued to request improvements in his daily life. In May 1922 he asked the superintendent for a set of chessmen to be sent to him. 'Of course I understand that play has to be confined to the yard, but one could improve one's game, and have a pleasant break from reading by playing over some of the games by acknowledged masters of which many are reported in the weekly papers.'[41] Just four days before Mackay wrote this letter, an order, signed by Matthews, directed that he be transferred to Waikeria Reformatory near Te Awamutu 'by first available escort'.[42] Mackay was there by June.

Known as Waikeria Reformatory Farm, this prison was set aside for reformative detainees and reformable hard labour men — 'well-conducted prisoners of the better class'. Given Mackay's string of discipline problems at Mount Eden, the move to Waikeria is puzzling. There is a possible clue in a speech given by Matthews in 1923: 'The nature of the work at Waikeria — breaking in land for cultivation, draining, ploughing, milking, &c — made it comparatively easy to prevent the association of any men of confirmed bad habits with the others.'[43] Perhaps the plan was to isolate Mackay from negative influences and to prevent him from being a negative influence on others.

The prison had been established in 1912 on 1570 acres of land. A prison farm followed, which by 1922–23 was milking over 200 cows, producing butterfat worth £3500 for the state.[44] Horticulture was also important, and Mackay was initially assigned to the potato-digging gang, but after breaking the gaol record — 'I mean for digging fewer' — he was allowed to work in the garden, 'the best pozzy here'.[45] Mackay's first job there was scaring the birds off the cabbages; he then moved on to looking after the tomato plants. 'We do things on a big scale —,' he told an ex-prisoner friend eight months after his arrival, '3 acres of onions, two of pumpkins, half an acre of garlic, 4 of cabbages, & so on; but our biggest job is the tomatoes. We have over 3 acres, about 20,000 plants. I spray, cut back & tie up & keep the plants clean round about & believe I give satisfaction. I can honestly say I know most of the plants by name now.' At lunchtime prisoners were allowed to swim in the river that flowed beside the garden.

WAIKERIA REFORMATORY FARM.

REFORMATORY BUILDINGS: ADMINISTRATION BLOCK.
Built throughout by prison labour.

BIRD'S-EYE VIEW OF WAIKERIA REFORMATORY BUILDINGS FROM RESERVOIR HILL.

The Waikeria Reformatory Farm, near Te Awamutu,
photographed in 1923. *Alexander Turnbull Library, Evolution
of the Prison System by Charles E Matthews, 1923*

Although Waikeria was 'freer and easier' than Mount Eden, for a social animal like Mackay it was still difficult and isolated: 'I keep in good health & sleep much better than I did at the Mount & seem to be a good deal easier in my mind, but I have no one here that I can call a mate. I read a good deal more than I did at the Mount.'[46]

Initially, however, Mackay was not allowed the same privileges as he had enjoyed in Auckland: in line with prison regulations, he was permitted only one or two books at a time in his cell. When he complained, his letter went all the way to the normally accommodating Charles Matthews, who told the Waikeria superintendent, Dr St L. H. Gribben:

> While I do not think Mackay should be given all the latitude he received while under Mr Vincent's control, I think he might be let down gradually. You might, for instance, let him have his fountain pen and writing materials, together with a reasonable supply of cheap paper, exercise book, or something of that kind. You might also let him follow up his French or Esperanto, cutting out which ever of them you think best. I do not think there will be any harm either in his being allowed a lead pencil and his penknife.[47]

Presumably alerted by Mackay, Baughan wrote to Gribben to ask about a book 'on the subject of auto-suggestion' that she had lent to Mackay while he was at Mount Eden:

> [He] tells me there is no book-shelf in the Waikeria cells. Is there any special reason for this? If not, would you have any objection to my trying to arrange for them? Books would seem to be a very important part of a reformative scheme if inmates [can] be got to value them? and it may often happen that one book in a man's little private stock may be needed to help with the

study of another. I am aware, however, that there may be special difficulties of which I know nothing — if so, pray forgive the suggestion.[48]

Mackay was allowed to continue with his Esperanto and kept in touch with Edmanson, who sent him stationery, books and magazines. The Esperanto work caused some consternation among Waikeria staff, who were suspicious about what he was writing. In August 1922 the superintendent forwarded to Wellington a letter from Mackay and four pages 'allegedly' written in Esperanto. 'There is no one here acquainted with this method of inter-communication and hence censorship is not possible. Are we to treat all such in a similar way to letters written in Maori? I shall be glad of your instructions in the matter.'[49]

Matthews allowed the material to be sent to Edmanson untranslated, and by the end of 1923 Mackay was granted permission to teach an Esperanto class at Waikeria. He was also allowed to continue sending his French translations for checking. Mackay kept up his reading, teaching himself a few verses of poetry every morning.

He also encountered someone from his former life: a fellow inmate who had been a steward at the Wanganui Club. Once, after staying there, Mackay had discovered that his dress cufflinks were missing. 'Putting two & two together, I have very little doubt where they went to. One day [in prison] I tactfully brought the conversation round to the topic of men's jewellery, but he changed the subject.'[50]

Mackay was discharged as a bankrupt while at Waikeria, and as early as February 1922 was considering a return to journalism when he was released. 'You know,' he wrote to his sister, 'when I was young I made good pocket money out of writing for the newspapers & I look upon that as one possibility when I get out again.'[51] However, continuing clashes with the Waikeria staff were making this a more distant prospect. If the isolation at Waikeria was intended to make

Mackay more compliant, it did not seem to be working. In March 1923 his privileges were withdrawn for a month after he was reported for urinating in front of the cottages, rather than 'retiring to the rear'.[52] Later that year, he complained to prison staff that since coming to Waikeria he had not been fairly treated, was more frequently searched than any other prisoner and was constantly watched.

Michael Hawkins, the inspector of prisons and director of works, rejected the complaint, arguing that the precautions taken were 'absolutely necessary in the circumstances . . . after hearing the prisoner's statement and taking into consideration the type of man he is'. The inspector also refused Mackay's request for a transfer either to a camp or to Paparua in Christchurch: 'In my opinion New Plymouth is the place to which he belongs.'[53]

After 1910, a new prison classification system had attempted 'to set apart a different institution for each group of prisoners ... At the same time, prison camps were developed as an alternative to the closed prisons.'[54] Invercargill Prison was used for offenders under 25; Waikeria and a tree-planting camp at Kaingaroa were for well-behaved prisoners; Auckland, Lyttelton and Wellington became general penal prisons; and from 1917 'prisoners who were sentenced for acts of sexual perversion', in other words homosexual men, were segregated at New Plymouth Prison.[55] Mackay was transferred there in November 1923.

When New Plymouth Prison closed in 2013, its cell blocks and exercise yard were largely unchanged from when Mackay was a prisoner there from 1923–24. Ann Shelton photographed the entrance to one of the cell wings.

7. PUNISHMENT

Mackay, by now aged 48, does not appear to have requested the move to New Plymouth, even though his mother and two sisters lived there, and his previous request to be sent to Paparua in the South Island, or to a camp, suggests that the move was against his will. Mackay's 'sexual perversion' was clearly more important in the minds of prison authorities than the attempted murder charge of which he had been found guilty. That was why, in a climate of hardening views about homosexuality, he was dispatched to New Plymouth.

In 1924, a Committee of Inquiry into Mental Defectives and Sexual Offenders was amassing evidence. It had been established because there had been 'for a considerable time . . . a growing feeling of anxiety among the public owing to the number of mental defectives becoming a charge upon the State, and also the alarming increase in their numbers', and because 'the frequency of sexual offences, many of a most revolting character, [meant] there was a strong demand that some action should be taken to prevent further acts of this nature; it being suggested that the law should be altered to make it possible for surgical operations to be performed upon these offenders'.[1]

The resulting report, presented in 1925, quoted the new controller-general of prisons, Michael Hawkins, who replaced Matthews after his sudden death in late 1924. Hawkins considered that there were two types of sexual offenders. The first were men who succumbed to sudden temptation and assaulted women and young girls; they could, on the whole, be cured and would seldom commit another crime. Men of the second type were quite different — sexual perverts who continued to abuse young children, especially boys.[2] Hawkins' next point illustrated how, in 1924, pederasts — men who had or desired sex with boys — were lumped in with what would now be called gay men. There was no legal distinction because all male-male sex was illegal, no matter the ages of those involved.

> The worst pervert of all is the one who flagrantly offers himself for the purposes of sodomy. Strange as it may seem, there are quite a number of such degenerates in our prisons to-day; middle-aged and elderly men being the chief offenders of this class. In my opinion segregation for life is the only course, and my years of experience among such a class have convinced me of this, their case being absolutely hopeless when this stage has been reached, and no cure is possible in such cases.[3]

The Waikeria superintendent also gave evidence to the inquiry. When asked by committee member Sir Donald McGavin whether children should be told anything about 'abnormal sexualities', Gribben said, 'It is the normal boy I am concerned about who becomes often the victim of such unscrupulous sexual perverts as Mackey [sic] & Holdaway,'[4] a reference, surely, to Charles Mackay and to Hubert Holdaway, who in 1924 had been sentenced to five years' imprisonment with hard labour for indecent assault on boys.

The committee of inquiry was ambivalent about compulsory castration of offenders, but several prisoners underwent voluntary castration in the 1920s.

At New Plymouth Prison, which had been a stockade and barracks and then a military hospital before it became a prison in 1871, 'men deemed morally untrustworthy'[5] worked in the prison's quarry, where Mackay was given the task of stone napping — serving the hard labour part of his sentence, possibly for the first time. There is no evidence that Mackay worked in the quarry at Mount Eden, where he was given a role in the library; at Waikeria he was gardening. To be put in the quarry at New Plymouth, and seen as 'morally untrustworthy' in the eyes of prison authorities, was a sign of how low his prospects had sunk.

ABOVE
The interior of New Plymouth Prison, photographed around
1900. The cell corridor is the same one photographed by
Ann Shelton in 2013 (see pages 130–31). *Auckland Libraries
Heritage Collections, Auckland Weekly News 29 June 1900*

BELOW
New Plymouth Prison, with Mount Taranaki in the
background, photographed around 1910. *Auckland
Libraries Heritage Collections, 35-R94, F. G. Radcliffe*

New Plymouth was a forbidding place. The whitewashed cement cells measured 7 x 10 feet, the smallest in the country when the prison was closed in 2013. The 15-foot ceilings added to their starkness. The wooden doors, sheathed in tin, each had a viewing porthole, covered with a swivelling iron plate. The cells were ventilated with a fanlight above the door and one window set high in the small wall opposite the door.

Mid-1924 marked a turning point in Mackay's fortunes, suggesting that he was managing to survive the system better. In June, after he had been in the quarry for about six months, Matthews approved his transfer to the garden gang, which worked on nearby Marsland Hill. According to historian Peter Boston, to gain work inside the prison or in its garden, men needed to demonstrate that they were amenable to discipline, or that they lacked the physical fitness required for hard labour.[6] Mackay was also given more privileges: he was permitted to receive the *Taranaki Herald*, where one of his sisters worked, and to buy a typewriter out of his earnings to help with the Esperanto class he was teaching. He may also have been helping other prisoners with their English.[7]

In November 1924, for reasons that are unclear, Matthews approved Mackay's transfer from New Plymouth to Hautū, the prison farm established in 1921 near Tūrangi, and directed that he be given 'light work, gardening if possible'.[8]

S et up as part of the Prisons Department's agricultural policy, Hautū Camp used prisoner labour to create farms from a 10,000-acre block of 'pumice land' on the south-east side of Lake Taupō. As well as developing the land for cultivation, Matthews believed the farm offered prisoners 'more congenial work' and 'a new occupation to follow after release'. [9] It was a bleak, austere environment for the inmates, who were housed in simple wooden huts.

Hautū Prison Farm, near Tūrangi, photographed around 1923. *Alexander Turnbull Library, Evolution of the Prison System by Charles E. Matthews, 1923*

Then, just 10 months after arriving at Hautū, Mackay was returned to Mount Eden. He was suffering from a varicocele, a varicose vein on one of his testicles, and in September 1925 he applied to be transferred to a town prison for surgery. The nearest hospital, at Raetihi, would not accept prisoners without an officer present for the whole time, so Michael Hawkins ordered that Mackay be sent to Auckland. The prison medical officer at Mount Eden, however, considered an operation 'unnecessary' for the 'quite small' varicocele: 'all that is required is a suspensory bandage'.[10] Despite the superintendent's strong recommendation that Mackay go back to Hautū,[11] he remained at Mount Eden.

His medical problem kept Mackay away from hard labour, as he told Baughan: 'The Doctor here refuses to operate, & without an operation I am unfit for any serious exertion. In the meantime I have been given light & not uncongenial work.'[12] In December 1925 the superintendent selected him to replace another prisoner as clerk in the Mount Eden quarry manager's office. As he told Hawkins, 'I thought that not only was Mackay capable, but also that it would give his active brain some chance of functioning in this capacity.'[13] The controller-general's response suggests that Mackay, who had already applied to be sent back to Waikeria, had a surprising amount of say over where he was detained: 'In view of your remarks, if Mackay is now willing to remain at Auckland, the Department will have no objection, but it would be desirable, I think, that he should forward an application to this Office, indicating that he wishes to withdraw his request for a transfer.'[14]

Mackay duly did so and in December 1925 enrolled in a correspondence diploma course in bookkeeping, perhaps with an eye to future work opportunities. At this stage he had another 10 years left to serve. Prisoners studying in this way were allowed a desk and an extra hour of light in their cells, so that may also have been an incentive. He continued with his Esperanto, but Edmanson had not had the same influence in the department following Matthews' death. 'It seems to me,' the Auckland superintendent informed Hawkins, that 'there is more in Mackay's Esperanto correspondence than meets the eye, and I would strongly recommend that some Esperanto expert other than Mr Edmanson should censor this correspondence.' Hawkins agreed: 'The privilege granted to Mackay to correspond with friends and others in Esperanto has been reviewed and it has been decided that the prisoner must cease communicating with esperantists outside New Zealand.'[15]

By now, Mackay was looking towards the time when he would be beyond the walls of Mount Eden, and appeals from friends and family for his release began to gain momentum. The rules for hard labour sentences meant that he could not appeal for release until around the middle of 1927 but, remarkably, in April 1924 he was allowed to write to Donald McBeth about his case coming before the Prisons Board.[16]

Set up in 1911, the board was part of New Zealand's first parole system. Previously, offenders whose conduct was reasonably good were released after serving three-quarters of their sentence, but in 1920 the law was changed so that all offenders serving finite terms, like Mackay, were eligible for parole after six months, or half the sentence, whichever was longer.[17] The board had the discretion to review a sentence earlier 'owing to special circumstances'. This may have been why Mackay's case was first considered in July 1924, some three years before the midway point of his sentence. Although the appeal was unsuccessful, it was carried forward to be reconsidered when the board met in October.

The report from the gaoler at New Plymouth Prison prepared for that meeting shows how Mackay was faring four years into his sentence:

If released Mackay will not look for employment in New Zealand, but intends to leave immediately for England. He is not the type of man one would expect to commit further crime.

Notwithstanding the fact that he studies in all his spare time, I think his mentality is becoming impaired by prison life. I am present nearly all time when he has visitors, and one cannot but notice how his memory is beginning to fail more especially in relation to events of recent date. He is a man who has practically no means of earning a livelihood other than by brain work, therefore it appears to me that if he is detained for the greater portion of his sentence he will become more or less a derelict on his release. For these reasons I recommend his case for favourable consideration.[18]

Baughan, too, had noticed Mackay's decline. 'No amount of prison life,' she later wrote, 'did this man the least good — far from it. He deteriorated visibly, and I have reason to fear that his practices were not less perverse on release.'[19] It is interesting to note even a sympathiser using the prevailing word 'perverse'.

Despite the gaoler's sympathetic report, Mackay's appeal was once again unsuccessful. In September 1925 the Prisons Board heard a further appeal for release. The report, from Hautū — he had only just arrived at Mount Eden — reiterated that Mackay, with the support of his friends, planned to leave New Zealand immediately after he was freed. 'His future conduct I think will be satisfactory,' wrote the officer in charge.[20] This appeal, too, failed.

ichael Hawkins announced his retirement as controller-general in January 1926, the same month that Robert Stout retired as chief justice. Because the Prisons Board president had to be a judge, Stout was required to step down from this role but stayed on as a member. When the list of board members confirmed in March 1926 included no Prisons Department staff, the newly appointed controller-general, Bert Dallard, threatened to resign. He seems, however, to have been part of the board when it considered Mackay's case on 27 May that year.[21] As well as Mackay's own petition, the board had a report from the Mount Eden superintendent: 'Compared with the past Mackay appears to have realised his position, and I am of the opinion that he has changed for the better. He certainly appears to have much more control of himself than in the past.'[22]

This time, just over six years into his 15-year sentence, the Prisons Board recommended to the governor-general that Mackay be released 'on probationary licence for the unexpired period of his sentence, with permission to leave the Dominion in the charge of his sister, and to remain out of New Zealand during the currency of his licence'.[23] The recommendation was confirmed and preparations began for Mackay to leave prison.

Memos in his file detailing the expediting of his passport indicate haste, and contribute to an impression that the department was acting covertly — an 'officer of discretion' was detailed to see Mackay off by steamer.[24] Mackay's probation licence, outlining the conditions of his release, is missing from the file, but a final memo indicates what happened next: Mackay was freed on 6 August 1926 'and sailed for England by the SS *Marama* under the charge of his sister, as directed'.[25] None of this was made public at the time, but a month later the news was leaked in spectacular fashion, via the front page of *Truth*.

After claiming frequent 'allegations of preferential treatment to prisoners who prior to conviction held prominent social positions', the paper stressed the need for a 'frank' public statement setting out the reasons for Mackay's early release. Without this, the paper argued, even though there may have been 'good grounds' for the decision, most of the general public would feel that Mackay had

N.Z.
Above all for New Zealand
Truth
THE PEOPLES PAPER.

Mackay, Ex-Mayor Of Wanganui, Released From Mount Eden Gaol

EIGHT YEARS AND NINE MONTHS OF FIFTEEN "YEARS' SENTENCE FOR ATTEMPTED MURDER REMITTED

Discharge Conditional On His Leaving The Dominion

GIPSY DOESN'T LIKE THE "TRUTH"

Article That Was Publicly Quoted To Him By His Congregation

When The Elijah Of Evangelism Gently Closed The Door

Practising What You Preach

The front-page story in *N.Z. Truth* decrying Charles Mackay's early release from prison and departure for Britain. *N.Z. Truth, 9 September 1926. Papers Past*

'been very leniently treated on account of the influence he at one time possessed'. Making leaving the country a condition of his discharge 'was equivalent to a declaration that Mackay was not a fit and proper citizen for the Dominion', and thus, said *Truth*, not fully redeemed.[26]

Ten days after Mackay sailed for London, another prisoner, Joseph Crook, died after an accident in the Mount Eden quarry. He had been serving a sentence of 14 years' hard labour for attempted carnal knowledge and indecent assault on a six-year-old girl. But, as *Truth* pointed out:

> whereas Mackay served only just over six years of a 15 years' sentence, Crook had served seven years of a 14 years' sentence, and he presumably would have served for a still longer period had not Death released him. The serious nature of Mackay's crime — had Cresswell not survived Mackay would have been sentenced to death — the very substantial reduction made in his sentence, and the fact that he was ordered to leave the country if discharged strongly suggests preferential treatment, and it is therefore the Government's duty . . . to see that a full statement of the case is made public.[27]

Mackay's case became linked in the media coverage with the early releases of two other middle-class prisoners later in 1926: all three were alleged to have received preferential treatment because of their connections. The appointment of Dallard, who was unpopular with Prisons Department staff, was also rolled into the controversy.

In August 1926, the Prisons Board recommended the early release of Erne Baume, a law clerk who, in 1925, had been sentenced to three years in borstal for his role in a fraud. Baume, who was from a wealthy, well-connected family (his stepfather was clerk of the House of Representatives), had used cheques to defraud the Post Office of £1100. Baume's accomplice, William Smith, was sentenced to 12 months' 'reformative treatment' in borstal. Baume was released after serving seven months of his sentence and was sent out of the country, leaving on 1 October 1926. Unlike Mackay, Baume's name wasn't on the passenger lists, but this didn't stop news of his release hitting *Truth*'s front page a few days later. This, said the paper, was yet another example of the justice system allowing 'favoured thieves' to go free; it demanded an explanation from the government.

The week after that story broke, Dallard was confirmed as head of the Prisons Department. News of yet another premature release then appeared in *Truth*. Selwyn Baker, a 17-year-old church organist, was released from borstal in October 1926 after serving only three months of a two-year sentence for five charges of indecent assault. Baker's case was complicated by a technicality by which he was sentenced in an adult court when he should have appeared in the Children's Court, where he would have been eligible for probation. Even *Truth* agreed that the offending — Baker lifted women's skirts 'and immediately afterwards, without making any indecent suggestion, jumped on his bicycle and rode away'[28] — was minor.

The controversy snowballed when the cases of Baume and, to a lesser extent, Mackay and Baker, were taken up by the Reverend Howard Elliott from the virulently anti-Catholic Protestant Political Association. A successful 'sectarian polemicist',[29] Elliott addressed a gathering at the Wellington Town Hall on the cases in November, alleging that Baume had received preferential treatment while in borstal, and criticising Dallard's appointment. This was part of a broader campaign to challenge senior public service appointments under the Reform Government, led by Joseph Ward, who was Catholic. Statements made by Elliott at the meeting hint at resentment among prison staff: 'The injustice of Mr Dallard's appointment to other older and more experienced officers in the Public Service who were eligible for the position is emphasised by the facts which reveal the unfortunate position which the present prison administration has placed the Government in.'[30]

Dallard challenged Elliott to produce affidavits 'of persons having direct and personal knowledge of the allegations which he made in his address'.[31] Elliott did not do this but continued to call on the government to initiate a full inquiry into Dallard's appointment, together with the circumstances surrounding the releases of Baume, Mackay and Baker.

Justice minister Frank Rolleston rejected Elliott's requests and confirmed his confidence in Dallard: 'If Mr Elliott refuses to produce the evidence which he said was in his possession the public can draw their own inference.'[32] But Elliott's agitation, and the surrounding publicity, had an impact. Rolleston approved a magisterial inquiry into Elliott's allegations about Baume and asked the Prisons Board for a report 'setting out the principles on which the board acts in recommending the release of prisoners, and dealing with the facts in regard to the cases of Baume, Mackay and Baker'.[33]

The board's report, released four days before Christmas 1926, was printed in newspapers across the country, including both the Whanganui papers. It included a summary of the facts of the three cases and reasons for the early releases.[34] In Mackay's case, the board's reasons focused on what had happened to him after he was sentenced.

Mackay had already suffered 'extremely severe punishment': he had been imprisoned for six and a half years, he had lost his status as a lawyer and become a bankrupt and he had been divorced by his wife and permanently separated from his three daughters. The board had also noted the positive reports about his conduct and industry in most of the prisons where he was held.[35] It had taken account, too, of increasing 'signs of degeneration, both in mind and body . . . the superintendent of one institution specially referring to his failing memory and health'.

In addition, there was the concern that were his release delayed Mackay might not be able to earn a living and would become a permanent charge upon the state. The board had also recorded the willingness of Mackay's sister, 'an intelligent and responsible woman of mature years', to accompany her brother to London and set him up in a new occupation 'in which he could earn an honest living in a new environment'.

Finally, the Prisons Board report made it clear that Mackay was seen as a homosexual: 'That Mackay, notwithstanding his high intelligence and great abilities, was sexually perverted there can be no doubt. It was so stated by his counsel when pleading for mitigation of sentence, and it is clear that Mackay recognised this perversion, and had consulted both doctors and metaphysicians for treatment and advice.'[36]

Once Mackay's release became known, *Truth* led the criticism. Mackay apparently had 'no intention of seeking the quiet glades of life, or of letting himself remain in the shades of any backwater, though he was on his release not thought a fit and proper citizen for New Zealand'. He had gone to England, where, perhaps, he intended to 'write a book on the Dominion Prison system, and some kind things about the New Zealand Prisons Appeal Board, who so courteously set him at large'. *Truth* even suggested a possible title: '"MONEY (or Position) TALKS." By One Who Knows.'[37]

The Strand, London, around 1920. *Alamy*

8. LONDON

n August 1926, Charles Mackay and his 52-year-old sister Margaret Jean Mackay, whom he called both Jean and Jeannie, boarded the SS *Marama* in Auckland bound for Melbourne, and then sailed on the *Moreton Bay* to London, where they arrived on 25 September.

It must have been a comfort to Mackay that his mother and most of his siblings had stood by him throughout his years in prison, but even so his exile had been brutal. As Hector Bolitho recalled, 'He had lost everything . . . His body was tired and warped when he arrived in London, and he was poor.' But 'slowly, the wonder of England enlivened his blood and smiles came to his melancholy face',[1] so much so that by 17 December that year, as an outraged *Truth* reported, Mackay was signing the visitors' book at the New Zealand High Commission on the Strand.[2] Mackay was also spotted a week later by Cranleigh Barton, a lawyer who had worked in Whanganui in 1915 and during the 1920s, and who was now using his wealth to travel the world, working as a watercolour artist. Entries in Barton's diaries indicate that the two men were well acquainted. They had spent some time together in Christchurch in January 1919, described by Cranleigh Barton in his diary, perhaps a code for an intimate encounter:

> I was on my way to the Cathedral when I met C. E. Mackay (Wanganui's Mayor) and he suggested I should join forces and go with him to New Brighton so we went out on the top of a car and spent an hour on the beach, such a lovely sunset and still glowing in the west when we returned to town. I notice the longer twilight Christchurch has after Wellington. We had supper at The Rendezvous. He was very amusing and had a large fund of stories — a curious mixture.[3]

It was a different story when the two men crossed paths in London in December 1926.

'I had a busy morning,' Barton noted that day, 'went to the NZ

LEFT
Cranleigh Barton,
photographed in
London by Howard
Coster in 1926.
*National Portrait
Gallery, Ax2250*

BELOW
The main entrance
hall of New Zealand
House, located
on the Strand in
London. *Alexander
Turnbull Library,
1/2-079236-F*

Office and who should come in but C. E. Mackay of Wanganui whose crime and punishment at the time of the Prince's visit was the talk of NZ. I think he recognised me but pretended he didn't so I didn't make a point of it. He looked quite prosperous.'[4]

On his arrival in England, Mackay had euphemistically listed his profession as 'retired solicitor', but, as he had planned while in prison, he returned to journalism and quickly found work as a freelancer, writing and cabling stories for Wellington's *Evening Post*, Auckland's *New Zealand Herald* and other papers in New Zealand and Australia. His business card read 'Mr. C. E. Mackay, *Waitara Daily News*, Waitara New Zealand'. No such publication has ever existed; in a risky move, Mackay had made it up in order to obtain the press pass he would need.[5]

In London Mackay also became involved in advertising, then in its infancy and regarded as a modish industry. It was a natural choice for someone of his background and personality and it also gave him an opportunity to work with 'artistic' types. In March 1927 he established the Adelphi Publicity Company in partnership with Hilton Simmons Maughan, a 32-year-old former army officer,[6] and they were soon joined by a third shareholder, 21-year-old Derek George Hooydonk, who had a Belgian father and English mother. All three men described themselves as advertising agents and contractors for the company, whose activities included the design and exhibition of advertisements of all descriptions.[7]

The company offices were at 12 York Buildings, Adelphi, a small district of Westminster south of Covent Garden, between the Strand and the Embankment, and bounded by Charing Cross Station and the Savoy Hotel. This area was then the centre of London's queer life. Its pubs and other venues catered for a large queer clientele, and the Adelphi, the Embankment, the Charing Cross arches and the railway station concourse were cruising sites.[8] Men would pick each other up and have sex in urinals, parks or, less commonly, back at their digs.

Not far from Mackay's office was the Adelphi Building, built in the years 1768 to 1774 by Robert and James Adam on sloping ground between the Strand and the Thames. Beneath the buildings was a series of vaulted brick arches, accessed by underground streets duplicating the street-level layout. The arches were originally used to store goods for transhipment to boats on the Thames and coal to be delivered to the West End, but in the nineteenth century they became associated with criminals, the homeless and prostitutes. By the 1920s, the queer men frequenting this rabbit warren of narrow alleyways and passageways, above and below ground, were attracting police attention. According to a local police inspector, 'it was a well-established "resort of persons of the sodomite class" because of its "position and surroundings" . . . and since "the locality is badly lighted" and housed several notorious urinals'.[9]

Over a period of 18 months in the late 1920s, a single policeman arrested more than 15 men for sexual offences in the urinals, known as 'cottages', in the Adelphi Arches. As well as police surveillance, blackmail was a threat for men using the urinals as a meeting place. Despite these risks, men seeking sex navigated this hidden geography, 'a network of sites at which homosexual desire could be expressed . . . until these urinals were cleaned up, London must have been about the most secretly *homosexual city* in existence'.[10] As a result of police repression, London's queer scene was directly sexual, and also hidden. As historian Florence Tamagne has noted:

> There was little time and opportunity for small talk and idle chat, much less a real exchange of information. In the bars, simply asking for a cigarette was enough to pick up a partner, without attracting the attention of anyone else. In essence, the English homosexual culture was an underground culture, closed to the uninitiated, inaccessible to the timid, and concentrated very closely in obscure districts of London and the ports.[11]

This covert world was populated by working-class men who loved and had sex with other men, but who did not see themselves as queer. As historian Matt Houlbrook has written, 'Such figures — known variously as men trade, rough trade, roughs, renters, or to be had — were an integral part of London's sexual landscape.' Guardsmen and sailors were among those offering their bodies for sale in this now vanished world, where 'sexual and emotional relationships between men were deeply embedded within the contours of everyday life'.[12]

Despite the illegality of homosexuality — classified as 'gross indecency' — the homosexual subculture in 1920s London was thriving, particularly in the West End. A long-standing tradition of pubs and cafés being taken over by queer men continued, and theatres, music halls and cinemas were also meeting places, together with private drinking clubs in Soho. There is little doubt that Mackay found the city sexually liberating — perhaps this was what Blanche Baughan was referring to when she wrote about his 'perverse practices' following his release from prison.

Also part of this underground world was D'Arcy Cresswell, who lived in central London for 12 of the 18 months Mackay was in the city. Although there is no evidence that they met, Cresswell had written to Mackay in prison, possibly in connection with the mysterious second statement about the 1920 shooting (see Chapter 5), making an encounter in London conceivable.

Mackay lived north of Adelphi, at 9 Coram Street in Bloomsbury — another part of London favoured by homosexual men. It is uncertain whether that address was then a private hotel or whether he boarded with others, but in either case the lack of privacy in his lodgings would have driven him, as it did many men wanting to meet other men, into public but risky spaces such as parks and urinals. The city's cruising areas included Trafalgar Square, Piccadilly Circus and Hyde and St James's parks.

One evening Hector Bolitho visited St James's Park with Mackay after dinner: 'We leaned over the railing of the bridge, smoking our cigars, until the forms and the noises were dimmed by the increasing night'.[13] In writing this, in his 1935 memoir, *Older People*, Bolitho was telling his readers that he and Mackay were checking out the men. 'Forms and noises' may be referring to the traffic and Buckingham Palace, but could also be something else altogether — men having sex in the royal park, which had been famous for this as far back as the 1700s. In 1791 the home secretary had been urged to lock the park gates at night in order to 'forestall "that most detestable and abominable Crime"'.[14]

Like sailors, guardsmen had an established reputation for soldier prostitution. 'To the soldiers, prostitution was a tradition; it seems that the young recruits were initiated by their elders as they were being integrated into the regiment.'[15] As evidenced in newspaper stories, court cases, official documents and memoirs, soldiers had been figures of erotic fantasy at least since the nineteenth century, and were involved in a number of gross indecency cases well into the twentieth. Among the well-known homosexual men attracted to them were poet and critic John Addington Symonds, Irish nationalist Roger Casement, homosexual law reform campaigner George Ives, the poet A. E. Housman and many others.[16] The writer J. R. Ackerley summed up their appeal: 'Young, they were normal, they were working class, they were drilled to obedience.'[17] Wellington Barracks, alongside St James's Park near Buckingham Palace, was one of the best spots to seek 'a touch of scarlet' — code for sex with a guardsman.

As Bolitho recalled, in the weeks after the pair's initial visit, Mackay went to St James's Park 'almost every evening and he celebrated his little journeys with a bombardment of gay postcards. One arrived almost every morning, with a joke, a verse, or a frank expression of the joy he had found over the beauty of the evening light or the scent of the flowers.'[18] It may have been on one of these visits that he met and got to know a Coldstream guardsman named

Montague Glover's photograph of men cruising in an area known as the 'Meat Rack' in Trafalgar Square, London, in the 1930s. According to historian James Gardiner, this is one of the very few images showing men openly cruising on the streets of London before the 1970s. *James Gardiner/Neil Bartlett Collection*

St James's Park

St James's Park, London, photographed in the 1920s, a liaison spot for gay men in this era. *Te Papa Tongarewa Museum of New Zealand, O.032083*

LEFT
Hector Bolitho,
photographed in London
by Howard Coster in
1937. *National Portrait
Gallery, x3016*

RIGHT
The Russian impresario
Serge Diaghilev (right),
shown here with principal
dancer Serge Lifar in
Venice, was founder
and director of the
legendary Ballets Russes
and one of the most
high-profile homosexuals
of the 1920s. *Alamy*

Chris Craggs, whom he later made a beneficiary of his will.

Mackay was not spending all his leisure time in St James's Park, however. He took a 'great interest' in what would be the penultimate London season of the Sergei Diaghilev's legendary Ballets Russes,[19] which performed in London more often than anywhere else. Its 1928 season included the premiere of works with music by Igor Stravinsky and Gabriel Fauré, and choreography by Léonide Massine and George Balanchine.

Diaghilev's relationships with handsome dancers in his company were well known. After the death of Oscar Wilde, he was arguably the most famous homosexual of his day, and his openness about his sexuality was an act of defiance in the wake of the persecution suffered by Wilde.[20] Diaghilev's sexuality found expression in the ballet *Les Biches*, first performed in Monte Carlo in 1924, and five times in the 1928 London season that Mackay followed. The title of the ballet, which had music by French composer Francis Poulenc and choreography by dancer and choreographer Vaslav Nijinsky's sister Bronislava Nijinska, can be translated as the hinds (does) or as darlings, but it has another slang meaning: a woman or man 'of deviant sexual proclivities'.[21] Featuring a group of men and women at a country house, the ballet had no storyline but was notorious for its sexual subtext and the choreography played 'with gender stereotypes, androgyny and homosexuality . . . In its open exploration of sexual perversity (or what was taken for it), this ballet went further than any other work Diaghilev ever produced.'[22]

Remarkably, sometime during the London season, Mackay wrote to Diaghilev with his own ideas for ballet scenarios.[23] The specifics of his letter are unknown, but he, along with many other homosexual men, 'took over' that 1928 season. Even *Vogue* magazine's dance critic noticed and felt emboldened to write about it: 'The Russian Ballet has returned to London, and once again in the long intervals . . . the corridors of His Majesty's Theatre are crowded with sweet seasonable

An alleyway leading from the Adelphi to the Strand,
a queer haunt in London in the 1920s. *Alamy*

young men . . . the beautiful burgeoning boys.'[24] The surrounding streets, 'now off-limits to women', were filled with 'young men in "strange raiment" crowding the promenade'. Male dancers such as Serge Lifar captured the attention of this audience: 'flowers ceased to be a tribute paid only to the ballerina'.[25]

The Ballets Russes would perform one further season before Diaghilev's death in 1929, but Mackay did not see it. He had left London to begin a European tour, basing himself in Berlin, where he arrived in late November 1928. A final glimpse of him, from Bolitho, suggests his time in the British capital had been restorative: 'For a year or more, England had given his life a benison, soothing him for all he had suffered. I think that in the end, he regretted none of the violence and punishment which had forced him to slink away and hide himself in London. His pride and his laughter came back to him . . .'[26]

A film industry ball in Berlin in 1929. Actor Hans Albers is seated in the foreground. *Alamy*

9 BERLIN

During the era of the Weimar Republic, from 1919 to 1933, Berlin had 4 million inhabitants, making it the world's third largest city after New York, with 8 million, and London with 7.5. The republic had 17 changes of government over its lifetime; Mackay arrived in Berlin during a period of relative economic stability after the hyperinflationary years of 1921-23. Although its inhabitants 'lovingly referred' to this apparently glamorous time as 'Berlin's golden twenties',[1] many people were still suffering economically. Housing was in short supply, and unemployment was high; meanwhile, others had accrued massive wealth and Berlin was an inexpensive destination for visiting foreigners with stronger currencies.

The contrast between these worlds was stark. British artist Francis Bacon was 'deeply affected by the palpable, intense contrasts of "high-bourgeois sophistication" on the one hand, and "Lumpenproletariat misery" on the other'.[2] But despite this edginess and instability, Berlin was 'irresistible', as historian Peter Gay noted in a famous essay about Weimar culture: 'To go to Berlin was the aspiration of the composer, the journalist, the actor; with its superb orchestras, its hundred and twenty newspapers, its forty theatres, Berlin was the place for the ambitious, the energetic, the talented. Whatever they started, it was in Berlin that they became, and Berlin that made them, famous.'[3]

The city's efficient and extensive public transport system, and the construction of innovative public housing designed by leading architects, attracted visitors from all over the world. Particularly for English intellectuals, however, visiting the capital of the former enemy was still regarded as daring.[4]

Among the many chroniclers of Weimar Berlin was Harold Nicolson who, in 1929, was close to the end of his career as a British diplomat and about to move into journalism and politics. Like Mackay, Nicolson was married but had relationships with men, facilitated by a posting to 'wicked' Berlin, where he took visitors for tours around the queer sites. It was convenient that his wife, Vita Sackville-West, hated the city — 'Oh, that filthy, filthy place. How I loathe it' — preferring to stay in England with her lover, Virginia Woolf.[5]

Nicolson's 1929 essay 'The Charm of Berlin' attempted to encapsulate the city's magnetism. As he saw it, that allure had two main elements: movement and frankness.

> There is no city in the world so restless as Berlin. Everything moves . . . At 3 A.M. the people of Berlin will light another cigar and embark afresh and refreshed upon discussions regarding Proust, or Rilke, or the new penal code, or whether human shyness comes from narcissism, or whether it would be a wise or a foolish thing to turn the Pariser Platz into a stadium. The eyes that in London or in Paris would already have drooped in sleep are busy in Berlin, inquisitive, acquisitive, searching, even at 4 A.M., for some new experience or idea. The mouths that in Paris or London would next morning be parched for bromoseltzer, in Berlin are already munching sandwiches on their way to the bank.[6]

As another observer recorded: 'No-one ever dreamed of going straight home and to bed from these affairs [parties and balls]. We either went to a dance restaurant or to one of the smoky overcrowded night spots, where a blind man tinkled a piano or a man-woman sang operatic arias in falsetto while the guests clapped and ate chicken soup.'[7] It is easy to imagine Mackay, described by a friend as possessing 'a great mental and physical vigour',[8] in that environment.

Then there was the frankness. According to Nicolson:

> London is an old lady in black lace and diamonds who guards her secrets with dignity and to whom one would not tell those secrets of which one was ashamed. Paris is a woman in the

After midnight at a cafe on the Kurfürstendamm, one of Berlin's great avenues. Photograph by Felix H. Man, 1929. NGA, purchased 1987. Accession Number: 87.1469. IRN: 72469

prime of life to whom one would only tell those secrets that one desires to be repeated. But Berlin is a girl in a pullover, not much powder on her face, Hölderlin in her pocket,[9] thighs like those of Atalanta, an undigested education, a heart that is almost too ready to sympathize, and a breadth of view that charms one's repressions from their poison, and shames one's correctitude. One walks with her among the lights and in the shadows. And after an hour or so one is hand-in-hand.[10]

Mackay originally intended to stay only six months in Berlin, but 'finding it so interesting he decided to stay longer'.[11] The man who had championed the building of the Sarjeant Art Gallery was no doubt intrigued by the work of the Bauhaus design school, and Berlin's expressionist architecture. It would be surprising if work by artists such as Ernst Ludwig Kirchner, George Grosz, Christian Schad, Max Beckmann, Otto Dix, Paul Klee and many others escaped his attention. He may also have been drawn to the movie industry — the films made at Ufa's Babelsberg studios south-west of Berlin launched the careers of Marlene Dietrich, Billy Wilder, Fritz Lang and many other luminaries; or to the music — *The Threepenny Opera*, with music by Kurt Weill and lyrics by Bertolt Brecht, had opened just before Mackay arrived. He certainly attended the Staatsoper, the Berlin State Opera, which had reopened the previous year after a big renovation. There was no shortage of other attractions in the Weltstadt, the Global City, that might have persuaded Mackay to stay.

On 14 November 1928 he moved from his first pension on Bülowstraße to Winterfeldtstraße 8 in Schöneberg, a middle-class area in the city's fashionable 'West End', which had developed into one of Berlin's three main gay areas in the 1920s. There he rented a furnished room from Frau Weissing.[12] He joined the Foreign Press Club, began to file stories for papers in New Zealand and Australia, and got a job teaching English at the nearby branch of the English Institute.

He was now well set up to explore 'the greatest and most differentiated homosexual infrastructure in the country — arguably the world — which attracted thousands of travellers from the provinces and abroad'.[13] The city had more than a hundred Dielen (locales) and entertainment venues — 'taverns or pubs; cafés, restaurants, casinos, ballrooms, clubs, dance halls, cellars, and shady private establishments'[14] — for homosexual men, lesbians and transvestites. Some of these catered for specialist tastes, like the Schnurrbart Diele, the 'moustache café', where men with magnificent facial hair would meet others similarly endowed.[15]

Visitors could navigate balls, parties and myriad other attractions using queer travel guides, while staying in queer-run and queer-friendly accommodation. There was also an extraordinary amount of queer media: 'From 1919 until February 1933, somewhere between twenty-five and thirty separate homosexual German-language journal titles appeared *in* Berlin, some weekly or monthly and others less frequently . . . there were practically no such journals published anywhere in the world until 1945.'[16]

And there was a huge number of male prostitutes, as many as 22,000, according to one estimate.[17] As a former garrison town, Berlin, like London, had a tradition of soldier prostitution. Numbers had grown rapidly after the war, following mass demobilisation and economic hardship. As well as bars and clubs, prostitutes could be found in popular cruising areas such as the Tiergarten Park, the area around the Friedrichstraße Station (where visitors from England arrived) and Unter den Linden, the grand avenue leading to the Brandenburg Gate. The Passage, also known as the Lindenpassage, or Kaiserpassage, an arcade running diagonally into Unter den Linden from Friedrichstraße, was notorious as a place to find prostitutes. The young men would take their clients to Stundenhotels or Absteigen, 'small discreet hotels or

British diplomat Harold Nicolson, husband of Vita Sackville-West, represented the British Embassy at Charles Mackay's funeral on 8 May 1929. *National Portrait Gallery, x24457*

Eldorado, the famous nightclub in post-war Berlin that catered for the gay community, was popular with locals and tourists. Audiences, straight and gay, queued up at the famed Jewish-owned nightclub where trans women and drag queens performed and gave paid dances to visitors. *Alamy*

An issue of the German lesbian magazine *Die Freundin* from May 1928. Twenty-five to thirty different weekly or monthly German-language periodicals for homosexual readers were published in Berlin in the 1920s. *Alamy*

private flats where a room could be used for an hour or less'.[18]

Although homosexuality was illegal, and discretion was often required, the authorities generally tolerated queer people, preferring to know where they were so they could have some control. From 1885 the Berlin police had maintained a Department of Homosexuals, set up to manage and keep an eye on queer activity in bars, brothels and other locations.[19] Later, the department's domain included blackmailers. These were treated more harshly than their victims, who were reluctant to report cases to the police. Police were deployed in cruising areas, to protect men who were looking for sex from potential blackmailers.[20]

English journalist Michael Davidson, who was in Berlin at the same time as Mackay, recalled the police officer who appeared when he was having trouble shaking off an offensive youth he had picked up. '"You know," said the policeman kindly, "you should be very careful about what boys you pick up — there are some bad ones about."'[21] Historian Robert Beachy has argued that the approach taken by the police actually 'contributed to the *creation* of Berlin's community of sexual minorities . . . allowing it to develop within a network of bars and same-sex entertainments'. In the late nineteenth century the police commissioner, Leopold von Meerscheidt-Hüllessem, even gave tours of the city's homosexual nightspots and escorted visitors to same-sex costume balls.[22]

Berlin also had the world's first homosexual emancipation movement,[23] which was campaigning for the abolition of Paragraph 175, the law that had made homosexuality illegal since 1870. Magnus Hirschfeld, a physician and sexologist who was also homosexual, was a leading figure in the movement. In 1897, with several friends, he founded the Scientific-Humanitarian Committee in his Charlottenburg apartment. The committee worked for the reform of Paragraph 175 and other legislation relating to homosexuality by publishing papers, giving lectures and organising conferences.

By 1919, Hirschfeld had moved to the Villa Joachim in Tiergarten, on the corner of Beethovenstrasse and In den Zelten.[24] The home of Hirschfeld and his lover, Karl Giese, this grand and elegant building also housed the sexologist's Institute for Sexual Science, which 'accommodated a research and teaching institute, a library, museum and archive, a lecture hall and a clinic for those seeking advice on sexual matters, including abortion and birth control, and treatment for venereal diseases'.[25] Extremely successful, the institute became very well known and a popular tourist attraction.

Hirschfeld was building on earlier work by other scholars. As early as 1867 Karl Heinrich Ulrichs, then a 42-year-old lawyer, had called for the repeal of laws forbidding sex between men. Other terms for same-sex love were used until the term 'homosexual' appeared in print in 1869 in two anonymous pamphlets published in Germany by Karl Maria Kertbeny, an Austro-Hungarian translator. Doctors became involved with defining homosexuality, notably Richard von Krafft-Ebing. In his 1885 work *Psychopathia Sexualis*, described as a 'medico-legal study for the use of doctors and lawyers', Krafft-Ebing identified four stages of homosexuality: the psychosexual hermaphrodite, who preserves some traces of the heterosexual instinct; the homosexual; the effeminate; and the androgyne.[26] He was the first to distinguish disease (perversion) from vice (perversity). Thanks to the work of German sexologists, homosexuality could be seen not as a moral lapse to which anyone was susceptible, but rather as a pathological difference of personality.[27]

The development of ideas regarding homosexuality was quite different in England, where doctors and others resisted studies of the subject. Havelock Ellis was able to publish *Sexual Inversion*, his medical textbook about homosexuality, in Germany in 1896 without difficulty, but when the English edition appeared the following year, a bookseller was prosecuted for selling the book, which was then banned. This was only a couple of years after the Wilde trials, which had fuelled public antipathy to any discussion about homosexuality.[28] It has been suggested that German newspaper reports of these spurred Hirschfeld and other activists to build a movement 'at whose centre was the idea of a persecuted, misunderstood, vulnerable, blackmailed martyr figure. In this sense, the spectre of Wilde . . . haunts the early German homosexual rights movement.'[29]

Germany had its own scandals associated with homosexuality, most notably a series of libel trials between 1907 and 1909 known as the Eulenburg Affair.[30] As in England, such events introduced homosexuality as a topic in the media, which could have a powerful impact on its acceptance and on discussions about it that could change attitudes and opinions.[31] Hirschfeld and others worked with publishers to print articles about homosexuality, which were sold throughout Germany and in other countries.

Film was also used to promote the movement's ideas. *Anders als die Andern* (*Different from the Others*), the first film to deal openly with homosexuality, was made by Austrian director Richard Oswald as part of a series to educate the public about social issues. It argued for the abolition of Paragraph 175, using research by Hirschfeld, who helped to fund the film and appeared in it as himself. The film was released in 1919, but public screenings were banned in 1920 and copies were destroyed.[32]

Anders als die Andern is about a case of homosexual blackmail, which has some similarities to what happened to Mackay in Whanganui. A violinist forms a relationship with a young pupil. The pair are seen together by a blackmailer hustler, who demands that the violinist pay

Magnus Hirschfeld (right) with Conrad Veidt in the 1919 film *Anders als die Andern*, the world's first known gay movie. © *Filmmuseum München*

him hush money. The violinist remembers meeting the hustler at a gay dance hall, and the hustler leading him on before turning on him and using his homosexuality to blackmail him.[33] Like Mackay, the violinist seeks a cure for his homosexuality, and undergoes hypnosis, which, as in Mackay's case, is unsuccessful.

Because this is Berlin, not Whanganui, the violinist can seek help from a sexologist, Hirschfeld, who outlines the argument underlying the homosexual rights movement: 'Love for one of the same sex can be just as pure and noble as that for the opposite sex. This orientation is to be found among many respectable people in all levels of society. Those that say otherwise come only from ignorance and bigotry.' Hirschfeld also explains the violinist's homosexuality to his parents:

> You mustn't think poorly of your son because he is homosexual. He is not at all to blame for his orientation. It is neither a vice nor a crime, indeed, not even an illness, but instead a variation, one of the borderline cases that occur frequently in nature. Your son suffers not from his condition, but rather from the false judgment of it. This is the legal and social condemnation of his feelings, along with widespread misconceptions about their expression.[34]

Anders als die Andern inspired a song in 1919, 'Das Lila Lied' ('The Lavender Song'), which became an anthem of the gay movement of the Weimar Republic. The chorus begins 'Wir sind nun einmal anders als die Andern, die nur im Gleichschritt der Moral geliebt . . .' ('We are just different from the others, who are being loved only in step with morality.')

The unusual visibility of homosexuals and homosexuality in Berlin has been seen as the model for the gay rights movement in the United States. Germany was where the concept of 'homosexuality' as an inborn condition took root; Hirschfeld and others had taken 'homosexual' — the term claimed by Mackay in 1920 — beyond the medical world.

All three of the pensions where Mackay lived during his five and a half months in Berlin were near one another in the Schöneberg gay area. Then, as now, Nollendorfplatz — where the underground station now has a dome marked out in rainbow neon — was the focal point, but after the Second World War the gay area was rebuilt elsewhere in the city.[35] Today it runs west from Nollendorfplatz to Kurfürstendamm, Berlin's Champs Élysées. In the 1920s, it extended for five blocks further east from Nollendorfplatz, along a boulevard called Bülowstraße. Mackay lived in two pensions in this part of Bülowstraße at the beginning and end of his stay in Berlin, but stayed longest in a third pension one block south in a street called Winterfeldtstraße.

Where Bülowstraße reached Dennewitzplatz — a small green triangle dominated by a red brick church called the Lutherkirche — the train line went through the middle of a nearby apartment building. Tourists came to photograph this remarkable sight. Dennewitzplatz marked the start of the 'homosexual pleasure mile', which had developed in the 1920s. The building with the train tunnel housed the Hollandais gay bar, famous for big parties and balls, and further along Bülowstraße was the Café Dorian Gray, which was both a meeting place for the homosexual movement and an entertainment venue. Named after Wilde's novel, the café 'announced its "Internationaler Verkehr!" (international clientele), and also that French and English were spoken on the premises'.[36] A few doors away was Oasis, a lesbian bar. There were more venues on the other side of Bülowstraße.[37]

Back along Bülowstraße towards Nollendorfplatz, the DéDé-Bar, a night-time venue for men only, was opposite Mackay's first pension. Known as the 'Bar of the International World',[38] it was named after a French novel with a cult following in Germany about the homoerotic relationship between two boys. 'Men came here to meet men and arrange one-night stands. They hung around for a few hours, looked at who was still available or went off with the words: "In der DéDé-Bar sehen wir uns wieder" (We'll see each other again in the DéDé-Bar).'[39] Other gay venues and bars could be found as the 'gay golden mile' continued further west into the Kurfürstendamm entertainment district.

Mackay may have chosen this neighbourhood because it was close to one of his employers, the English Institute — at Bülowstraße 93, two doors away from the DéDé-Bar — but he was still living in the midst of the world's most vibrant gay culture. British writer Christopher Isherwood, famous for novels that have become emblematic of Weimar Berlin — one inspired the play, musical and film *Cabaret* — lived in Schöneberg, in a pension on Nollendorfstraße, a couple of streets away from Winterfeldtstraße. Like Mackay and many other expatriates, Isherwood taught English.

Although the bars and venues in Mackay's neighbourhood reflected the more refined nature of Berlin's west, they were still places where older men chased boys, and payment, or some sort of exchange, for sex was often involved. According to the queer traveller and Oxford don Maurice Bowra, who visited Berlin's 'night resorts' in 1927, 'The old (60 and over) are the most successful as all young Germans are gerontophiles.'[40] In terms of age, Mackay, as a 53-year-old man, had the odds in his favour. A bar described by Isherwood in *Goodbye to Berlin* featured foreigners like Mackay who lived in Schöneberg:

On Saturday and Sunday evenings the Alexander Casino was full. Visitors from the West End arrived, like ambassadors from another country. There were a good number of foreigners —

Adolf Hitler makes his first speech in the Berliner Sportpalast in November 1928. Following the speech, there was street fighting between the Nazis and left-wing protesters. This led to the reimposition of a ban on Hitler speaking in Prussia imposed three years earlier, and a ban on demonstrations, triggering the protests and fighting later remembered as Blutmai (Bloody May). *Alamy*

Dutchmen mostly, and Englishmen. The Englishmen talked in loud, high, excited voices. They discussed communism and Van Gogh and the best restaurants. Some of them seemed a little scared: perhaps they expected to be knifed in this den of thieves . . . [Some rent boys] sat at their tables and mimicked their accents, cadging drinks and cigarettes.[41]

I n the midst of all this easy sociability, Mackay could not have avoided noting the tone of menace that was developing in Berlin as the Nazis began their ascent. Not far away from his Winterfeldtstraße pension stood a huge brown brick building, the Fernamt Berlin, Europe's largest telephone exchange when it was completed in 1929. Built over the entire block behind the phone exchange was the Sportpalast (Berlin Sports Palace), used for cycle marathon races, boxing matches and other popular entertainments. It was also a venue for political rallies, most infamously those held by the Nazi Party and orchestrated by Joseph Goebbels, who became the party's head of propaganda and was responsible for creating Hitler's image. Goebbels had arrived in Berlin in 1926, as the party's Gauleiter for the city,[42] and Mackay was living in Winterfeldtstraße when Hitler gave his first speech in the Sportpalast on 16 November 1928.

Both the political situation and the queer scene he inhabited, in which older men interacted with younger men in bars, were combined in a long newspaper article on 'Young Germany' written by Mackay in 1929 and printed that year in the *Dominion*, the *New Zealand Herald* and the *Wanganui Herald*.[43] Mackay's focus echoed a contemporary obsession with German youth among English intellectuals, which stemmed both from British notions of Germany as a new, dynamic nation and a wider concern about the morals of the young in the interwar period.[44] The article consists of a series of vignettes of Mackay's life in Berlin, revealing how he operated as

The beer house Neue Welt in Neukölln, Berlin, photographed in 1930. *Alamy, Sueddeutsche Zeitung Photo*

a freelance reporter and who he was meeting — apparently always younger men. Mackay refers to his other job, as an English language teacher: 'I speak as one whose work brings him into day-long contact with the youth of all classes here.'

The piece begins with a reference to a soldier, his friend Sergeant Gerd Hauptmann, of the North Prussian Cavalry, who has four horses in the barracks: 'Gerd may have somewhat exaggerated the number of his horses, as I fancy he does that of his love affairs. But the spirit in which he spoke is that animating not merely the army, but also young Germany, or at least young Germany that counts.' He quotes from a letter sent by his very first acquaintance in Berlin, a 'lad' studying in Heidelberg whom he encountered while visiting Berlin: 'We met in a beer-house, got into conversation and exchanged cards.' The letter, in English, concludes with these words: 'Why is England so jealous of us? Why cannot she be our friend. England shall never be the Rome to our Carthage. Mark my verity.'

Another beer-house conversation follows, with Mackay drinking Berliner Kindl in the company of a tailor's assistant. When the beer arrives, the waiter puts it on a cardboard coaster, printed not with the usual advertisement, but rather a patriotic statement: 'England's colonies are a hundredfold as big as she and have nine times her population — and Germany?' Mackay described how when he 'smiled and turned the inscription down the little tailor turned it up again and, slapping his chest, exclaimed, "Not yet, but soon."'

Mackay reported evidence of the closeness that still existed between Britain and Germany after 1918. King George V may have changed the name of the British royal house from Saxe-Coburg and Gotha to Windsor, but he was still the first cousin of Germany's last Kaiser, Wilhelm II. 'When I open my London paper in a restaurant,' noted Mackay, 'someone, usually a woman, is bound to ask me how the King is.'

'Quo Vadis — Young Germany?', as the *Dominion* headlined it, is a strange, chatty piece, and becomes even odder at the end, where Mackay shares his theory about how 'Young Germany' is revealing the underlying instability of its country:

> The nervous state of every German youth is reflected by some involuntary twitch or inability to keep his facial muscles under control. This physical instability may at any time be transmitted into rash political action. Young Germany is liable to go off at half-cock.

> Like most things in Germany this has its ludicrous aspect. In England the ability to move one's ears is so rare as to be a gift of price among school-boys. But here half of them seem able to move their ears. Of course it must be admitted that generally they have more to do it with.

> Do not despise such a detail as frivolous and vain. The nervous twitch of some German boy may yet be deeper fraught with human destiny than ever was the profoundest nod of Lord Burleigh.[45]

When it published the piece, the *New Zealand Herald* left off the last two paragraphs about the ear twitching, together with Mackay's final observation, from Christmas 1928, when he was the guest of a 'delightful family' in Prague, 'probably the most Francophile city in Europe, and where the large German element has at present to keep very quiet':

> The son of the house, just home from Bonn University, told me that in twenty years Bohemia would be German. 'But are not the Czechs in Bohemia much more numerous than the Germans?' 'Maybe they are, but is the butcher afraid of one sheep or of ten?'

It is a little ironical that next year the Czech Government will be at the expense of giving this youth a year's military training, of which he will well know how to profit. To do them justice, I believe they have sufficient sense to bar subjects of German extraction from joining their air force.

Mackay's summary of 'Young Germany's intentions', however, was pretty accurate. Gone was the 'dream of an overseas empire', replaced by this 'programme':

The incorporation into the Republic of all the surrounding territory that can be considered Germanic, including Austria. The overlordship of the countries further East, such as Poland. The re-establishment of German influence in Russia, and the development of her riches by German capital and skill. After that a final settlement of accounts with France and the incorporation in the Republic of Alsace-Lorraine — and more — and Lombardy. In fact the Empire of Charlemagne once more.

Mackay wrote his article in 1929, four years before the Nazi Party seized power, but even then its characteristic political violence was becoming evident. Being a newspaper man put Mackay closer to this rising tension, even if he was, apparently, about to move to a less dangerous occupation: he told a friend that he had obtained a job as an English lecturer at a Berlin university.[46]

Like many other English-speaking expatriates, Mackay seems to have operated in Berlin without being fluent in spoken German. As Ruth Hethke, the 18-year-old chambermaid at his pension, said, 'If I am asked how well Mr Mackay spoke German, I can only testify that he spoke somewhat broken German, however one could communicate well with him.'[47] Mackay had gone further in the New Zealand

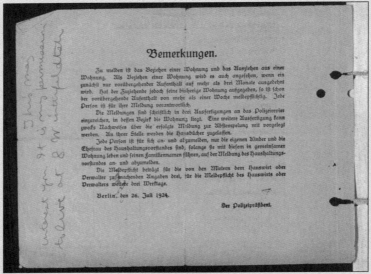

As is still the case today for anyone living in Germany for more than three months, Charles Mackay had to register his address. In 1928 the registrations were handled by the local police station. On the back of his registration form (included as part of the police investigation file) Mackay wrote, in pencil, in his looping script: 'This may interest you. It is my permission to live at 8 Winterfeldtstr.' *Geheimes Staatsarchivs PK, I. HA Rep. 219 Prussian State Criminal Police Office, Nr, 55*

education system than many of his generation, and he had excelled at Wellington College, where the curriculum may have included German, though possibly only written.

He spent time with people learning or teaching English, and with foreign journalists who were more likely to speak English as one of their languages. As his stories indicated, he frequented restaurants, shops and hotels, the places where English was spoken,[48] though it would not have been so common in the beer bars. Christopher Isherwood learnt enough German to proposition men for sex, and Mackay perhaps managed to do the same.

Berlin police clear a street at Hermannplatz in Neukölln during the clashes of May 1929. AKG Images, AKG3955343

BLUTMAI

A s a foreigner, Adolf Hitler, who was Austrian, had been banned from speaking publicly in Prussia, and therefore in Berlin, since September 1925. After the ban was lifted in September 1928, his first speech in the city, made on 16 November that year, led to 'a number of clashes between Communists and Nazis, resulting in three deaths. The Berlin police then banned all demonstrations in the city.'[1]

But a bitter division continued between two political factions, the communists and the Social Democrats. The split had its origins in changes in the make-up of the working class, 'between the employed and the unemployed and, more specifically, between the highly skilled and relatively secure minority and the fluctuating industrial population of the semi-skilled'.[2] The police were closely aligned with the socialists — the Minister of the Interior, Albert Grzesinski, and Berlin's police chief, Karl Zörgiebel, were both Social Democrats — and regarded the communists as enemies. The Social Democrats argued that the revolution in Russia could spread to other countries, and used this as a pretext to suppress the Communist Party, whom they accused of taking orders from Moscow. The Nazis, of course, were the beneficiaries of this internecine war within the left, which enabled Goebbels to step up his attacks on 'Marxists'.

These tensions were the background to the police decision to expand its ban on demonstrations to include any planned for 1 May 1929, the fortieth anniversary of the first May Day, or International Workers' Day. (Ironically, in 1919 the socialists had voted, unsuccessfully, for the day to be a public holiday.)[3] The decision was a provocation to the communists who, in defiance of the ban, organised demonstrations under the slogan 'Straße frei für den ersten Mai!' ('Streets free for the 1st of May').

The police clearly expected violence. On the eve of May Day, officers were issued with rifles more lethal than their standard issue firearms, as well as a large quantity of ammunition. Banned from having a regular army, Prussia had a militarised police force, which was spoiling for a fight with the communists.[4] The entire Berlin police force — about 16,500 men — was mobilised and put into 'a state of extreme readiness' from 7 a.m. on 1 May.[5] Armoured vehicles with machine guns were ready, together with high-pressure hoses, and spotter planes were used for the first time in a non-military context.

The communists rallied at assembly points in the city, including Potsdamerplatz and Alexanderplatz. The fighting between police and communists began near Alexanderplatz, in Münzstraße, 'a narrow grey-faced street' in the Scheunenviertel, then a working-class area in the old city centre.

Minutes after the police started attacking communists and anyone else who happened to be on the street or by an open window, the British reporter Sefton Delmer was part of the crowd swept along to the nearby Bülowplatz: 'At one end of the square was an overturned lorry. Police were firing at it, and from behind it Communists were firing back. I was lucky not to be hit. Bullets zipped up the gravel in little spurts of dust around me as I ran. A few yards away from me a schoolboy fell badly wounded,' he later wrote. [6]

Delmer was the head of the Berlin bureau of the *Daily Express*, the conservative London newspaper with a reputation for sensational reporting. Aged just 24 when he got this job, he had been born in Berlin in 1904 to Australian parents and spoke English with a slight German accent. Educated in Germany and England, he identified strongly with both countries, taking care not to lose his 'cachet of being an Englishman, and an Oxford man to boot, which even today [he was writing in 1961] gives you a certain status among Germans'.

Ignoring his mother's protests — 'I don't want my boy filling his mind with all those nasty murders' — he had followed his father to work at the *Daily Express*. The tumult of Weimar Berlin was catnip for someone like Delmer, who went on to become intimately involved in the British propaganda war against the Nazi regime during the Second

World War: 'Berlin in 1928 had just about everything which the editor of a popular daily yearns for — sex, murder, political intrigue, money, mystery and bloodshed. Particularly bloodshed', he wrote in his 1961 autobiography.[7]

On Thursday 2 May things were quiet initially but then flared up in the evening. Fighting became concentrated in two communist strongholds: 'Red' Wedding in the north and Neukölln in the south. A state of siege developed in both districts, and the police imposed martial law from 2 p.m. on the Friday. Wedding and Neukölln were to be isolated from the rest of the city by a wall of police and armoured cars; from 9 p.m. until 4 a.m. no traffic, including the underground, was allowed to pass through their streets.

All shops, public houses and places of entertainment had to be closed by nine o'clock. Doctors, nurses and midwives were the only people allowed to be out. All windows fronting onto the street had to be kept shut and no lights were to be turned on. With immediate effect, the police were authorised to fire at any buildings not complying with these regulations. Most, but not all, evening newspapers published the regulations, but a large part of the population did not read these and radio was not very widespread. Many people, therefore, knew nothing whatever of the prohibitions imposed for the night, especially not in Neukölln, where they were particularly extensive.

Confined to their apartments, residents flew red flags from their windows as the fighting broke out around them and bullets lodged in the plaster walls. Within the restricted areas, police searched houses for weapons. It is now known that the aggression was overwhelmingly on the police side, who shot randomly and maimed innocent bystanders rather than protesters, including some who had been standing on their balconies. Six Neukölln residents were killed between midday and five o'clock that afternoon.

Friday 3 May was only the second morning Mackay had woken at his new pension at Bülowstraße 22. At 7.30 a.m., the chambermaid Ruth Hethke brought coffee to his room. He then left to teach at the English Institute, a few doors away across the road. Just after 9 a.m. Mackay was back and Hethke heard him typing while she was cleaning the adjacent rooms. The pair had a conversation when Hethke brought in Mackay's second morning coffee, between 10 and 10.30. He asked her whether she could use a typewriter. When she answered no Mackay said he would have to teach her.[8]

Mackay then went to the Russischer Hof in the neighbourhood known as Mitte, where the Foreign Press Association was based and from where he sent his stories. He tried to meet the association secretary, Dezsö Vértesi, who was too busy to see him. Mackay then went to order American books from the Asher & Co. bookstore in Behrenstraße, a few streets away, before returning to his pension. Around 2 p.m., he travelled from Bülowstraße to the home of the Melnitz family, just over a kilometre away towards the Tiergarten. There he gave an English lesson to the children of Curtis Melnitz, the representative in Germany of the American film company United Artists, until about 4 p.m.

From there, as arranged earlier, Mackay went to Sefton Delmer's flat in nearby Viktoriastraße. The violence was expected to continue, and Delmer, who had been reporting on his own, needed help to cover what had become a big, constantly changing story in which there was worldwide interest. Mackay's press pass would enable him to get through the police cordons. The pair agreed to meet again at the flat at 9 p.m.

Mackay returned to Schöneberg to collect mail from his old pension in Winterfeldtstraße and then gave lessons at the English Institute from just after 5 until 9 p.m. In the staffroom, Mackay told his teaching colleagues that following the declaration of an emergency in Neukölln, 'there would be the greatest night', and an escalation of the

RIOTERS KILLED DURING MAY DAY DEMONSTRATIONS IN BERLIN.

The German police were compelled to fire on Communist demonstrators during the recent May Day riots in Berlin. Eight rioters were killed and over 200 persons arrested. The picture shows arrests being made. —Keystone

conflict. He wanted to go there that evening and expected something 'unusual'.[9]

From the English Institute, he headed to Delmer's flat, where the two had dinner. Around 9.40 p.m., the two men went by taxi to the Wedding district and then to Hermannstraße in Neukölln, several blocks north of the area where the fighting was happening. This was apparently Mackay's first visit to Neukölln, which would have put him at a disadvantage, especially as the cordon had altered the customary rules about access.

After moving around the area of unrest, Delmer and Mackay caught a taxi back to Delmer's flat, arriving about 11.20 p.m. Ten minutes later Delmer sent Mackay back in the same taxi to Hermannstraße to get the latest news, while Delmer phoned a story through to London. 'Call me up as soon as you have had a look around, Charles,' Delmer told Mackay as he climbed into the taxi. 'Also los! An die Barrikaden!' ('Off you go! To the barricades!')[10]

The Deutsches Filmarchiv, the German Film Archive, contains a compilation of hand-camera footage of the riots, less than eight minutes long, taken from trams, roofs and windows. The piece of film is famous because of its use as propaganda by three groups: communists, Nazis and socialists. For a few seconds, the camera lingers on a scene in which lengths of wood are lying on the ground, and on a fence, part of the barricades that prevented Mackay's taxi going any further when he returned to Neukölln to check on the fighting.

The fighting was happening in a very small area of Neukölln, covering 12 blocks, or about 1.5 square kilometres. In Hermannstraße, protesters had used wood piled up on the street for the construction on Berlin's underground to build barricades, as well as trees, toppled Litfaßsäulen (advertising columns), barbed wire and cobblestones. In

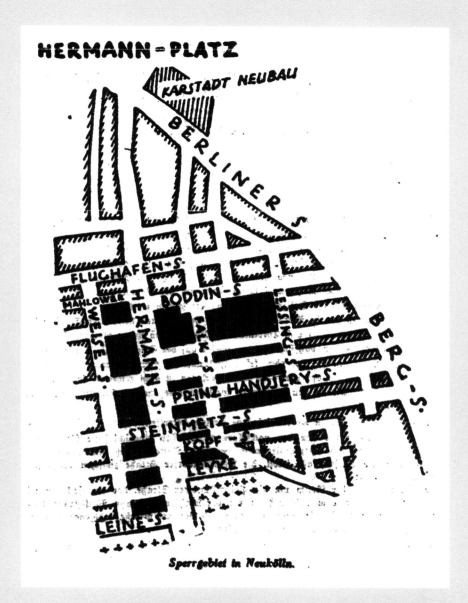

A map showing the exclusion zone (Sperrgebiet), marked in black, in Neukölln. *Berliner Morgenpost, 4 May 1929*

Berlin-Neukölln Herrfurthstr.

OPPOSITE ABOVE
A postcard showing the view down
Herrfurthstraße from Hermannstraße,
Neukölln, 1935. The Hirschowitz clothing
store, outside of which Charles Mackay
was standing when he was shot, is
on the ground floor of the building
on the right. *Museum Neukölln*

OPPOSITE BELOW
A group of police stands in front
of Hirschowitz's clothing shop in
Hermannstraße, while one runs towards a
Panzerwagen (armoured car) used during
the fighting. *Geheimes Staatsarchivs
PK, IX. HA, SPAE, VII Nr. 2940-2*

ABOVE
Police and barricades in front
of the Hirschowitz clothing
store. This image shows the
view of Hermannstraße towards
Hermannplatz, with Herrfurthstraße
on left. *Still from Kampfmai 1929,
from archive of the Deutsche
Kinemathek — Museum für
Film und Fernsehen, Berlin*

retaliation the police had built their own barricades to confine the protesters and prevent vehicles from entering the area.

Mackay got out of his taxi and walked around the block and back down Hermannstraße to the barricades. He was standing near the Hirschowitz clothing store, on the corner of Herrfurthstraße and Hermannstraße, when he was shot by a police sniper operating from a flat on the corner diagonally opposite, about 110 metres away. The clashes of Blutmai had claimed 32 lives. Charles Mackay was the thirty-third and last of the Blutmai fatalities.[11]

D
elmer waited until 1.30 a.m. for Mackay to return before concluding that he must have gone off for a drink. The next morning he phoned Mackay's landlady, who told him that he had not returned home. Delmer then started ringing hospitals. He eventually found his friend stretched out on a marble slab in the mortuary of the Neukölln District Infirmary, his head resting on a support, a white sheet pulled up to his chin.

'There he lay, his mouth gaping open, his smashed spectacles at the foot of the slab with his papers. His wispy, greying hair was ruffled and sticky. His shoes pointed stiffly skywards showing the holes in their soles. On the slabs beside his I counted seven Germans, the other Neukölln victims of the quiet night.'[12] The archive holding the investigation file into Mackay's death contains several photos of Mackay's body. The police ordered autopsies for all who had been killed in the street fighting. The two doctors who completed Mackay's confirmed that he had died from bleeding caused by a shotgun wound: 'The bullet entered the middle of the abdomen immediately above the pelvis in a left, backward and upward direction and came out at the back above the left main trochanter [the bones connecting muscles to the upper part of the thigh bone].'[13] No bullet was found, making it difficult to tell whether he had been shot with a police weapon.

The police listed the items found in Mackay's pockets at the time of his death:

> 1 letter — four pages
> 1 talisman
> 1 pencil
> 1 cigarette-holder
> 1 pocketknife
> 1 box of matches
> 1 rubber
> 2 used tickets of the Berlin State Opera
> 1 small dictionary
> 1 small cigar-holder (cardboard)
> 1 business card of the firm Asher & Co.
> 3 used public transport tickets.[14]

The 'talisman' on the list, also described in some press reports as an 'amulet', was a greenstone tiki. It had, it seems, been given to Mackay by Māori in Whanganui but, as Delmer noted, 'If the token charm exercised any influence over the life of Mackay it can be said to have brought him nothing but bitter sorrow and disappointment.'[15] After his death, Mackay's friends in Whanganui wrote to the New Zealand Embassy in London, asking about the tiki. The letter was passed to the British Embassy in Berlin, which reported that the tiki had been handed to Philip Pembroke Stephens, the Vienna correspondent for the *Daily Express* (whose son was Mackay's godson and who inherited the portion of Mackay's estate not left to others) and the sole executor of Mackay's will. Sefton Delmer later described what happened to Stephens and the tiki:

> Eight years later, Philip Stephens too was wearing the Maori charm around his neck when he was hit in the head and

A photo montage using an image of police during the 1929 riots superimposed on a photograph of the same location in 2019. *Geheimes Staatsarchivs PK, IX. HA, SPAE, VII Nr. 2940-2, and Markus Stein*

A map drawn as part of the police investigation into Mackay's death. The words 'Standort des Mackay' show where he was shot. The arrow shows the location of the sniper. *Geheimes Staatsarchivs PK, I. HA Rep. 219 Prussian State Criminal Police Office, Nr, 55*

killed by a Japanese sniper's bullet in Shanghai, as he stood on the platform of a Chinese water tower, peering out over the Japanese lines. Like Mackay before him, Philip Stephens was killed doing his duty as a newsman, trying to find out whether there was anything new to report.[16]

Even before Delmer's first story about Mackay's death appeared in the *Express*, he was taking action to put pressure on the Berlin police. At 1 p.m. in London, just over 12 hours after Mackay had been shot, Delmer, or another representative of the paper, contacted the Foreign Office. A note from a diplomat in the file gives an idea of the tenor of the call: 'It was clear that the Sunday Express would make a "headline story" of this [Mackay's death] and would accuse us of apathy if we had no comment.'[17] Within the hour, the Foreign Office sent a telegram to the British ambassador in Berlin, Sir Horace Rumbold: '*Daily Express* inform us that C. E. Mackay, one of their correspondents, was shot today in street riot. Please report facts.'[18]

The embassy confirmed the story, adding that 'the police state that Mackay had already received warning to leave the scene of the disorders'.[19] This was a reference to a statement circulated by the police to German newspapers that Mackay was shot dead at 9.10 p.m. Unfortunately for the police, this could not be true, as Delmer told his readers the next day in the front-page story in the *Sunday Express*: 'At 9.10 p.m. Mackay was having a bite of supper — the last he was ever to take — at my flat in the Victoriastrasse, twenty minutes by motor-car from the Neukoln [sic] area . . . Mackay had no intention of entering the danger zone. If he did enter it it was by an accident.'[20]

There was enormous press interest in the riots, and many other journalists had risked their lives in Neukölln that night. This account is from the *Berliner Tageblatt*:

The car drives around the cordoned area. Always the same darkness, which is so unaccustomed in the city, thus uncanny. Floodlights which suddenly illuminate facades. Nowhere is movement seen, a head, a spying eye. It is as if the plague had waged here and killed everyone . . .

Close by the border of the area, however: joie de vivre . . . In the big dance-palace the colourful light-ball turns. Despite Friday, well-attended. As the cowboy band plays, tales are told of the cruel acts perpetrated on policemen. If you reply that, agreeably, there have been no casualties in the police force, you meet unbelieving listeners.

With no surprise I hear next day of the death of a British colleague. He must have fallen the same time as we too were driving round in the area of the Hermannstraße. It was apparently before the time when lights and traffic were prohibited. But if here and there in such lively streets shots ring out — one doesn't know, is it for you or is it for me? — then people must perish.

A journalist who does this kind of external service must reckon on everything. Whether such consequences were avoidable, however, seems to this one not to be beyond all doubt.[21]

Mackay's death and the resulting publicity, in Germany and overseas, sparked a diplomatic incident, causing embarrassment for the Prussian government. In total, the police came up with three different versions of a story that Mackay had visited the Neukölln area that day and had been warned not to return. The police argued that this meant he was responsible for his own death. Delmer, however, was able to account for Mackay's time and prove the police stories false. The police then used Mackay's lack of German to suggest that he did not understand the commands yelled at him and was therefore culpable.[22] None of those killed were found with weapons, and all but Mackay were Berlin civilians. The first fatality in Wedding, a man called Gemeinhardt, shot by the police while standing at his apartment window, was a Socialist Party leader. No police were killed during the Blutmai fighting.

The Associated Press sent a report back to Mackay's family in New Zealand, to whom condolences were sent from the German government. Because Mackay had no relatives in Europe, the international media community stepped in and worked with the embassy and the British church in Berlin to arrange his funeral. Mackay belonged to the Verein der Ausländischen Presse in Deutschland, the Foreign Press Association in Germany, which collected his body from the hospital mortuary and took it to the chapel at the New St Matthew's Cemetery (Neue St Matthäus Kirchhof) at Priesterweg, in the southern part of Schöneberg. This was a second graveyard for St Matthäus Church, opened in 1899 after it was decided that only parishioners could be buried in the old graveyard.

The British chaplain, the Reverend R. H. Cragg, led Mackay's funeral service on Wednesday 8 May. A German government official placed a wreath on the coffin, as did representatives of the Foreign Press Association, the Association of the Foreign Free-lance Journalists and the Association of Teachers of Foreign Languages. The British consul-general to Germany, George Lyall, and counsellor, Harold Nicolson, attended on behalf of the British Embassy. There were also people from the German Foreign Office, the Berlin police and the German press. Many foreign journalists attended: according to Delmer nearly all countries in the world were represented. And at least one New Zealander was at the funeral: Tom Sullivan, the New Zealand oarsman, who had been working in Berlin for several years as a rowing coach.[23]

After Mackay's death, his last stories were published under his by-line in newspapers on both sides of the Tasman. Other stories, including a profile of Sullivan, which appeared in the Christchurch *Press* as being 'By a New Zealander in Berlin', had no attribution. After leaving New Zealand, Sullivan became an international professional champion sculler.[24] Following the Great War he had been club captain and trainer for the Berliner Ruderklub, described by Mackay as 'the most fashionable and exclusive of the many rowing clubs of Berlin'. His sketch of Sullivan captured his personality:

> I found Sullivan as hale and hearty as ever . . . he likes his job and is well looked after. Even after all these years, he only speaks a few words of German, but, said he, 'They have to get on with me, and I find I can manage all right without German. Put plenty of energy into your language and they understand it alright.' I may mention that the highest compliment you can pay a German is to speak English to him.

Mackay went on to describe Sullivan shouting at a stout German banker he was training. The interview must have taken place just before Mackay's death; the report was read in New Zealand the day before his burial.[25]

Coverage of Mackay's funeral was overshadowed by the funeral for several other victims at the Friedrichsfelde Central Cemetery in the east of Berlin. The communist leader Ernst Thälmann told the huge crowd that 'The Communist Party show[ed] its full solidarity with those who stood on the barricades.'[26] But not everyone was mourning the Bloody May losses. The conflict was a boost for the Nazi Party, keen to exploit the division between the socialists and communists and build support among workers, by drawing them away from the other two parties. Political violence escalated and the city began to drift into what some described as civil war — an atmosphere that intensified through to 1933, when Hitler was appointed chancellor in January. The Reichstag was set on fire in February, and by March Hitler had proclaimed the Third Reich.[27]

On 12 May 1929, just four days after Mackay was buried, the Nazi Party won its first election victory in Saxony. As historian Léon Schirmann, author of a book that examined the riots, has noted, 'The Bloody May marks a significant point in the history of the visible rise of the National Socialist Movement.'[28]

W. H. Auden wrote about the riots in his poem '1929', originally known as 'It was Easter as I walked in the public gardens', one of his famous poems from the period when he lived in Berlin. The vivid description of the fighting sits uneasily alongside Auden's apparently unsympathetic response to the violence.[29]

Charles Mackay had made a will on 13 December 1927, nearly a year before he moved to Berlin. Because he died in the city, the will was opened and executed there. This took some time, however; the file was not completed until 1933, perhaps because the lawyer handling the case had trouble contacting Alastair Campbell, who was named as a beneficiary.

Twenty-eight-year-old Campbell was a New Zealand architect who had been living in London since 1924. It is not clear how he had met Charles Mackay, but back in Whanganui in March 1920 Campbell had been commissioned by Mackay to paint two watercolour views of buildings at Wanganui Collegiate, which Campbell's firm had designed, for a portfolio of paintings to be presented to the Prince of Wales during his visit to the city. The pair had kept in touch while Mackay was in prison and Campbell had visited him at Mount Eden.[30] It is possible that Campbell was the person Ruth Hethke mentioned in her police statement, after Mackay's death:

> His friend (I can't remember his name at the moment), who had already moved in to our pension a week before Mr [Mackay], and had spent some days away from Berlin, came to us on Saturday 4.5 at about 10.30 am. He enquired whether Mr [Mackay] had moved into our pension, and at the same time informed us that [Mackay] had been shot in Neukölln on Friday. He had learnt this in the Language Institute at Bülowstraße 93.[31]

After appointing Philip Pembroke Stephens executor, the will turned to the beneficiaries:

> I give to my friend Alastair Campbell Compton St London W.C.1 my wristlet [watch] to my friend Walter Harrison of Queen's College Oxford my typewriter and to my friend Guardsman Chris Craggs 2651809 — 2nd Battalion 4 Company Coldstream Guards my clothes, boots and shoes. I give all the rest and remainder of my property to my godson Pembroke Stephens son of said executor but I direct that there shall first be paid out thereof the sum of five guineas to each of my sisters and brothers which I ask [them] to expend in some little memento of me and especially request my said executor to keep my ring, studs and spirit flask ... for my godson.[32]

Mackay had met Harrison, an Australian Rhodes Scholar, on the boat trip to London in 1926. The pair had kept in touch and Harrison had visited Mackay in Berlin with another Australian Rhodes Scholar, John Hardie Lavery.[33]

Charles Mackay's will, held by the Amtsgericht (local court) in Schöneberg, Berlin. The file itself has been in the wars, perhaps literally. The bottom part of each page has been singed by fire, and the document has survived some sort of water damage. Given how badly Berlin was bombed during the Second World War, it is remarkable that the file survived. *Amtsgericht Schöneberg II, 64/29 VI 1574/305 and 65/29 IV 1185/305*

Mackay's grave cannot now be found in the New St Matthew's Cemetery. When the author first visited in 2007, there were no headstones earlier than the 1940s, and the graveyard had more green space than would be expected. The reason is that in Germany graves are rented. Only those of prominent people, like the Grimm brothers at the original St Matthäus cemetery, for example, are retained. When Mackay died the rental period was 25 years; it was later reduced to 20. After the end of that term, unless the plot is renewed — and sometimes it cannot be — the headstone is removed and the grave begins a 'Ruhezeit' or resting period before it can be reused. Embalming is uncommon in Germany. When a whole cemetery is closed, the resting period is 30 years; the last burials at New St Matthew's Cemetery took place in 2005 and it is scheduled to become a park some time after 2035.

German burial records are well maintained, for reasons that once included the Nazi interest in proving racial ancestry, but because the ownership of the cemetery has changed, records of Mackay's burial are difficult to track down. The register is written in Sütterlin, an alphabet script no longer used in Germany.[34] The cemetery has been reduced in size twice, once during the Nazi period and again in the 1970s for a motorway. This means that Mackay's grave may not even be within the current cemetery area. And even if it is, it would only be an unmarked grassy plot.

There is, however, photographic evidence of Mackay's grave before the headstone was removed. The image is held by his great-nephew, Rod Mackay, grandson of Charles's brother Frank, who farms the family property in Te Kauwhata. Topped by a large cross, the stone had just two lines of text, unusually for a German grave, in English:

CHARLES EVAN MACKAY
MAY 3RD 1929

Rod Mackay can recall his mother saying 'that the person involved died under suspicious circumstances (shot as a spy in Germany was the impression I had), and that there was something shady'.[35]

Some of the newspaper coverage following Mackay's death referred to his controversial past. A Sydney newspaper ran an article under the headline:

TRAGIC LIFE OF CHARLES MACKAY
SHOT IN BERLIN; HAD BEEN IN PRISON
CRIME IN N.Z.[36]

It was sent by the German consul in Sydney to the Auswärtiges Amt (Foreign Affairs Department) in Berlin and explained how Mackay's career as mayor and lawyer ended when 'under unsavoury circumstances, he shot a man and put a revolver into the victim's hand in order to suggest suicide'. Among the New Zealand papers reporting Mackay's death, *Truth* savoured the chance to allude to an unmentionable subject.

> Mackay's career as mayor of Wanganui came to an abrupt end when he was arrested on a charge of attempting to murder a returned soldier named Walter Darcy Cresswell on May 15, 1920. He pleaded guilty and was sentenced to 15 years' imprisonment . . . The case, which created considerable interest at the time, was marked by sordid features, recapitulation of which after such a long lapse of time would serve no good purpose, especially now that Mackay is dead.

> Cresswell's connection with the affair showed him in a highly creditable light, his determination to expose Mackay animating the latter in attempting to kill him.[37]

Charles Mackay's grave in the New St Matthew's Cemetery, Priesterweg Schöneberg, Berlin. *Rod Mackay*

Once the generation of New Zealanders who remembered the 'Wanganui Sensation' and its strange Berlin coda had died, the memory of Mackay and his story would disappear from view, just like his German grave. And even before this, Mackay's in-laws and others in Whanganui were taking steps to ensure that he was not just forgotten, but also eliminated from history. At the same time, Cresswell's fondness for 'Greek love' changed the view of his role in the 1920 shooting, complicating efforts to conceal the story.

Cresswell's patron, the Bloomsburyite Lady Ottoline Morrell, photographed in London by Philip Edward Morrell in 1931. *Alamy*

11. CRESSWELL

After recovering from the shooting, D'Arcy Cresswell returned to England in 1921. An account of his life (written by literary scholar John Weir for a collection of prose by Cresswell's contemporary James K. Baxter), sourced from Cresswell's own writings, is a litany of relationships with men. During six months spent in Germany, for example, 'he fell in love with Otto Gugenheim [sic], a seventeen-year-old lad ("handsome, serious and reserved") and an army sergeant ("a wild and reckless fellow")'. After going to Wales in November 1922, he formed a relationship with a young Aberavon miner 'who promised to follow Cresswell to London but did not . . . "he is a man I shall never forget, nor ever cease to love"'.

Back in London, and living above a butcher's shop, he was 'poor and friendless' until Guggenheim arrived from Cologne to study medicine. 'Cresswell could not see enough of him, remarking "We were devoted to each other." He also wrote "I took but a limited interest in women."' Nevertheless Cresswell frequented bars and cafés searching for someone else and found 'an unnamed South African who had fled from home for some reason. He had other affairs with men . . .'[1]

Cresswell later recorded that 'for men I had more and more the utmost liking and intimacy, even for those illiterate and rough kinds I had formerly been thrown amongst, some of whom I loved dearly . . . Nevertheless the temper and attributes most favourable to this passion are to be found where men are segregated to themselves and pursue one calling in common, as soldiers, sailors and students, particularly soldiers and sailors . . .'[2]

But then there was an affair with a woman, Freda Dacie, who worked as a nurse in a London hospital. She was four months pregnant when the pair married on 28 August 1925. The marriage certificate lists Cresswell's occupation as 'poet'. Their son, David, was born in January the following year; shortly afterwards Cresswell abandoned Freda and the child. When she met someone else, Cresswell refused to agree to a divorce, so David's half-sister from his mother's subsequent

THE POET'S PROGRESS

BY

WALTER D'ARCY
CRESSWELL

WITH A PORTRAIT BY
WILLIAM
ROTHENSTEIN

LONDON
FABER & FABER LIMITED
24 RUSSELL SQUARE

relationship was born illegitimate. Interviewed many years later, David Cresswell said, 'My father was a homosexual and that dominated his life. The mysterious thing to me is how I came to be begotten . . . D'Arcy was an attractive man and had opinions about everything and some of his opinions were outrageous. I think she just fell in love with him, I think he was attractive, [with] strong opinions, and interesting. She was in a set of fairly wild friends . . . in London, in spite of being a nurse.'[3]

David believed that Cresswell's family put pressure on him to marry — 'no way were they going to have an illegitimate grandchild' — and threatened to cut his allowance. Circumstances were challenging in the new household: determined to be a poet, Cresswell was selling his poems door to door and Freda had had to give up work to look after David. Cresswell's father was unhappy about his son's career decision but had agreed to match the money he earned from his poetry sales.

The family did not talk about D'Arcy. When David asked about him, he was told his father was abroad, 'away in New Zealand'. He was 12 when he finally met D'Arcy, who was back in England after six years in New Zealand. Later, when he was a student and out one day with friends, he saw his father in Piccadilly Circus:

> I said, 'Gosh, there's my father', they were all very intrigued . . . Shall I try and go after him and contact him? Anyway, he'd vanished before I could make up my mind. He looked as though he was prowling, there was something about him, the way he was slinking along, he looked as though he was looking for homosexuals . . . his sexuality manifested itself in a physical way.[4]

They had intermittent contact but maintained a relationship; David stayed with his father several times, and not long before his death D'Arcy stayed with David and his wife Ruth and met his grandchildren.

In the 1960s, Charles Carrington gave an interesting insight into his friend's sexuality around the time of the shooting in 1920:

Darcy always used to twit me with being immature. I wasn't a man of the world like him. I lived a sheltered life. But the heart of the matter lies in homosexualism. In those days, even intimate friends, as we were, rarely broke the taboo by talking about it. And I don't think Darcy had yet admitted to himself that he was a homosexual. Later, of course, he gloried in it.[5]

Cresswell's large opinion of his own talent as a poet was not shared by others. In the words of the English professor William Broughton, 'his great failure, though, perhaps even his tragedy, was his unfulfillable wish to be recognized as a fine poet, which he patently was not'.[6] The poet Denis Glover criticised Cresswell's poems for their 'cloyingly anachronistic style' and 'neo-classical pastiche', and described them as flat, mannered and irritating. It is hard to disagree.[7]

> O England! why do you hasten to fall and forget your spring?
> Like the leaves that hurry down from the trees in the autumn,
> To whirl away over the earth with the following wind,
> To lead the way for the year's load of snow,
> Which is death that follows forever the marching summer
>   of life,
> Having now only the weak sun of remembered song,
> Only cities that are shrouds, only poets that are tombs![8]

As a gay history website observed of another example of Cresswell's poetry, with a gift like that, it is hardly surprising that he had to live off his family.

> Dear books, be all the nourishment I need!
> I am so poor I scarce have means to buy
> One meal a day. Alas! I must rely

On your fair thoughts for all my winter feed.
(Throw him a bale of silage!)
One day at last, like Venus' doves, you'll draw
My happy soul t' the star-empurpl'd glen.[9]

Cresswell's prose is more highly regarded and caught the attention of people associated with the Bloomsbury Group of writers, artists and intellectuals who, as Dorothy Parker memorably quipped, 'lived in squares, painted in circles and loved in triangles'. The group began at 46 Gordon Square, the London home of Virginia Woolf and Vanessa Bell, and included their spouses, Leonard Woolf and Clive Bell; Bell's lover, the painter Duncan Grant; Woolf's lover, Vita Sackville West; bisexual economist John Maynard Keynes; the critic Roger Fry; and the painter Walter Sickert.[10]

Cresswell's entrée to Bloomsbury was through the artist William Rothenstein, whose wife introduced him to Arnold Bennett, best known for his novels. When Cresswell sent Bennett his draft memoir and poems, the latter managed to dodge giving an opinion on the poetry — 'I am very pleased with the poems, but I will say nothing about them (because I am not a judge of verse) except that I am quite sure that they have distinction'[11] — but he persuaded Faber & Faber to publish the memoir, against the advice of T. S. Eliot, a director at the firm. *The Poet's Progress*, with a portrait of Cresswell by Rothenstein, came out in 1930. The anthologist and translator Edward Marsh, 'a well-connected, gay taste-maker', liked the book and took Cresswell under his wing.[12]

From late 1928 until he left for a visit to New Zealand towards the end of 1931, Cresswell's lodgings were in Stourcliffe Street, near Marble Arch. To reach his rooms visitors had to walk through the landlady's sitting room, where she would often be sitting by the fire knitting. Cranleigh Barton, who had met Cresswell (whom he nicknamed 'Pussy') when the pair were sailing to London in 1914, visited one of Cresswell's rooms in March 1925. 'On Wednesday at 4pm,' he wrote

in his diary, 'I went and had tea with Darcy Cresswell at his room — 12 Lexington St, Soho — it is tucked away in a most unpretentious house and he meals for himself. After tea he showed me some of his favourite points of view about the neighbourhood.'[13]

Further north in Bloomsbury, at 10 Gower Street, stood the residence of Bloomsburyite Lady Ottoline Morrell, who was impressed by the first volume of Cresswell's autobiography and who maintained contact with him until her death in 1938.

D'Arcy Cresswell arrived in New Zealand in January 1932 with a reputation for having made it in the London literary world, but back in London the relationship with his patron had soured. An exasperated Edward Marsh had paid for Cresswell's passage home to get him off his hands, having become 'gravely concerned' at his protégé's 'apparent inability or refusal to continue with the solid labouring required for a continued literary life of worldly and steadily developing achievement'.[14]

During the voyage back to New Zealand a ship's doctor removed the bullet lodged in 1920 from Cresswell's back: 'The lung which it had passed through had given trouble, but the bullet had not. Lately it had started to move about, and the ship's surgeon removed it,' he told the Christchurch newspaper *The Sun*, not long after his arrival.[15]

Cresswell then went south to stay with his family at their farm, Barnswood, in South Canterbury until the end of May 1933, and also spent time with friends in Christchurch. A letter to Marsh in February 1932 reported the effects of the Depression were being felt, even among wealthy landowners like the Cresswells. 'The slump here is awful, & unlike that in England it chiefly devastates those who were formerly rich & who led the country's social life, that is the big landholders.'[16] By late October Walter Cresswell was 'all but bankrupt, and his mortgages are threatening to sell him up. He has lost steadily £10,000 a year on these properties, since the slump, and from being wealthy is now penniless,' Cresswell told the British writer Maurice Baring.[17]

While in New Zealand, Cresswell was working on the essays that became the second volume of his autobiography, *Present Without Leave*, published in London in 1939. Some of the book was reproduced in the Christchurch *Press* in five instalments between February and March 1932, but the series was stopped following protests from scandalised readers angry at seeing themselves and their region satirised.[18] During his previous return to New Zealand, Cresswell had 'caused some astonishment by describing Christchurch as a "most un-English looking City" in which his impressions were those of entering a Wild West show'.[19] Although it is not difficult to see what might have irritated readers in 1932, Cresswell's prose writing is wry and sharp.

> They [New Zealanders] have no political talent, but a great desire to be governed, lest they be thought savages. Even so they desire to be artists and poets, yet there are none among them, and few persons of taste. Their statues and monuments are among the worst to be found; yet so eager they are they prefer a bad taste shall flourish than none. All they do is savage and violent, in accordance with nature around them; and this exercise of their passions they mistake for progress. In all things they exhibit immense energy; and in this alone they show they are subject to the titanic and terrible presence about them.

He admitted that, faced with disaster, New Zealanders 'show themselves a truly great people. In short their failings are such as enlightenment may remove; while their virtues another people might long in vain to acquire.' Interestingly for a man who spent so much of his life in England, he felt that their 'present condition depends on the state of peoples a great distance off and their communication with these. They have as yet no future their own, and when at length that confronts them they shall awake to find where they lie, and what realm it was they so rudely and rashly disturbed.'[20]

The controversy over his newspaper articles did not deter Cresswell from working, and the nearly eight years he spent in New Zealand during the 1930s were productive: 'Half the Cresswell there is got written here'.[21] He returned to England in 1938, and apart from one short visit to New Zealand in 1949-50, was based in London for the rest of his life.

Writing in the literary magazine *Landfall* after Cresswell's death in 1960, its editor Charles Brasch argued that New Zealand literature, in a real sense, began in the 1930s under Cresswell's banner.[22] This bold claim rests on Cresswell's contact with key figures during his time back in New Zealand, including the Christchurch poet Ursula Bethell, who knew Cresswell's mother. Cresswell admired Bethell's work and spent time at her house, Rise Cottage, on the Cashmere Hills, which was a hub for artists and writers and a refuge when 'almost no other house in Christchurch was open to me after the *Press* began to serialize *Present Without Leave*'.[23] Cresswell was an advocate for Bethell's work, advising her on the selection of poems for publication, helping her to get published and reviewing her work.[24]

In 1934 Cresswell moved to Auckland, where he spent time with other writers, including Frank Sargeson, Robin Hyde, Jane Mander and Roderick Finlayson, and lived in several baches owned by the Stronach family in Castor Bay on the North Shore. He was a regular at Gleesons Hotel near the Auckland waterfront, a meeting place for sailors and gay men.[25] Cresswell remained determined to be a poet, but his criticism, published in the new literary journal *Tomorrow*, and his prose continued to be more highly regarded. Some of his poems were included in Allen Curnow's ground-breaking *Penguin Book of New Zealand Verse* in 1960, but not in later editions. As John Newton and others have noted, interest in Cresswell's autobiographies has grown, and they continue to find readers.[26]

Although there are only passing references to the Whanganui incident in Cresswell's published writing and surviving letters, homosexual themes permeate his life and work, including the two volumes of his autobiography. Among his projects was *The Forest*, a verse play idealising Greek love and misogyny, eventually published in 1952. Cresswell connected his sexuality with the Whanganui shooting in a 1939 letter to his friend Ormond Wilson, whom he had met in London in 1928, while Wilson was studying at Oxford University. From a privileged background, Wilson had attended Christ's College, as had Cresswell and Carrington. He went on to become the youngest MP in the 1935 Labour government, representing the Rangitikei electorate, and was one of New Zealand's leading left-wing intellectuals.

In 1939 Cresswell was in the running for a job with the New Zealand Public Relations Council in London, but the application process hit a snag when his contact, the general manager Gilbert McAllister, was warned by the New Zealand High Commission that there would be 'strong objections' to Cresswell's nomination. Cresswell described to Wilson what happened next:

> I told him [McAllister] of my writings, & the opposition they raised in N.Z. — of the suppression of the Progress II in the Ch-ch 'Press' & the outcry. I told him all about Mackay shooting me in Wanganui, & the absolute freedom I took on sexual matters since. I hinted at low company & all that, & we discussed homosexuality, tho' without reference except my hints, to myself. At all this he rather laughed, and said it must be due to something else.[27]

Given Cresswell's openness about his sexuality, it is interesting to speculate how widely known his role in the Whanganui incident was in the decades after 1920. Historian Alison Laurie has argued that Ursula Bethell and her companion Effie Pollen must have been aware,

RIGHT
Charles Carrington,
photographed in 1921.
*Alexander Turnbull
Library, 88-252-3*

LEFT
George Hamish Ormond
Wilson, photographed
around 1938. *Alexander
Turnbull Library,
1/2-043440-F*

and could therefore have regarded him as 'unreliable': 'perhaps they were worried Cresswell would recognise their relationship was lesbian if he met Pollen, and could not be trusted to keep this confidential'.[28] For her part, Bethell told Brasch that when Denis Glover reported Cresswell's 'homosexual goings on' she thought the 'references in D'Arcy's writings were just a pose, but Denis says not at all. I feel it's a dip down for D'A. & a thing he's deceiving himself about.'[29]

The homosexual composer Douglas Lilburn, who was born in Whanganui, certainly knew about the case. He warned artist Douglas MacDiarmid to keep his friends in New Zealand 'happily ignorant' of where he was living because it would undoubtedly raise eyebrows when, at Lilburn's suggestion, MacDiarmid moved into Cresswell's London flat after Christmas in 1946.[30] The New Zealand poet Count Geoffrey Potocki De Montalk, who knew Cresswell in London in the 1930s, mentioned the Whanganui incident in his *Recollections of My Fellow Poets*:

> There was, of course, the business about the Mayor of Wanganui! In a way, through his Sir Galahad goings-on, Cresswell was responsible for [Mackay's] death . . . Certain of the literati in New Zealand know all about it, and would perform a better service to New Zealand literature and history, by putting it on record, than by pontificating about me and Fairburn, and by breaking the world record in split infinitives.[31]

Once his allowance from his family ended, around 1950, possibly following the deaths of his parents, Cresswell had to support himself.[32] Unable, or unwilling, to make a living from his writing, in 1951 he became a night watchman at Somerset House in London, a large Georgian building on the south side of the Strand then used to house various government offices.

As he told Ormond Wilson in 1959, Cresswell was looking forward to turning 65 in January 1961: 'This post ends in 18 months when I finish the night watching & pick up the old age pension, & thus face the world for the final 30 years of doing what I was sent forth to learn to do. For the whole job I need 100 years.'[33] His ambitious plans were thwarted when, on 21 February 1960, aged 64, he died in his flat at 8 Abercorn Place, St John's Wood, of gas poisoning. Some suspected it to be suicide, but the coroner ruled his death accidental.

After Cresswell's death, friends contributed a series of tributes that were published in *Landfall*. They were led by historian Charles Carrington, who described Cresswell's 'strange experience in Wanganui' and how being shot through the body was an influence on his make-up.[34] Ormond Wilson's tribute was acute and honest:

> There never was the ability to write great poetry . . . and yet his friends have all, at one time or another, and for shorter or longer periods, believed in him. But their belief was rather in the man than what he had done. And he, despite his selfishness and bigotry, his squabbles and his odd secretiveness, poured himself out to them in his letters, disclosing all his hopes and aims, his intrigues, his sordid affairs and his revelations. It is the letters which need to be published, to complete the always promised but never fulfilled continuation of his autobiography.[35]

These glancing references mark the beginning of the re-emergence of the story of the 1920 shooting. Initially this, understandably, happened in a circumspect fashion, given that homosexuality was still illegal. Several decades later, Wilson dubbed Cresswell 'that most eccentric of nonconformists' and credited him with providing insights into the homosexual underworld.[36] As discussing homosexuality grew easier, this aspect of his personality became associated with Cresswell's reputation as a writer, and fuelled interest in the story of the 1920 shooting.

Charles Mackay (front centre) was president of the Wanganui Trotting Club, a key establishment in an era in which horse racing was a sport of the elites. This image is of the club members at its annual meeting in March 1920, not long before Mackay's dramatic fall from grace. Donald McBeth, Mackay's friend and fellow lawyer, is third from left in the back row. *Alexander Turnbull Library, G-16645-1/1*

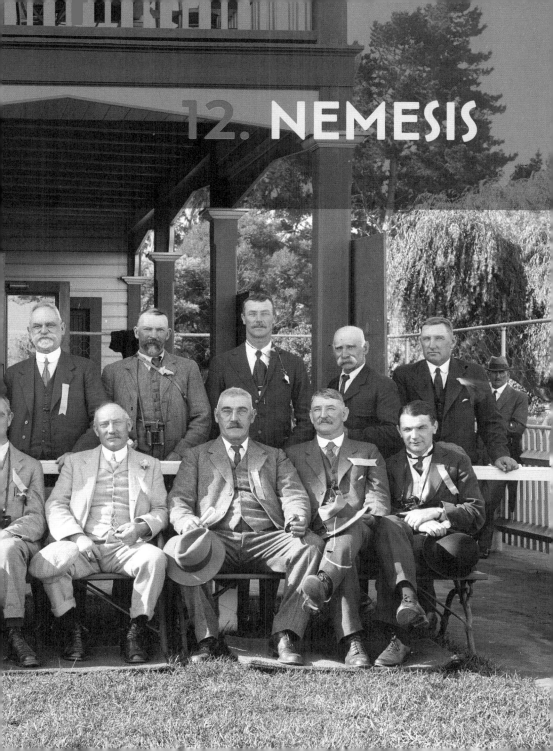

n the mid-1960s Ormond Wilson decided that D'Arcy Cresswell's letters should be edited and that the editor should be Helen Shaw, the poet and writer who, in 1955, had edited *The Puritan and the Waif*, the first collection of critical essays about Frank Sargeson's work. Historian Tim Shoebridge has pointed out similarities between the work of Cresswell and Shaw, 'an "organicist poet", or a romantic writer who rejected modern thinking and technology in favour of spiritual intuitions'.[1] Shaw had been aware of Cresswell's writing for some time. In 1949 she wrote to her friends Jean and John Bertram: 'I've been reading . . . Darcy Cresswell's The Poet's Progress. Heaven knows why not before. I think it is terrific. That amazing ego, that astonishing outpouring.'[2] Shaw assiduously took up the cause of promoting Cresswell's work.

Writing to Shaw in 1965, Wilson said he was impressed with her research to date, 'But if you are going into everything so thoroughly, then you'll also have to study the Wanganui affair.'[3] She was prompted, too, by another correspondent, the Labour MP John A. Lee, who had helped Cresswell — in his words 'a distinguished dead-beat' — to get a job in a forestry camp near Auckland during the Depression. 'Don't forget,' Lee wrote, 'that D'Arcy was the boy in the Mayor of Wanganui case of long long years ago. The Mayor served his sentence and later died in Germany.'[4] Lee could not remember when the shooting happened, but suggested that Shaw write to the Whanganui library and town clerk to get the dates so she could find newspaper coverage.

When Shaw followed Lee's advice, the town clerk suggested she omit any reference to the incident. The city librarian was more helpful, telling her the date of the shooting and passing on references to newspaper articles. Shaw wrote an account of the shooting in a biographical essay that was part of the manuscript she submitted to Auckland University Press.

The Whanganui incident, she suggested in that essay, may have created the first public image of Cresswell and it also 'gave an

LEFT
Hella Hofmann (Helen Shaw) photographed by Frank Hofmann. *Te Papa Tongarewa Museum of New Zealand, A.027502. Gift of the Frank Hofmann Estate, 2016*

BELOW
Retired schoolteacher Bill Mitchell began researching the 'Wanganui Affair' after being told about it by his friend Frank Sargeson. Mitchell's drafts of his work, 'Resign or Else: The "Wanganui Affair"', have been important sources for later researchers. *Alison Morrison*

indication of the strangely inexplicable and highly individual nature of his temperament and aim'.[5] And it highlighted the centrality of Cresswell's homosexuality in his life: 'The Wanganui incident must be looked upon as a motivating force affecting Cresswell's future behaviour and lending weight to his intense belief in the ideal he was, all his life to approve . . . "that affection of men for each other which so delighted the Greeks" which coloured so much of his thinking.'[6] Auckland University Press rejected Shaw's manuscript 'on moral grounds'. It was later accepted by Canterbury University Press, and Cresswell's edited letters were published in 1971 but without Shaw's essay. The compromise was a chronology, with one brief reference to 1920: 'Attempt made on his life in the "Wanganui Affair".'[7]

This was not the end of Shaw's work on Cresswell or of her interest in the Whanganui affair. In 1983, *Dear Lady Ginger*, her edited selection of letters between Cresswell and Ottoline Morrell, was published in New Zealand and England. This included a rare reference by Cresswell to what happened in 1920, in a 1933 letter that mentioned 'being shot thro' the lung here on my return from the war (a matter which earned me a letter of thanks from the Chief Justice of N. Z.)'. Shaw included a summary of the shooting in a footnote, drawn from 1920 newspaper reports.[8] She died in 1985, leaving behind plans for a biography of Cresswell.

In the mid-1960s, while Shaw was beginning her research into the shooting, William Broughton, then an English literature student at the University of Auckland, had also come across the affair while working on a PhD thesis about the life and work of Cresswell and his fellow poets A. R. D. Fairburn and R. A. K. Mason. During his research, Broughton discovered the real reason Cresswell returned to England in 1921: the 'wish to escape the sensational publicity which resulted from his being assaulted and wounded in an attack made upon him in Whanganui'.

Broughton included more details in a footnote: 'This occurrence,

Lady Ottoline Morrell, photographed in London in
1929. National Portrait Gallery, Ax143222

often referred to by Cresswell's friends as "the Wanganui incident" (for example in the *Landfall* memorial) was, according to Messrs. Roderick Finlayson and Ormond Wilson, one in which Cresswell was attacked and shot by the then mayor of Wanganui as the result of a private quarrel. The mayor was later arraigned for attempted murder.'[9]

More than 30 years after completing his thesis, Broughton was commissioned to write the essays about Mackay and Cresswell for the *Dictionary of New Zealand Biography*.[10] In his essay about Mackay, Broughton deliberately treated Cresswell's behaviour as a separate, standalone matter.

> Cresswell was a returned soldier who had come from his home in Timaru to visit relatives near Wanganui. The two men became friendly and met on several occasions. On 15 May after an argument at his office Mackay shot and seriously wounded Cresswell. It was later alleged that Mackay had made homosexual advances to Cresswell, who then attempted to extract a letter of confession and resignation from the mayor. Cresswell stated that he had led Mackay on, 'to make sure of his dirty intentions.' Mackay was arrested and charged with attempted murder; he pleaded guilty, acknowledging the factual truth of an unsworn evidential statement that Cresswell made from his hospital bed. No defence was called, though a plea in mitigation was made when Mackay was sentenced to 15 years' imprisonment, which he began serving in Mount Eden prison.[11]

As Broughton explained to one of the dictionary staff, 'I hope some day to do some further work on Charles Mackay, because he seems to me to be a significant figure in Wanganui's history who was unjustly expunged from the town's annals and perhaps then I will get a little closer to the truth behind the whole sorry business.' When he was working on his thesis, 'the suspicion that [Cresswell] was blackmailing Mackay in 1920 was hard to resist though of course it was unproveable.'

While writing the essay, 'and looking at it now from the perspective of Mackay', Broughton found it 'tempting to think that Mackay's political opponents and the RSA were in collusion and set the whole thing up, with Cresswell the willing decoy who would be presented as a "wholesome" young returned soldier who was prepared to risk his chastity to expose the mayor's perfidious behaviour, etc.' Although such an interpretation seemed 'rather horrifyingly possible', he knew that 'without more evidence, which won't be easy to document after 75 years, it can be nothing more than a glint in a researcher's eye at present'.[12]

The conspiracy theory came up again the following year, when Broughton's essay about Cresswell was edited. In a report on the entry, one of the editors, Ross Somerville, neatly summarised the conundrum faced by anyone who came across the story of the shooting: 'Doesn't this make the reader want to know what interest Cresswell could possibly have had in the Wanganui Mayor's resignation? Could we not introduce a suggestion at least of the likely scenario — that Cresswell was being willingly used as a provocateur by the Mayor's opponents.'[13] Although this makes sense, no evidence to support the conspiracy claim has ever emerged and the final dictionary text reflected this:

On 10 May 1920, when visiting relatives, he [Cresswell] was introduced to the mayor of Whanganui Charles Ewing (Evan) Mackay. The two men quickly became friendly, but five days after their first meeting Cresswell was shot and injured by Mackay. Cresswell later alleged that the mayor had made homosexual overtures to him, to which he responded by demanding a letter of resignation. The real motivation behind Cresswell's actions remains unclear.[14]

Somerville mentioned a source that *did* suggest there was a conspiracy: 'I think Michael King's *Sargeson* might provide more info than we had when the Mackay essay was researched.'[15] In *Frank Sargeson: A Life*, published in 1995, just before the Cresswell essay, the historian and biographer was definitive:

> Cresswell's case had taken place in Wanganui in May 1920, shortly after the visit there of the Prince of Wales. The town's long-time mayor, a distinguished lawyer named Charles Evan Mackay, was known by some of Wanganui's other leading citizens to be an active homosexual, and they wanted to be rid of him. Using a Cresswell cousin as an intermediary, they hired D'Arcy, an unemployed returned soldier, to act as *agent provocateur*. He travelled to Wanganui from Timaru, was introduced to Mackay by his cousin at a hotel dinner, and behaved in such a way as to encourage intimacy from the mayor.[16]

King's source for this claim was research by Bill Mitchell, an 'erudite and warmly witty retired principal from Belmont',[17] whose home had been within walking distance of Frank Sargeson's Esmonde Road cottage on Auckland's North Shore, where Mitchell, Sargeson and another friend, Ian Hamilton, used to gather on Friday afternoons. At these 'Frank's Fridays', the three septuagenarians would chat and drink Lemora, a fortified citrus wine. On one occasion, Sargeson told the others about the shooting. The story was a gift for Mitchell, a bright man in need of a project. As he explained to Michael King, 'Frank who was on speaking and argumentative terms with Cresswell excited me over this "Wanganui Affair" and I decided to investigate it.'[18]

After Sargeson's death in 1982, Mitchell began researching the incident and writing an essay about his memories of Sargeson. There was no shortage of information on Cresswell, but Mitchell was frustrated by the lack of material concerning Mackay. 'What Mackay was really like as a bloke . . . a father, a husband, a lawyer, a mayor, a president and chairman of this and that I have difficulty in discovering. No Wanganui archive has even a photo or reference.'[19] He completed one draft, 'an infuriatingly long & repetitive account of the Cresswell–Mackay business called "Resign or Else!"', and tried to persuade the writer and art historian Eric McCormick to write up his research, but the latter told Mitchell he could do it himself.[20] Graeme Lay, a younger writer mentored by Sargeson, also refused Mitchell's invitation.

Mitchell deposited his first draft with the Alexander Turnbull Library in 1982 but kept researching. He visited Whanganui, where he made an unsuccessful attempt to meet Mackay's surviving daughter, Josephine Duncan, and a woman who had worked in Mackay's office. When Mitchell's second draft was deposited at the Turnbull in 1985, it caught the attention of librarian Phil Parkinson, who was part of the collective that produced *Pink Triangle*, a national gay magazine that had begun as a National Gay Rights Coalition publication.

Parkinson decided to write a feature-length article about the Whanganui affair, based on Mitchell's essay, but with additional research. Mitchell checked the draft — 'I have "diabolized" — or proof read your article' — but did not want his name associated with the finished feature, which was published in *Pink Triangle* in 1985.[21] Parkinson included Mitchell's theory about why Cresswell blackmailed Mackay, but also added a rationalisation of Mackay's behaviour.

> Cresswell's motives, as indicated in his statement, are palpably false. It seems probable that Mackay's political enemies had become aware of the Mayor's secret and made use of their handsome visitor (who was probably just as unwilling to have

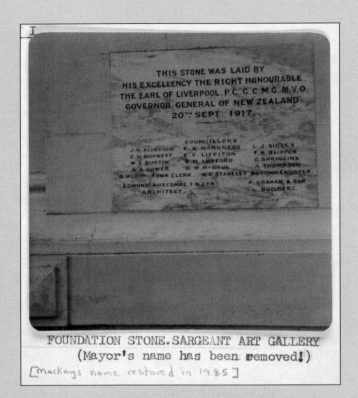

THIS STONE WAS LAID BY
HIS EXCELLENCY THE RIGHT HONOURABLE
THE EARL OF LIVERPOOL. P.C. G.C.M.G. M.V.O.
GOVERNOR GENERAL OF NEW ZEALAND
20TH SEPT. 1917

COUNCILLORS
J.W. ALDERTON   F.A. HARKNESS   L.J. SIGLEY
C.H. BURNETT   E.F. LIFFITON   T.B. SLIPPER
W.S. DUSTIN   W.M. LUXFORD   G. SPRIGGINS
A.A. GOWER   G.W. McCAUL   A. THOMPSON
G. MURCH TOWN CLERK.   N.C. STAVELEY BOROUGH ENGINEER.

EDMUND ANSCOMBE F.N.Z.I.A.   P. GRAHAM & SON
ARCHITECT.   BUILDERS.

FOUNDATION STONE. SARGEANT ART GALLERY
(Mayor's name has been removed!)

[Mackays name restored in 1985]

RIGHT
In 1985, Colin Whitlock, the Wanganui Borough Council town clerk, directed that Mackay's name and title be restored to the Sarjeant stone. Subsequently, while in Whanganui for the Tylee Cottage Residency, artist Ann Shelton discovered the original historic specifications for the stone actually stated that the lettering should be gilded. In her artwork *Double Dawn, freshly gilded foundation stone, the Sarjeant Gallery Te Whare o Rehua, 8 July 2013* (gold leaf on existing foundation stone, 2013) Shelton commissioned a stonemason to re-gild the lettering for Mackay's name and title.

THIS STONE WAS LAID BY
HIS EXCELLENCY THE RIGHT HONOURABLE
THE EARL OF LIVERPOOL. P.C. G.C.M.G. M.V.O.
GOVERNOR GENERAL OF NEW ZEALAND
20TH SEPT. 1917.

MAYOR
C.E. MACKAY
COUNCILLORS
J.W. ALDERTON   F.A. HARKNESS   L.J. SIGLEY
C.H. BURNETT   E.F. LIFFITON   T.B. SLIPPER
W.S. DUSTIN   W.M. LUXFORD   G. SPRIGGINS
A.A. GOWER   G.W. McCAUL   A. THOMPSON
C. MURCH TOWN CLERK.   N.C. STAVELEY BOROUGH ENGINEER.

EDMUND ANSCOMBE F.N.Z.I.A.   P. GRAHAM & SON
ARCHITECT.   BUILDERS.

his own sexual orientation discovered) as bait. Refusal by Cresswell to cooperate might have drawn suspicion to himself and he might have warned the Mayor . . . The mere knowledge that his secret was known may have been enough to destroy any hope Mackay had of resisting blackmail . . .

As Parkinson points out, 'Faced with his limited options for defence against blackmail, [Mackay's] choice of murder (if indeed his actions were the result of deliberation), seems reasonable after his attempts at persuasion and procrastination were unavailing.'[22] While Parkinson was working on the article, another collective member contacted the Wanganui Gay Rights Group and asked for a photograph of the Sarjeant Gallery foundation stone, from which Mackay's name had been removed but recently restored, and this was used to illustrate the article.

In 1989 Bill Mitchell wrote to Michael King, mentioning his Sargeson essay and his manuscript about the Whanganui incident: 'The irony of the whole thing is that a supposed Sir Galahad rids Wanganui of a capable, cultured mayor for his "dirty practices" and then he himself enters upon a life even more notorious and "dirty" as a gay . . .'[23] It was the shooting that interested King, who had discovered Sargeson's own hidden homosexual scandal. Until King's biography appeared, Sargeson's homosexuality had been largely hidden — 'an irregular but committed homosexual life that was not secret from his friends, but not seen', as the writer C. K. Stead put it.[24] Those friends did not, however, know about a court case in 1929, when Sargeson was living in Wellington and working at the Public Trust Office. He had spent 1927-28 in Europe, where he had been freer as a homosexual man and had relationships with men in England and Italy. These had continued on his return to New Zealand.

Sargeson's sister told King that the police surprised Sargeson, then still known by his birth name of Norris Davey, and another man, Leonard Hollobon, while they were masturbating each other in a Wellington boarding house. Davey gave evidence against Hollobon, who was sentenced to five years' reformative detention, while Davey got a two-year suspended sentence and was released into the care of his uncle, Oakley Sargeson, who farmed a remote King Country property. After 18 months there, Norris Davey re-emerged as Frank Sargeson.[25]

Hollobon's trial file, located by Chris Brickell while researching *Mates & Lovers*, his major history of gay life in New Zealand, told a different story. There was no police sting, and it was Hollobon who, under duress, dobbed in Davey:

> The saga began when Hollobon called Wellington police and said he was being blackmailed by a man for five pounds. Two detectives went to talk with him: 'We asked him what was the reason for the man demanding money from him. He then explained that for some time past he had been indecently interfering with men, and that they were then afterwards demanding money from him.' They asked him for the names of men who he had been 'indecently interfering with'. He gave them the names of two sailors; it seems they left New Zealand before the police could get to them. He also named Norris Davey.[26]

The story of Sargeson's arrest in 1929 was the big revelation of King's book, and triggered a major reassessment of the place of homosexuality in the writer's work. It explained why the subject was written about in such a coded, careful way. King made the connection between Sargeson and Cresswell: 'Both were involved in traumatic court cases which had accentuated New Zealand society's abomination of homosexual behaviour in the 1920s.'[27]

Sargeson knew about the Whanganui incident first hand because of his friendship with Cresswell, who was seven years older and had a big impact on the younger man. According to Charles Brasch, Sargeson 'had the utmost respect for D'Arcy Cresswell as a man who has given his life unswervingly to what he believes in'.[28] Sargeson's impressions of Cresswell, recorded in the second volume of his memoirs, are among the most vivid images of 'that slight figure of a man[29] who conceived of himself as a poet':[30]

> although Cresswell was kind enough to grant that he had derived some literary benefit from knowing me, my own debt was much the larger. If I had never met him I doubt that I would have had the confidence, after an interval of nearly ten years, to begin sustained work . . . no matter how ardently I wished to think of Cresswell as a Poet I was unable to: and perhaps what disconcerted me most of all was his inability to see that it was his prose that brought him closest to becoming the Poet it was his life's ambition and purpose to be.[31]

Sargeson, who was 17 when Cresswell was shot by Mackay, remembered 'a sensational happening in a New Zealand provincial town while I was still a schoolboy: there had been an attack upon Cresswell's life during the time he was briefly back in the country after his war service: I remembered from the newspapers [sic] reports the full name, and I thought there was also some reference to a poet.'[32] He found out more in the mid-1950s, sending Janet Frame, then living in an army hut on his section, to the library to find copies of the newspaper coverage.[33] Kevin Ireland, who lived in the hut after Frame, noted that Sargeson was fascinated with the story, and told everyone about it, including Bill Mitchell.[34] By 'exciting' Mitchell about the story, Sargeson was indirectly responsible for the story emerging as it did.

In his phenomenally successful *Penguin History of New Zealand*, which was published in 2003 and sold over 250,000 copies, King repeated Mitchell's claim that Cresswell was hired to blackmail Mackay. More than any other retelling, this was the one that alerted most people to the Whanganui story. Mackay's experience, King argued, illustrated the high risks of involvement in active homosexuality when it was illegal.[35] Brickell used King's and Mitchell's versions of the story in *Mates & Lovers*, published in 2008.[36]

Mitchell himself admitted that his draft manuscripts, which he described as 'a miscellany of facts, opinions, suspicions, prejudices, convictions, conjectures and hearsay', were 'long-winded and poorly organised'.[37] Unable to comprehend how Cresswell — who 'enthusiastically practised the very same aberrant way of life he so savaged, condemned in the mayor of Wanganui' — could punish Mackay for being gay, he speculated about the conspiracy.[38] Mitchell's account includes some factual inaccuracies, which is why Broughton did not use it in his *Dictionary of New Zealand Biography* essay.[39]

It is also odd that none of Mitchell's three drafts mentions that he was born in Whanganui, lived there until around 1923 and met Mackay before his imprisonment. As he explained in a 1987 letter to the journalist Derek Round, who was also working on a book about the shooting, 'I . . . was much impressed by his urbanity, confidence & social poise.'[40] A first-hand memory like this would have been gold to other writers, but strangely did not find its way into Mitchell's work.

n a 1984 letter, Mitchell made a prediction: 'Some day someone will write a novel, article or play about the "Wanganui Affair".' He hoped it 'would not exonerate Cresswell or too unfairly castigate the mayor'.[41] He was right: the incident has inspired several novels, four plays and numerous articles, plus podcasts and artworks.[42]

In 2015 the F4 Art Collective created a work called *The House Guest*, which focused on the trauma suffered by Mackay's daughter, Josephine

Duncan, creating a narrative around the doll's house replica of the Totarapuka homestead that she loaned to the Whanganui Regional Museum in 1959.[43] The artists installed soundtracks that could be heard by visitors to the doll's house, including a song — 'You'd never believe/All the hurt she's seen,/All the pain that a lie has caused' — and an imagined 1959 interview between Duncan and Maxwell Smart, a former museum director and local historian. In this interview, Duncan recalled playing with the doll's house while her parents were arguing in an adjoining room. With her was 'a young actor from a big city. My father entertained and supported the arts with great passion.' Reflecting on this and all that happened to her family in the years that followed, the young man, Duncan told Smart, was probably the source of the argument she overheard.

The first play to respond to the 1920 shooting took a more literal approach to the story. *One of Those* was written by David Charteris, who was part of the Whanganui theatre scene. He had heard about the story in 1970 and incorporated it into a play about Whanganui artist Edith Collier, *A Moment with Edith*, which premiered in 2000. For *One of Those* he researched at the Turnbull, where he read Mitchell's papers. Josephine Duncan refused to talk to him but sent friends to report on *One of Those* when it was first performed as part of the Wanganui Art Festival in 2002.

A solo work performed by Charteris, the play begins with Cresswell in a coffin, addressing the audience. This picks up on a point noted by Mitchell: 'Mackay had a big funeral in Berlin and Cresswell went out unknelled and unknown in a London Crematorium.'[44] 'Who ever would have thought that death would be so, I don't know, ordinary, when I have spent my whole life trying not to be . . . A private funeral. Why a private funeral? Where is the New Zealand Embassy?'[45] Mackay features as a character — meeting Cresswell and talking to his lawyer after his arrest — and ponders how the young man is connected with the mayor's many enemies: 'Who set me up?'

Sir Robert Stout appears briefly, but the focus is firmly on Cresswell, who ruminates on the course his life has taken. The play culminates with his death, alone in his London flat. When *One of Those* was performed in Whanganui for the third time, in 2008, the venue was the Sarjeant Art Gallery. White plastic chairs were arranged facing each other in the magnificent dome at the centre of the gallery. When the play started and the lighting changed, the coffin was revealed in one of the plaster alcoves and Cresswell began to speak.

The first of the novels appeared in 2003. In *The Scornful Moon: A Moralist's Tale*, Maurice Gee moved the setting to Wellington and forward a few years to 1934, but some of the dialogue and details are identical to the Whanganui case. The story is narrated by Sam Holloway, part of a group of Wellington literary men who are writing a mystery novel together, one chapter each. This actually happened in the 1930s, and the manuscript of the novel is held at the Turnbull, where Gee's wife Margareta worked. Known as 'Murder by Eleven', the murder mystery was written by 11 of the 'bookmen' profiled by Christopher Hilliard in his 2006 book *The Bookmen's Dominion: Cultural Life in New Zealand 1920–1950* (Auckland University Press).[46]

She also told her husband about Mitchell's research, which was a starting point for what had begun as a subplot but became more prominent. Owen Moody, a headstrong young homosexual poet, blackmails Oliver Joll, a businessman standing for Parliament. Moody threatens to reveal Joll's homosexuality unless he withdraws his nomination: 'I understood that he had dirty intentions. For a short while I led him on in order to be sure. Then I told him that his behaviour disgusted me. I was angry to have been subjected to advances of such a foul nature and raised my voice several times as I denounced him.'[47] Moody works for Joll's enemy and political rival, James Tinling, who is also Holloway's brother-in-law. The twist in Gee's novel is that Tinling is also secretly homosexual and is being blackmailed by his driver, Lennie Ferrabee, whom he picked up some years earlier.

Although Gee quoted from newspaper reports of the Whanganui case, this was just a starting point, and he resisted finding out too much about Mackay and Cresswell: 'I put them both aside as characters and invented others to take their place, making it fiction.'[48] Mitchell had given a copy of one of his drafts to C. K. Stead, who was considering writing a play or something else based on the story, but stopped when *The Scornful Moon* appeared.

The story of what happened in Whanganui has intrigued writers and artists but, interestingly, they do not really engage with the nature of the homosexuality at the heart of the story. The focus on Mackay's enemies is understandable; there was a campaign of some sort to unseat him, and it concerned his sexuality. The determination of people in Whanganui to suppress this information had the opposite effect, and the story became a source of intrigue for those who encountered it.

Maria Place looking towards the Sarjeant Gallery, 1920s. *Whanganui Regional Museum Photographic Collection, 1999.50 WHS Coll*

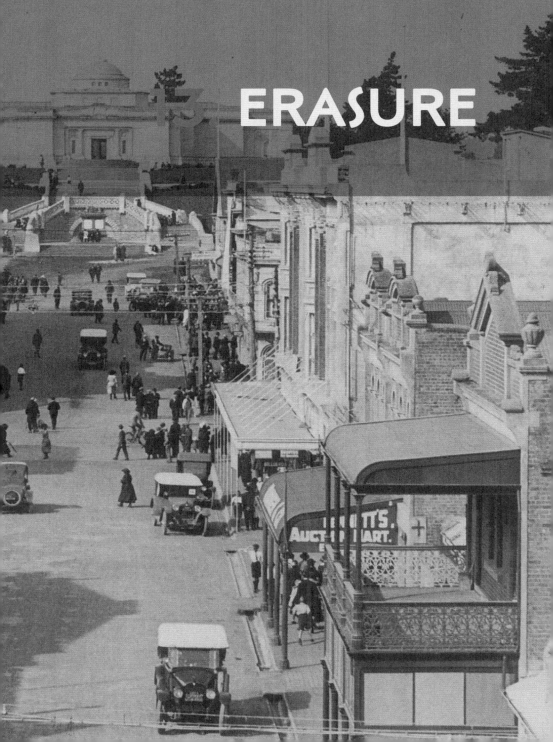

ERASURE

Whanganui's identity, history and fortunes are bound up with its namesake river. The city was built mainly on its right bank, about 5 kilometres from where the river reaches the sea. For a long time, the river has been central to the way in which Whanganui presents itself: the River City, the Rhine of New Zealand or Maoriland and so on. The pepeha, or proverb, which Whanganui iwi use in connection with their awa — 'Ko au te awa, ko te awa ko au' ('I am the river and the river is me') — has been widely embraced.

Once Whanganui was also known as the City of the Sandhills. This seems strange today — the city's urban form has obscured this geography — but there are clues about two giant sandhills that used to enclose the central area, where the town was first established. One is a phantom presence; the other is hiding in plain sight.

Despite its grassy appearance, Pukenamu, on which the Sarjeant Gallery stands, is a huge dune, formed out of wind-blown black sand from the nearby west coast.[1] Long before the gallery was built, there was a wooden stockade on Pukenamu, built during the New Zealand Wars to defend the town during fighting further north, but never occupied. The Rutland Stockade, as it was known, was dismantled in 1887 but remains on Whanganui's coat of arms.

On the other side of the town centre a second stockade stood on an even larger sandhill, known to Māori as Patupuhou/Patupuwhao. Today this is the site of Cooks Gardens, a running track in an amphitheatre. Where did the sand go? Some of it was moved to reclaim Taupō Quay, the foreshore of the Whanganui River in the town centre. What was not moved was sowed with lawn seed.

Nothing in the material used to promote the city ever mentions these sandhills, once so obvious that they were used to name the town. This erasure of something so sizeable, with no hint that it was ever there, works as a physical metaphor for the way in which Whanganui keeps its secrets, among them Charles Mackay.

The Rutland Stockade (below) and York Stockade, photographed as part of a panorama in 1872. *Alexander Turnbull Library, 1/1-000215-G, 1/1-000101-G*

In the twenty-first century, the people of Whanganui seem to have two reactions to the 1920 shooting: those who know about it are not keen to discuss it, unless they are recent arrivals to the city; others have never heard of it. An Auckland woman connected to one of the powerful land-owning families from the 1920s, and who was born in Whanganui in the 1930s, is unusually candid: 'In those days Wanganui [was] very closed. You shut up, unless you were actually of the other side that wanted to make a fuss, and get in the paper. A lot of stuff in Wanganui got shovelled under.'[2]

Her husband's uncle had to leave Whanganui in the 1920s after he was caught in men's toilets with a taxi driver. 'His father dropped him.' That earlier generation regarded sex the way people now think about death — as an unmentionable, uncomfortable, taboo subject. After Mackay was sent to prison, people in Whanganui went to unusual lengths to erase him from the story of the city and of his family. This was not because he had been found guilty of attempting to murder D'Arcy Cresswell but because he had publicly declared himself to be a homosexual.

The historian Barbara Brookes argues that tracing changes in what is shameful over time 'illustrates how people once lived in very different emotional communities, in which shame provided the glue that bound together individual desires and family responsibilities'.[3] She identifies three types of shame: national, familial and individual. If 'civic' is substituted for 'national', Mackay's case exemplifies all of these. Changes in what is regarded as shameful have allowed for a shift in the association of homosexuality with shame.

Eventually, this was transformed into gay pride, with associated law changes altering the status of gay people. For this to happen, as gay activist Bill Logan has noted, 'extinguishing the shame required breaking the secret'.[4] This is exactly what Mackay did by publicly declaring, through his lawyers, that he was a homosexual. He opened himself up to condemnation from his family and other people in Whanganui. It did not take long for them to react.

n June 1920, around a fortnight after Mackay's sentencing, a discreet paragraph appeared in newspapers throughout the country advising that 'as a result of recent disclosures and subsequent court proceedings, an action for divorce has been commenced by Mrs C. E. Mackay of Wanganui'.[5] Isobel Mackay had actually begun divorce proceedings much earlier, while her husband was still on remand and about 10 days before his trial for attempted murder.[6] Initially, her lawyers petitioned for divorce on two grounds:

> On the 1st day of May and on divers other dates the said Charles Ewing Mackay committed the offence of sodomy at Wanganui.

> On or about the 1st day of January 1920, the said Charles Ewing Mackay committed adultery at Auckland with some person whose name is unknown to the petitioner.[7]

The sodomy charge was, according to Isobel's lawyer, based solely on Treadwell's remarks during the sentencing hearing after Mackay was found guilty of attempted murder. In fact, Treadwell did not speak of sodomy in that hearing, only of his client's homosexuality. Sodomy was also never mentioned during the trial the previous day.[8]

The date of the alleged sodomy was two days before the Prince of Wales arrived in Whanganui, and nine days before Cresswell came to town. This meant the latter was not involved, though it was never clear who was. On 2 August 1920, Isobel's lawyers withdrew the sodomy grounds, as 'no further evidence in support of such allegation . . . has since been discovered'. As a result, the alleged adultery remained as the sole grounds for divorce.

In a letter held in the divorce file, Mackay wrote from Mount Eden Prison four days later to admit that 'on or about December 30th 1919 I committed adultery with a lady whose name I decline to state.'[9] Perhaps the sodomy ground was dropped as a result of discussion not

Isobel Duncan. *Whanganui Regional Museum
Photographic Collection, 2008.60.708 b*

reflected in the file. It may have been less shameful to admit to adultery than sodomy.

Once finalised, Isobel Mackay's petition for divorce was heard in Wellington, by the ubiquitous Sir Robert Stout, with no jury. Because of the age of the couple's three daughters, the case was heard in camera and publication of the evidence was forbidden. Stout recorded Isobel Mackay's evidence of her husband's adultery in his judge's notebook. This included additional information not included in the divorce file.

In December 1919, he recorded, Mackay had travelled to Auckland, where the J. C. Williamson opera company was performing. When he returned, he would not sleep in the same room as his wife and was prescribed various medicines and a special diet. The suggestion is that he had contracted a venereal disease from someone in the opera company.[10]

Stout granted the divorce in September; it was made final in February 1921, and Isobel Mackay was granted custody of the couple's three daughters. She then changed her surname by deed poll, reverting to her maiden name of Duncan, effective from 6 September 1920. Her three daughters also became Duncans.[11] Isobel stayed on in Whanganui, living at the Totarapuka homestead in Whanganui East until her death in 1946.

Mackay's collection of books was sold and the contents of the house were purged of items associated with him. After Josephine Duncan died in 2008, aged 95, the surviving contents of Totarapuka came to the Whanganui Regional Museum.[12] The large collection of more than 400 items — furniture, ceramics, jewellery, decorative arts, paintings and textiles — spans six generations, and includes furniture brought out to New Zealand by her grandfather, Andrew Duncan. Despite the purge of anything to do with Mackay over the previous eight decades, some items had clearly slipped the net before the collection arrived at the museum: a small silver cup won by Mackay for junior double rowing sculls in 1903, the year before his marriage; a monogrammed handkerchief; and a copy of *Pride and Prejudice*, inscribed by Mackay with his name and the date, 29 June 1907.

Isobel Duncan and her daughters Sheila (left) and Josephine, photographed in the 1920s. *Whanganui Regional Museum Photographic Collection, 2008.60.314*

sobel was well set up to manage life as a divorcée. In 1911, Totarapuka and its lush gardens had been featured in a promotional book about the town produced for the coronation of George V. In a section headed 'Some Pretty Homes', it was described as 'Mr C. E. Mackay's Residence', but the homestead was in fact owned by the Duncan family: by Andrew Duncan's widow and then, after her death in 1917, by her daughters — Isobel and her sister, Elizabeth Young.

Isobel's wealth enabled a life of privilege, but she was also unconventional. Remembered by her daughter Josephine Duncan as attractive, with a 'nice voice and figure', she was a good horsewoman who hunted and a keen golfer. Before her marriage she had spent time in the United States, before being sent 'Home' to England to be presented at court. Isobel did not spend time in the kitchen — the family had a cook, Harriot [sic] Shaw, who arrived at Totarapuka aged 16 and 'died on the place aged 93' — but she loved gardening, working alongside Jack the gardener in the 4 acres of grounds that remained after Totarapuka was subdivided. Josephine described her mother's occupation as 'socialite'; she always ran everything she was connected with. 'People liked my mother . . . and she liked people. Everybody was just the same to her.'[13]

Given her background, Isobel might have been expected to be Tory, but she stood up for workers' rights and was once asked by railway workers to stand for Parliament. She also, like her father, spoke te reo and was the only person able to persuade local Māori to go to hospital during the 1918 influenza epidemic. She challenged leaders Apirana Ngata and Te Rangi Hīroa (Peter Buck), arguing that Māori should be taught in schools. Contracting the flu in 1918 had left her with a weak chest, and after her marriage ended, during the 1920s she spent winters in California.[14]

It is not hard to imagine this confident, independent, forthright woman as mayoress, one who shaped the role, not content merely to cut ribbons and present prizes. During the Great War she had run fêtes, bazaars and garden parties to raise funds, organised socials for

Isobel Duncan and an unnamed boy in the garden at Totarapuka in the 1920s.
Whanganui Regional Museum Photographic Collection, 2008.60.679

departing troops and helped to set up local branches of the British Red Cross Society and the Women's National Reserve. In August 1919, her war service was recognised with an OBE. Her intelligence, determination and independence may explain why she and her daughters were able to stay in Whanganui after her husband's fall from grace.[15] It helped that the town was united in its determination to suppress and expunge any reference to Mackay.

Traditionally, photos of former mayors were hung in the Whanganui council chamber, but no portraits of former mayors were on show when the council moved to a new building in 1968. Perhaps they had had enough of leaders with strong personalities. After he was elected mayor in 2004, Michael Laws directed that the portraits be reinstated. Museum staff could find representations of all the former mayors except Mackay. Eventually a damaged 1919 photomontage of Mackay with his councillors was discovered behind a wall. This image, which had also been used in newspapers when Mackay's death was reported, was enlarged.

Mackay was expunged in another way. At some stage, his name and title were sanded off the Carrara marble foundation stone beside the entrance to the Sarjeant Gallery, though other plaques featuring his name seem to have been left untouched. In the weeks after his death the alteration to the stone was mentioned in some papers, including Sydney's *Daily Guardian*: 'His name appears on no list of past mayors. It has been erased from foundation stones, and future generations will know him not.'[16] As mayor for a long period, Mackay had opened numerous buildings, but he was intimately involved with the genesis and realisation of the Sarjeant. This particular erasure was therefore very significant.

More is known about another deletion of Mackay's name: early in 1921, Mackay Street in Wanganui East was renamed Jellicoe Street,

The Wanganui Borough Council members and officers, photographed in 1919. *Alexander Turnbull Library, 1/1-016124-G*

after Viscount Jellicoe, who was New Zealand governor-general from 1920 to 1924. The street, named after Mackay when it was created around 1907, made up one side of a triangle of land bought by Andrew Duncan after he arrived from Scotland in 1840.

A book about the history of street names in the city, first published in 1978 and reprinted in 1989, tried to obfuscate the story. *Streets of Wanganui* was the work of Athol Kirk, who wrote other books and newspaper articles about local history, and who would have been nine when Mackay shot Cresswell. Kirk may have remembered the incident, but he managed to omit any reference to it: 'In a patriotic gesture after World War I many street names were altered. MACKAY STREET, named after a former Mayor, became JELLICOE STREET after Lord Jellicoe . . .'[17] This explanation is both misleading and factually incorrect. Whanganui's two daily newspapers recorded what actually led to the decision to change the name.

The idea had been mooted in a letter to the editor shortly after the 1920 shooting and trial. 'Cockney' suggested 'that very few citizens would object to the small inconvenience caused by changing the name of Mackay Street to that of Princes Street or Prince Edward Avenue'.[18] The suggestion was stoutly rejected by 'Pharos', who criticised 'Cockney' as belonging 'to that class of person which believes in kicking a man when he is down'. The letter is a rare show of public, albeit anonymous, sympathy for Mackay:

> Despite his failings [he] has served Wanganui well for thirteen or fourteen years . . . Mr Mackay has broken the law and will suffer the penalty, but it is neither for him nor for any other private person to sit in further judgement . . . 'Cockney' would do well to revise his obvious opinion of a man in whom the public has reposed its confidence for so long a period and who now requires 'more to be helped than hindered.'[19]

At its final meeting for 1920, on 21 December, the council adopted a recommendation included in a report from its Works Committee:

> Re Changing names of streets. We recommend that the following names of streets be changed:
> Krull Road to Oakland Avenue
> Mackay Street to Jellicoe Street.[20]

Krull Road was named after Frederick Krull, the first German consul to New Zealand. Although some councillors spoke strongly in support of the Krull family and their loyalty to Britain, the anti-German sentiment expressed during the war years had evidently not quite faded. It was noted that ratepayers' wishes should be respected. As the minutes of the meeting record, councillors' comments about Mackay Street were less clear-cut and more equivocal:

> Cr. Aitken — did not consider that the change in the name of Mackay Street was a great compliment to Lord Jellicoe. They should wait until they got a new street to name. Surely they could find another name for Mackay Street.
> Cr. Spriggens: Call it Aitken Street!
> Cr. Aitken: What about Sigley Street?
> Cr. Sigley: No thank you!
> Cr. Aitken: Well, there you are . . .
> Cr. Donaldson — The change in the name of Mackay Street would be a compliment to Lord Jellicoe.
> Cr. Richardson: A back-handed one.
> Cr. Donaldson said it was not a back-handed one at all. There were some disreputable streets in Wellington which had been named after Wellington Mayors. There were worthy citizens in Wanganui whose names could be given to streets.
> Cr. Luxford considered that the new names were good ones.

It was finally decided that the names of the two streets should be changed as suggested.[21]

From the 1920s, books about Whanganui and its history omitted any mention of Mackay and his career, apart from including his name in lists of former mayors. The preface of *Wanganui from 1856 to 1929* seemed to express the general approach: 'In this book I have refrained from making any unpleasant remarks about any citizen, old or new . . .'[22] A decade later, the history produced for the city's centenary covered major projects in which Mackay was a key figure — the establishment of the first tram system outside of the major cities in New Zealand, and the building of the Sarjeant Gallery — without mentioning him.[23] And, as noted earlier, in 1965 the town clerk made it clear to Helen Shaw that 'As the incident was not a very savoury one in the history of this city, and also as members of the family of the late Mr Mackay are still residing in Wanganui', she should 'either tone down the matter in your writings, or omit the incident altogether'.[24]

When Jim McLees arrived in Whanganui in 1968 to become chief sub-editor at the *Wanganui Chronicle*, he was warned not to tangle with the families of the Rangitikei Hunt or the Duncans. Any story involving the local gentry would need to be approved by the newspaper board, which they controlled.[25]

In the 1960s, the closest family members would have been Mackay's two surviving daughters: Sheila, who died in 1972,[26] and Josephine, who had a reputation in Whanganui as a redoubtable figure, an independent single woman who was respected and sometimes feared.

Encouraged by her mother, Josephine took up golf at 16, and with a handicap of 1 became one of the best young golfers in Australasia. Her selection for the New Zealand golf team was thwarted by the Second

World War, but she continued playing golf in England and Scotland while serving with the New Zealand Army as part of the Voluntary Aid Detachment. Back in New Zealand, Josephine took charge of running a 500-acre sheep and cattle farm on family land in Mangaweka. After the farm was sold in 1971, she returned to Whanganui and started the Wanganui Women's Emergency Refuge — one of the first refuges to be set up in this country. In a 1993 oral history interview her voice contains more than an echo of her strong-minded, energetic parents. Michelle Horwood, a curator from the Whanganui Regional Museum, tried to get Josephine to talk about her father, who was barely mentioned in the two-and-a-half-hour interview.

> MH: And what about your father, can you remember anything about him?
> JD: Nope.
> MH: Not at all . . .
> JD: The only thing I can remember is going to look at the art gallery when it was being built.
> MH: But you have got memories of him as a father?
> JD: Well, I was so young when he went, you know.[27]

Josephine told the interviewer she was born in 1917, four years later than recorded in her passport, and in newspaper reports of her birth.[28] Since the Sarjeant was erected between 1917 and 1919, Josephine is unlikely to have recalled seeing the building under construction if she had been born in 1917, but it would make sense for her to remember the gallery being built if she was between four and six years old. The altered date would also have meant that she was only three when her father went to prison, not seven. It may have been a genuine mistake, but perhaps she fudged her age in order to avoid difficult questions about her father.

When the author first went to Whanganui with a radio colleague,

Prue Langbein, to research the story for a feature, he was warned that Josephine did not like people asking about Mackay. She was not keen on the project. She did not seem to be ashamed about what had happened, but wanted to protect the reputation of her father — 'It's not a crime to be homosexual' — and mother — 'Well you're not going to bring her into it?' Again there was the confusion about her age — 'I was only four when it happened' — but she did have a view about what took place.

> PL: Do you think he was set up?
> JD: Of course he was.
> PL: Why would someone do that?
> JD: Don't be silly. It happens all the time.
> PL: Was he set up by the RSA?
> JD: Of course not. That was a distraction.
> PL: But what was in it for him [Cresswell]? He was homosexual too, why would he do it?
> JD: Well, it happens all the time. Could have been some dollars (or pounds?) in it.[29]

Paradoxically, the Duncan collection has been a catalyst for the emergence of the story of Charles Mackay and the rehabilitation of his reputation in Whanganui. A selection of items from the collection featured in a major 2019 renovation of the Whanganui Regional Museum's displays, which included reconstructed rooms from Totarapuka, with the gifted items illustrating 'the pioneering spirit and entrepreneurship of Whanganui residents and the legacy of this family'.

The exhibition text included a summary of Mackay's career and covered the shooting in a straightforward manner: 'His achievements were overshadowed, however, in 1920 when Mackay was found

Josephine (left) and Elizabeth Duncan. *Whanganui Regional Museum Photographic Collection, 2008-60-177-a*

guilty of attempted murder after seriously wounding Walter D'Arcy Cresswell and sentenced to 15 years' imprisonment. It was later alleged that Mackay had made homosexual advances to Cresswell. Mackay's sensational disgrace all but expunged his career from local history. Mackay St became Jellicoe St and his name was gouged out of the foundation stone of the Sarjeant Gallery . . .'[30]

This short account at last told a fuller, more rounded story. It also signalled, nearly 100 years after the shooting on Ridgway Street, that the prohibition was well and truly over. As Colin Whitlock, a much more recent town clerk, said about the Sarjeant Gallery foundation stone in 2009, 'If you hold things back, and make a big deal, secrecy out of them, when they see the light of day, then they get a bigger currency than they would have had otherwise. I think if the thing had been part of Wanganui's history, even folklore, all the way through . . . there'd be probably less curiosity about it.'[31]

When the gay liberation movement reached Whanganui in the 1970s, the foundation stone became a target for a protest highlighting Mackay and his contribution as part of the city's first Gay Pride Week. From 1972, the week, organised by the National Gay Rights Coalition initially in the main centres and later in smaller towns, allowed gay people a presence and a means of calling for law reform. Among the activities were wreath-laying ceremonies at war memorials to commemorate gays who had died through persecution in the past.[32]

In 1978 Whanganui joined Wellington and Auckland in laying a pink triangle wreath, although not on the war memorial. On the evening of Sunday 25 June, members of the coalition and their straight supporters watched as a man and a woman placed the wreath on the foundation stone at the Sarjeant Art Gallery. As well as remembering the homosexuals who had died in concentration camps, the wreath drew attention to the loss of Mackay's name and title from the stone, as Des Bovey, one of the organisers explained:

An important principle is involved . . . whether or not the man is homosexual is irrelevant. What we want to emphasis [sic] are the enormous pressures experienced by homosexual people especially those in public positions. This [man's] contribution to the city was considerable, particularly in the arts. He was a popular Mayor but recognition of this has been withdrawn … We have called on the Council to reinstate the name of the Mayor in recognition of those services, and in the recognition of the right of Homosexuals everywhere to dignity and self-respect.[33]

In a comic twist, the wreath made a circuit of Queens Park, before ending up back at the gallery. The Sarjeant custodian thought vandals had removed the wreath from the Whanganui cenotaph, 100 metres away, and so he returned it there. But then, according to a report in a gay magazine, by 11 p.m. the wreath was back at the Sarjeant, 'only to be found at 4.30am in the flower garden. From there it travelled to the gardener's shed from where it was last retrieved and replaced on its first site.'[34]

This agrees with a story from Bill Milbank, who was the gallery director at the time. He remembers that the wreath-laying angered the RSA, who phoned the mayor, Ron Russell, who then asked Milbank to remove it. Russell was also blasted by the gay group, annoyed that its wreath had been shifted.[35]

Unbeknown to the group, Russell, after prompting from town historian Arthur Bates, was in the process of quietly persuading the council to reinstate Mackay's name on the stone. But as a returned serviceman he was irritated by the protest and, according to Milbank, said he was not going to be pressured by the gay rights group. The idea was then put on hold. The restoration of the stone had been raised previously, but Dr H. D. Robertson, the Sarjeant's second curator, allegedly said that Mackay's name would go back on the stone over his dead body.[36]

Robertson died in 1980, and it was not until Doug Turney replaced Russell as mayor in 1983 that the matter was broached again. The restoration took place in 1985, after the sixtieth anniversary of Whanganui's city status the previous year. The decision reflected changing attitudes, as Colin Whitlock's memo to the gallery director showed:[37]

> It is noted that the name of the Mayor of the Borough of Wanganui at the time of laying the foundation stone, Charles Evan Mackay, has been removed. It is understood that this transpired following his incurring the displeasure of the then Wanganui City Council. In view of the time that has passed and a change of social attitudes it is believed that his name should be reinstated. He was the presiding Mayor at the time and despite any subsequent events in his personal life the reality of the situation should be recognised.
>
> Would you please therefore arrange for his name to be reinstated and at the same time to have freshened up the remainder of the inscription.
>
> Please note that no publicity is to be given to this matter.[38]

The memo is interesting because it suggests the council knew about the stone's alteration and may have even been responsible for it. Despite Whitlock's instructions, the restoration of Mackay's name and title *was* noticed. When the Sarjeant celebrated its seventy-fifth anniversary in September 1994, art historian Janet Paul wrote: 'It is good to know that Mackay's splendid work on behalf of the gallery project has once more been recognised by the restoration of his name to the foundation stone by a less prejudiced, better informed and more appreciative council.'[39] The month before, Phil Parkinson's *Pink*

Triangle article had been reprinted in the *Wanganui Chronicle*, nearly a decade after it was first published.[40]

And Mackay began to have a presence in the town in other ways. When the Dublin Street Bridge had opened in 1914, celebrations had been muted because of the war. In 2014 a local Rotary club suggested to the council that the centenary be marked by a re-enactment. Mackay had not been mayor when the bridge was completed, but he was part of the re-enactment as the MC, a role played by Mike Street, a retired teacher who was involved with Whanganui theatre groups.[41]

Mackay's story also inspired artists. In 2012 the photographer Ann Shelton spent three months in the city as part of a residency awarded by the Sarjeant Art Gallery. The resulting body of work, *the city of gold and lead*, was inspired by both the 1920 shooting and the Wanganui Computer Centre bombing in 1982.[42] As part of her research, Shelton discovered the original specifications for the marble foundation stone for the gallery. The letters were to be 'oil painted, gold sized and gilded'.[43] It is unclear whether this was how the stone was originally prepared, but by the time Shelton was in Whanganui, the black paint in the cut lettering for Mackay's name and title had disappeared, making it look as if he was still erased. Shelton persuaded the Whanganui District Council to gild the stone and retain it after her exhibition had ended. The exhibition of Shelton's work at the Sarjeant included a looped video of the lettering on the stone being covered over and revealed.

New Plymouth artist Katerina Smoldyreva, moved by Mackay's story and keen to pay tribute, used her 2018 residency in the city to produce a ceramic 'distorted monument' inspired by the mayor, a 'figure of authority collapsing into one of tragedy'.[44] As she noted, 'Equine statues . . . invariably depict a man on a prancing horse, proudly displaying his power, authority or political strength.' She chose to reveal 'the aspect of a fall from grace — literally and metaphorically — "screaming with emotions"'.[45]

Local artist Mike Marsh used a photo portrait to produce a painting of Mackay, presenting his tie in rainbow colours. The painting was bought by a gay man who owns a modernist house in the city that he rents to visitors, who could not miss the portrait, which is mounted on a wall outside the house beside an explanatory sign.[46] In its 2017 edition, the promotional magazine *Celebrating Whanganui* included a page of 'Interesting Facts about Whanganui'; one of them was the 1920 shooting.[47]

There were calls, too, for Mackay's name to be restored to Jellicoe Street. In a 2018 *Chronicle* editorial, Zaryd Wilson, co-producer of a podcast about the shooting, argued that there was no better way to honour Charles Mackay's contribution to Whanganui and that reinstating the street name would complete his redemption.[48] When Whanganui celebrated Gay Pride Week in 2019, Paul Chaplow, of Whanganui's economic development agency, declared that he wanted to make the city the LGBTQ capital of New Zealand. 'Whanganui is . . . unique. For a provincial town, there is a lot of diversity.'[49] It was a far cry from 1920.

EPILOGUE

For Blanche Baughan, the evidence of Charles Mackay's homosexuality — 'his perverse practices', in the language of her day — was central to who he was. Her account of him ends on a sombre note: 'Death has claimed him now. He has gone beyond the reach of our ignorances whether of heart or head, and who can mourn?'[1] What does it mean, to be less ignorant of Mackay's homosexuality? Or, put another way, what do the traces left by Mackay tell us about his homosexuality?

Charles Mackay's story illustrates the potentially devastating effects of the exposure of a person's homosexuality, and the establishment of 'the homosexual' as a social category to be punished and vilified. 'Although Mackay had ended up in court because he shot someone, his homosexuality seemed to be equally on trial.'[2] This was partly because he had made it a feature of the case by producing evidence of his 1914 treatment. There were reminders, too, if unexpressed, in the nationwide press coverage of the Mackays' divorce early in September 1920.

At the end of that month, when Mackay was struck off and declared bankrupt, most papers noted that he was serving a 15-year sentence for attempted murder. Unsurprisingly, *Truth*'s report was far more sensational, reminding readers that the victim had been 'the returned soldier Cresswell, who exposed the one-time Mayor's hideous double life of sexual perversion'.[3] Such language spoke of wider social attitudes towards homosexuality.

This did not mean that Mackay — and Cresswell, for that matter — necessarily identified as homosexual, and it may be wrong to focus on one aspect of their lives. This was a point made by Gregory Woods about the 'Homintern', a supposed network of homosexual influence: 'Notwithstanding the new sexual definitions of the era [early twentieth century] many of the individuals in question did not identify as homosexual at all, or even bisexual, but merely went about their lives without taking the contingencies of desire as an identifying factor.'[4]

But the traces left by Mackay and Cresswell suggest that their homosexuality, as they lived it, *was* a significant part of their lives. In Mackay's case, his decision to relocate to London, and then Berlin, is a major piece of supporting evidence. He was punished harshly, to deter other homosexuals. And he was not the first well-known public figure to endure this treatment for his homosexuality.

As with the Oscar Wilde trials in England and the Eulenburg Affair in Germany, the 'Wanganui Sensation' named and publicised homosexuality in New Zealand to an unprecedented extent. Homosexuals were able to read about themselves in the newspapers, but the case also gave ammunition to those who sought to pathologise and condemn homosexuality.

Truth made the Wilde/Mackay connection for its readers early in June 1920:

> The evidence which was adduced makes the case one of the most sensational in the annals of the New Zealand courts. Indeed, it would be hard to imagine a more extraordinary sequence of happenings. Charles Mackay, in his public business life, was a popular and successful man, but there was another and hideous side to his nature — a Jekyll as well as a Hyde to his character, and Cresswell, a returned soldier, unmasked the debonair Mayor and discovered him to be another Oscar Wilde, morally unclean; a pursuer of PERVERTED AND PUTRID 'PLEASURES'.[5]

As British historian Matt Cook has suggested, Wilde's conviction was 'the point at which diffuse indicators of homosexuality cohered into a fixed stereotype and the long parodied aesthetic and decadent pose became a more serious threat'.[6] Mackay was tried and found guilty of attempted murder, but also came to represent homosexuality in the public mind.

Mackay and Wilde had other things in common. Their wives, Constance Wilde and Isobel Mackay, changed their surnames and that of their children. On the days they were released from prison, Oscar Wilde and Charles Mackay left their home countries, never to return. Their arrests caused other homosexual men, like Hector Bolitho, to move overseas.

Both Wilde and Mackay used medical explanations of homosexuality in an effort to reduce their prison sentences. In 1896, Wilde cited such arguments in letters requesting the home secretary to reduce his sentence of two years' hard labour:

> The offences of which he was rightly found guilty . . . are forms of sexual madness and . . . are diseases to be cured by a physician, rather than crimes to be punished by a judge . . . It is under the ceaseless apprehension lest this insanity, that displayed itself in monstrous sexual perversion before, may now extend to the entire nature and intellect, that the petitioner writes this appeal which he earnestly entreats may be at once considered.[7]

Both men summed up their situations in letters from prison. Mackay wrote to a friend in December 1920: 'As to myself, I should tell you that since I last wrote I have been divorced, made bankrupt, & struck off the rolls, so that I will leave jail without a penny, a family or a profession. It is a bit hard, but it can't be helped.'[8] In his appeal to the home secretary, Wilde said of himself: 'He has lost wife, children, fame, honour, position, wealth: poverty is all that he can look forward to: obscurity all that he can hope for.'[9] Although he died in poverty, Wilde escaped obscurity. His works continue to delight readers and audiences, and interest in his life has only grown since his death. Mackay is also remembered, not just for his achievements as mayor of Whanganui but also for shooting a man who threatened to reveal his homosexuality.

This is a reminder that in a time when all same-sex love between men was illegal, the dangers of active homosexuality came as much from other gay men as anyone else. New Zealand writer Bill Pearson was a gay man who knew about the story of the shooting in Whanganui and spoke about it in interviews. Despite being from a later generation than Mackay and Cresswell, Pearson understood the world they lived in, where 'the need to avoid exposure could lead to strange postures and actions'.[10]

First published in 1954, Pearson's *Fretful Sleepers*, with its trenchant criticism of New Zealand society, has become a classic. Written when Pearson was in London, where he was able to live more freely as a gay man, the essay, according to his biographer, Paul Millar, was penned 'with one reality at the forefront of his mind, that discrimination against homosexuals occurred at every level of New Zealand society, and in seeking to express his sexuality there "[he] wouldn't have anything like the opportunities that [he] had in London"'.[11] Pearson is also remembered for deciding not to make the central character of his celebrated 1963 novel, *Coal Flat*, homosexual, because of New Zealand's Puritan climate, and to avoid the risk of exposing his own homosexuality.[12]

In such a homophobic society, Pearson believed, closeted gay men would 'go to very unpleasant lengths to protect that false identity'.[13] He saw this as a way to understand what Cresswell was up to, but that it also applied to Mackay. Both men were examples — admittedly extreme ones — of how gay men behaved at that time. For Pearson, the only gay men who could be condemned were those who betrayed other homosexuals: 'As far as I've ever felt the only betrayal that one had to avoid was being self-righteously moralistic, pretend[ing] to be one thing, and condemning the very thing one was.'[14]

Pearson's comment helps us to understand the shifts in the story of what happened when Mackay met Cresswell, and in the roles of the two men. In 1920, *Truth* was quite clear about who was the villain and who was the victim:

> Cresswell, being a wholesome-minded young man, on making his discovery, determined to force Mackay to resign from the Mayoralty, and Mackay, after pleading in vain with Cresswell, goaded into the desperation of a cornered rat, determined to make an end of his accuser. He induced Cresswell to call at his office, where he turned on the unsuspecting man and fired a pistol point blank into his breast, then, as the stricken man fell to the ground, Mackay, thinking him done for and dying, and seeing the end of his threatened exposure in sight, coolly and callously placed the pistol in his apparently dying victim's hand.[15]

By the beginning of the twenty-first century, the roles had switched and D'Arcy Cresswell was seen as the villain. Many modern eyes see him as a hypocrite, one homosexual man condemning another. The affair has become, wrote John Newton, 'Cresswell's monument to infamy. It could hardly be otherwise: on Cresswell's part, it reads as a story of mind-boggling iniquity.'[16]

Exactly what Mackay and Cresswell's homosexuality meant to them remains opaque and mysterious. What is more certain is that the society they lived in treated them in a certain way because of their sexuality — and how this was perceived at that time. This process did not stop with their deaths, and it supports Michel Foucault's argument that sexuality is socially produced and constantly contextualised.[17]

After Mackay's death in Berlin, a tribute by an unidentified writer appeared in both Whanganui papers. It reminded readers of Mackay's contribution to the city: 'He had a great vision of Wanganui's possibilities and planned accordingly.' Now, thanks to 'another revolver shot in far-off Germany, Charles Evan Mackay has achieved world fame'. As well as noting the passing of a brilliant man, the article emphasised, as Baughan had done, that this was a tragic story.

It was not accidental that Baughan, a classical scholar, hid Mackay's identity using the name of a Greek tragic hero, grappling with, but unable to overcome, an unavoidable destiny.[18] The anonymous writer observed the operation of Nemesis, the goddess associated with retribution, divine punishment for wrongdoing or hubris. Mackay's was a universal story, in which the wheel of fortune lifts people to power and then propels them to an inevitable downfall.[19]

As the 1929 tribute noted, in the latter part of his career as mayor, Mackay's 'power began to waver'; he was mocked as 'Sir Charles', and criticised for his focus on the royal visit at the expense of Whanganui's development:[20]

> But nerve-wracking as were the cares of office it was nothing to the toll being taken by Nemesis. Then one day the word of Tamocles [sic] which had been hanging over his head fell, severing all rights to public citizenship and office in a moment of time, severing appreciations of previous past sacrifice and effort, satisfying those who were of the 'told you so's' section severing the friendships in circles high and low . . . But the shot of a revolver and crash! Henceforth to the majority there was no worse than he. The desertion and opprobrium on all sides expressed were scarcely less comparable with an incident of centuries long past save that on [sic] was innocent and in this case there was no cross to hang this unfortunate on. They had found the only really bad person in the city, so to speak; so away with him.[21]

LATE C. E. MACKAY

A BRILLIANT CAREER

A contributor writes:—

For some it is that they live their lives as dead stars in a living firmament; for some their light shows as a clear, bright flame from youth to death; for some to flash suddenly as a meteor into full flame, only to fade away with a trickle of dust. For some it is to live quiet, self-contained lives, professing nothing in particular, seeking no great place in the affairs of the community or the larger world in which they have their being. For some it is to be called—it may be unwillingly—though possessing all the attributes of leadership and for all their effective years of life holding positions of leadership and trust. For some it is born with the inherent power to lead their fellow men, yet possessing little save the brains with which they were endowed, called in a time of sudden need to take up office, with responsibility dressed with the frills and furbelows with which they are decked. Yet great, a little Nemesis follows them all—heredity, greed, desire for power, the inherent demand for what they feel they are unjustly deprived of in some form or fashion the skeleton that hangs in every cupboard.

It is now moving into the years of history when a young man came to Wanganui. His had been a brilliant record at his college. He had graduated and with a splendid degree then not known so frequently as it is to-day. He looked out upon the future of his adopted profession with reasonable hopes of achieving outstanding success. It was a time when Wanganui was seeking a new chief Magistrate, and the choice of an opponent to the powers then in office fell to Charles Evan Mackay. His advent to office was heartily acclaimed on all sides.

Several days after Charles Mackay was buried in Berlin, a tribute by an unnamed author appeared in both Whanganui newspapers. *Wanganui Chronicle, 11 May 1929. Papers Past*

The article also acknowledged Mackay's contribution to his city, describing him as 'a brilliant meteor thrown into public life'. As Hector Bolitho noted in his book about Whanganui, 'There is no finer material work in which men can engage themselves than that of city building.'[22] Mackay's terms as mayor were marked by his energy, enthusiasm and an internationalist perspective.

When Mackay died, an American journalist colleague included a biographical sketch in a report of his death: 'He was quiet and unassuming and although not widely known was well liked. His hobby seemed to be art.'[23] The family of one of his friends has a story about Mackay looking at an exhibition of Modernist art and remarking to someone standing nearby that he did not know what the artists were trying to get at. The other person obligingly tried to explain the aims of the movement to him. A week or so later Mackay, visiting another art gallery, saw a portrait of the man who had spoken to him and learnt that it was Aldous Huxley.[24]

Mackay's interest in art is memorialised in the Sarjeant Gallery, a Whanganui treasure of national significance. In his survey of the gallery's history, Chris Cochran is clear about Mackay's central role. After Henry Sarjeant's death in 1912, the gallery project did not take off until after 1915, when Mackay was re-elected mayor. The next five years 'were crucial in terms of the establishment of the gallery. His position as both Mayor and as a member of the Sarjeant Art Gallery Committee enabled him in association with the Neames, to see through the planning, competition and construction of the Sarjeant Gallery with acumen and flair.'[25]

As noted earlier, his involvement did not end once the gallery opened: Mackay commissioned Frank Denton, a major New Zealand photographer who worked in Whanganui from 1899 to 1927, to start building a collection of international Pictorialist art photography. 'Probably the most significant collection of such photography in the country, it made the Sarjeant one of the first art museums in the world to collect photography as fine art — certainly the first in New Zealand by almost fifty years.'[26]

As the story of the shooting in Whanganui enters its next 100 years, a fuller picture of Mackay has been restored, along with his name on the Sarjeant Gallery stone.

A wry account by the *New Zealand Herald*'s London correspondent, printed in various New Zealand papers, painted a vivid image of this dynamic man on the make in the big city: 'He displayed tremendous energy and enterprise, and he attended a great many public functions, especially those where no invitation was needed. It is probable that he wrote for some New Zealand papers under a nom de plume. It is known that he had impressed his individuality upon a number of acquaintances, among whom were some interesting people.'[27]

The use of a nom de plume means it is unclear how many of Mackay's articles were published in New Zealand and Australia. Several weeks before his death, the *Manawatu Standard* printed Mackay's report of the Rhinelanders' Ball, by 'a New Zealander in Berlin'. The ball was a Berlin celebration of the annual Kölner Karneval, Cologne's carnival, famous for its costumes. Mackay did not go in fancy dress, deciding instead to 'wear a half-face mask and a small Maori "tiki" hung over my shirt like a decoration . . . My Maori tiki was the sensation of the evening. Every woman stopped me to touch it for luck, one even insisting on dipping it into her glass.'

The account of the ball, attended by 5000 people, like his other reports, takes the reader into the heart of Weimar Berlin, illustrating why the city fascinated visitors. Around 2 a.m. at the ball, Mackay was hailed by a familiar voice: 'It was my landlady, about forty and not too thin, dressed as a jockey . . . She asked me what was the English name of her costume. So I told her she would be called a "welterweight," and she was so pleased, she ran round clapping her hands and telling people, "Ich bin eine englische veltervetin".'[28]

After Mackay was killed, his employer Sefton Delmer described him as 'one of my best friends, and one of the most brilliant men I have ever met'.[29] Later, in his memoir, Delmer later recorded a different, less upbeat impression of the New Zealander: 'Charles Mackay was a tall spare man with a balding head and a lined and haggard face in which, behind steel-rimmed spectacles, whimsical optimism and humour were fighting a constant battle with self-pity and tragic despair.'[30]

German newspapers referred to Mackay as an Abenteurer (adventurer), and Weltenbummler (globetrotter). As a friend later told a London paper, 'I am not at all surprised that Mr. Mackay ventured alone into the danger area of Berlin so late last night. Beside the strong urge that he would have from duty, his adventurous spirit would have called him to risk his life in order to see for himself what was occurring . . .'[31] Perhaps his decision also said something about the sense of freedom and potential for reinvention that he had found in Berlin.

He could be irrepressible and courageous — qualities evident in 1915 when he faced down the anti-German riots in Whanganui. His head bleeding from where a stone and a firecracker had hit him, Mackay faced the angry mob on his own.

Mackay survived six harrowing years in prison, undoubtedly marked, but then reinvented himself following his period of recuperation in London. When he left London in 1928 he was 53, but managed to get a passport showing his age as 45. The eight-year gap was the length of time from the shooting in New Zealand to his arrival in Berlin. Perhaps the move to Berlin was a new start, a bid for reinvention?

Charles Mackay's story is one of resistance — of refusing to settle, of continually challenging norms, of being knocked down and getting up again. Perhaps this is what connects his story with the story of gay liberation: the determined push by queer people throughout history to live their lives, on their own terms.

CLOCKWISE FROM ABOVE
Looking for bullet holes in Charles Mackay's former office in 2012. *Leigh Mitchell-Anyon*; The author outside Werbellin Apotheke, near the spot where Charles Mackay was shot, in 2010. *Conor Clarke*; Former Sarjeant Gallery Director Bill Milbank, Wanganui Gay Rights Association Founder Des Bovey, photographer Ann Shelton and Paul Diamond toasting Charles Mackay outside the Sarjeant Gallery, just before the gilded lettering was uncovered in 2013.

NOTES

ABBREVIATIONS

AA: *Auswärtiges Amt Archive, Berlin*
ANZ: Archives New Zealand
ATL: Alexander Turnbull Library
DNZB: *Dictionary of New Zealand Biography*
GStA: Geheimes Staatsarchiv, Preußischer Kulturbesitz, Berlin-Dahlem
LA Berlin: Landesarchiv Berlin
MCH: Ministry for Culture and Heritage
WDC: Whanganui District Council Archives

INTRODUCTION

1   Peter Wells and Rex Pilgrim (eds), *Best Mates: Gay Writing in Aotearoa New Zealand*,
    Auckland: Reed, 1997.
2   Ibid., p. 16.

PROLOGUE: DEATH IN BERLIN

1   Statement by Police Senior Constable Kurt Worm in police investigation file, Ref: 219/55, GStA,
    39–42.

1: RIDGWAY ST

1   The following dialogue and descriptions are taken verbatim from statements in trial file, Rex v.
    Charles Evan Mackay: Attempted Murder, W3559/314 11/1920, R20558725, ANZ.
2   'A Painful Sensation', *Wanganui Chronicle*, 17 May 1920, p. 5.
3   'A Wanganui Sensation', *Te Puke Times*, 18 May 1920, p. 3.
4   'Wanganui Mayor Arrested', *N.Z. Truth*, 22 May 1920, p. 6.
5   From statement in trial file.
6   When Mackay appeared in the Police Court on 24 May, police lawyers said they would
    know by Wednesday 26 May whether Cresswell would be well enough to give evidence.
    This suggests that the statement was given between 24 and 26 May.
7   https://treadwellgordon.co.nz/about-treadwell-gordon/ (accessed 16 February 2022).
8   From statement in trial file.

2: BLACKMAIL

1   Whanganui District Council, *Wanganui Heritage Study – Volume 1 – Study*, p. 12, WDC 00363:0:48. WDC, https://archivescentral.org.nz/whanganui-district-council/record/ wanganui-heritage-study-volume-1-study (accessed 21 March 2022).

2   https://whanganuiregionalmuseum.wordpress.com/2018/03/26/whanganui-forgotten-capital-of-the-arts-and-crafts-movement/ (accessed 16 February 2022).

3   Bruce Attwell, *The Wharves of Wanganui: How Maritime Commerce Built a City*, Whanganui: Hilltop Publishing, 2006, p. 98.

4   L. J. B. Chapple and H. C. Veitch, *Whanganui,* Hawera: Printed by the *Hawera Star* [for the Wanganui Historical Committee], 1939, p. 252.

5   Quotes taken from Cresswell's statement in trial file, with verbatim spelling. Rex v. Charles Evan Mackay: Attempted Murder W3559/314 11/1920 R20558725, ANZ.

6   Whanganui historian Wendy Pettigrew passed on information that Mackay did not pay invoices (sent in February, March, April and May) for work in December 1919 by a local architect, Clifford Newtown Hood. Wendy Pettigrew, email to author, 19 October 2009.

7   'A Painful Sensation', *Wanganui Chronicle*, 17 May 1920, p. 5.

8   For another reference to strangers' rooms, see https://www.stuff.co.nz/southland-times/ news/73281481/invercargill-club-a-favourite-haunt-for-generations-of-gentlemen (accessed 4 May 2022).

9   Letter to Wanganui District Council Mayor and Councillors, from Farm Equipment Company Ltd, 20 November 1934, Maria Place Conveniences File (AAF 72 195), WDC. The urinals were built some time after 1917.

10 Matt Houlbrook, *Queer London: Perils and Pleasures in the Sexual Metropolis, 1918–1957*, Chicago: University of Chicago Press, p. 50.

11 Chris Cochran, *Heritage Assessment for the Wanganui District Council*, Wanganui District Council, 2012, pp. 39–40, https://sarjeant.org.nz/wp-content/uploads/2016/08/Heritage_ Assessment_FINAL.pdf (accessed 17 June 2021).

12 The Gallery Committee was chaired by Councillor William G. Hall until October 1916. According to the minutes, Mackay was attending committee meetings from 31 January that year. After October 1916, there were two committees: a building committee chaired by Councillor Sigley, and a gallery committee chaired by Mackay. Reports of Sarjeant Gallery Art Committee, seen at Sarjeant Gallery, 2009. The original plan was much grander, envisaging 'that the Art Gallery shall form part of a scheme including a Museum corresponding to the Art Gallery, and a central block of Municipal Offices and Town Hall', *Competition for Sarjeant Art Gallery Wanganui*, Wellington: Harry H. Tombs, December 1916, p. 1.

13 Seager believed Hosie had drawn the designs but was unable to prove this. The Wanganui Borough Council received conflicting legal opinions about who was the author of the designs and ended up engaging Anscombe as the overseeing architect. Hosie was not credited with the design. See Cochran, *Heritage Assessment*, pp. 5–7.

14 Charles Mackay, letter to Featherston Military Camp, 13 January 1917, Mayoral Letterbook, AAF 123:7, WDC.

15 *Competition for Sarjeant Art Gallery Wanganui*, p. 1.

16 'Sarjeant Gallery', *Wanganui Herald*, 8 September 1919, p. 2; 'Sarjeant Gallery: The Opening Ceremony', *Wanganui Chronicle*, 8 September 1919, p. 5.

17 Whanganui District Council, *Wanganui Heritage Study – Volume 2 – Study*, p. Q/5.

18 See Sarah McClintock, 'Cartoons used in battle for minds', *Whanganui Chronicle*, 3 May 2014, https://www.nzherald.co.nz/whanganui-chronicle/news/cartoons-used-in-battle-for-minds/

J6VD4OP73YHZGOYV4ZYYJQXJBM/# (accessed 21 March 2022); WWI Cartoon Collection, https://collection.sarjeant.org.nz/highlights/3/objects?page=2&sort=accession_no (accessed 21 March 2022).

19   'Ellen was also insistent that she be involved in the selection of paintings and with her new husband was twice authorised to spend, in one case £500 and in another £1000, on buying art work for the gallery during Grand Tours to the Old countries', Jock Phillips, 'Henry Sarjeant and the tradition of art patronage in NZ', Inaugural Henry Sarjeant Memorial Lecture, 20 November 2016, Sarjeant Art Gallery.

20   http://collection.dunedin.art.museum/search.do?view=detail&page=1&id=37101&db=object (accessed 16 February 2022).

21   Letter from John Armstrong Neame to Wanganui Town Clerk, 26 March, 1914, quoted on Sarjeant website: https://collection.sarjeant.org.nz/objects/43244/the-wrestlers (accessed 17 June 2021).

22   Robert Aldrich, The Seduction of the Mediterranean: Writing, Art and Homosexual Fantasy, London: Routledge, 1993, p. 222.

23   As depicted in Mates and Lovers, the play by Ronald Trifero Nelson based on Chris Brickell's Mates & Lovers: A History of Gay New Zealand, Auckland: Godwit, 2008, performed in two versions in 2009 and 2011.

24   Pers. comm., Karl-Heinz Steinle, Schwules Museum Berlin, June 2010.

25   Arousal was the aim of photos in a 1942 court case concerning indecent behaviour (the charge covering homosexuality). A 36-year-old Wellington barman named Robert Samways told a 15-year-old department store assistant he had 'pretty hot' French photographs, which would 'give him a stand'. The younger man went to the police. Samways pleaded guilty to an attempted unnatural offence and was sentenced to five years' reformative detention. Evening Post, 14 October 1942, p. 5. See also Sentencing File, RS, 13 October 1942, AAOM W3265, ANZ; and Chris Brickell, 'Court Records and the History of Male Homosexuality', Archifacts, 2008, p. 34. There is also at least one literary reference to photos being used to 'test' homosexuality. In William Golding's 1967 novel The Pyramid, 18-year-old Oliver, back in his home village after his first term at Oxford, accepts a role in a local operatic society production and is befriended by the director, Evelyn De Tracy. During one rehearsal, Oliver and De Tracy duck out to the nearby pub, where the older man, misreading Oliver's comment about wanting 'the truth of things', shows the boy photographs of himself dressed as a ballerina. Oliver roars with laughter.
'What on earth's this?'
'Just making a point, Oliver. To the perceptive. Give it back, will you?'
But I was looking through the sheaf. The costume was the same in each and so was Mr. De Tracy. In some of the photographs he was supported by a thick, young man; and in each of these, they gazed deep into each other's eyes. I laughed until it hurt.
'Give them back, now, Oliver.'
'What was it?'
'Just a farce, that's all. Give them back, please.'
'I don't think I've ever seen —'
'Oliver. Give them back. And run along.'
— The Pyramid, Faber & Faber, London, 1967, pp. 148–49.

3: THE TRIAL

1   The *Wanganui Chronicle* was owned and edited by Gilbert Carson and later owned by the Young family. The *Wanganui Herald* had been established in 1867 by John Ballance with his partner A. D. Willis. Ownership of both papers was merged in 1971.

2   'The Ridgway Street Sensation', *Wanganui Herald*, 17 May 1920, p. 5.

3   'Shooting Sensation', *Wanganui Chronicle*, 28 May 1920, p. 5.

4   The sketch has survived, but the photos are no longer part of the trial file. Trial file, Rex v. Charles Evan Mackay: Attempted Murder W3559/314 11/1920 R20558725, ANZ.

5   'Fifteen Years in Gaol', *New Zealand Herald*, 29 May 1920, p. 8.

6   'C. E. Mackay Sentenced', *Wanganui Chronicle*, 29 May 1929, p. 5. Comments by Treadwell and Stout taken from reports of this hearing in *Wanganui Chronicle*, *Wanganui Herald* and *N.Z. Truth*.

7   'The Ridgway Street Sensation', *Wanganui Herald*, 28 May 1920, p. 5.

8   'Mayor Mackay: Malefactor', *N.Z. Truth*, 5 June 1920, p. 5.

9   Matt Cook, *London and the Culture of Homosexuality, 1885–1914*, Cambridge, New York: Cambridge University Press, 2003, p. 94.

10 According to Chris Brickell, reporting of the Wilde case in 1895, which came from overseas, referred to homosexuality indirectly: 'vile', 'bestial' and 'unprintable' practices, and 'vices of imperial Rome'. Subsequently, other terms appeared such as 'perversion'. 'In 1907 *Truth* called Oscar Wilde a "homo-sexual sinner", and a year later the *New Zealand Times* told its readers of a German nobleman who "had an aversion for women, was inclined to the society of men, and gave every sign of homosexuality".' *Mates & Lovers: A History of Gay New Zealand*, Auckland: Godwit, 2008, pp. 72–75, 143.

11 Rex v. Charles Evan Mackay: Attempted Murder, AAOG, W3559, 11/1920 Box 217, ANZ.

12 Ibid. Albert Mackay's statement was dated 24 May 1920, several days before Mackay signed Cresswell's statement. This would appear to show that Mackay's lawyers were planning to use this medical defence before they knew what Cresswell was going to say.

13 Marijke Gijswijt-Hofstra, 'Introduction', in *Cultures of Neurasthenia From Beard to the First World War*, Amsterdam: Editions Rodopi, 2001, p. 2.

14 Cook, *London and the Culture of Homosexuality*, p. 80.

15 Email from Barbara Drinkall, 16 December 2009.

16 Conditions Albert Mackay claimed to be able to cure included haemorrhage, rheumatism, asthma, anaemia, neuralgia, neurasthenia, muscular troubles, constipation, neuritis, indigestion, chronic pains, disorders of the circulation, stammering, goitre, dyspepsia, sciatica, cigarette smoking and 'bad habits of all kinds', which perhaps covered homosexuality. His outline of his treatment of Charles Mackay in 1914 is reminiscent of a fictionalised story of medical treatment for the same 'condition', written in the same year, though not published until 1971, the year after the author's death. In E. M. Forster's novel *Maurice*, the protagonist, in an effort to 'cure' his homosexuality, goes to his doctor, who refers him to psychologist-hypnotist Lasker Jones. After several visits, Maurice finds the treatment is not successful.

17 Email from Barbara Drinkall, 16 December 2009; pers. comm., Barbara Drinkall, 7 December 2009. For example, see report of a fundraising show, 'Grand, Polite Vaudeville and Hypnotic Entertainment', at His Majesty's Theatre in Whanganui in June 1914, a couple of months before Mackay sought treatment. 'His Majesty's Technical College Benefit', *Wanganui Chronicle*, 5 June 1914, p. 8.

18 Teri Chettiar, '"Looking as Little Like Patients as Persons Well Could": Hypnotism, Medicine and the Problem of the Suggestible Subject in Late Nineteenth-Century Britain', *Medical History*, Vol. 56,

No. 3, 2012, pp. 335–54, n. 48, notes that Richard von Krafft-Ebing, Albert von Schrenck-Notzing, and Albert Moll all made extensive use of hypnotism as a means for 'curing' homosexuality.

19   'Suggestive Therapeutics', *Wanganui Herald*, 17 May 1919, p. 2. The same advertorial appeared in the *Wanganui Herald* between March and September 1919.

20   C. Harry Brooks, *The Practice of Autosuggestion*, London: George Allen & Unwin, 1922, pp. 19, 57, 68, 66.

21   'Mayor Mackay: Malefactor', *N.Z. Truth*, 5 June 1920, p. 5.

22   'The Prince's Visit', *Wanganui Herald*, 14 May 1920, p. 9.

23   'The Mayor and R.S.A. — The Recent Controversy', *Wanganui Herald*, 14 May 1920, p. 4.

24   'Mayor Mackay: Malefactor'. *N.Z. Truth*, 5 June 1920, p. 5.

25   'C. E. Mackay Sentenced', *Wanganui Herald*, 28 May 1920, p. 5.

26   When Frank Bennier was charged with murder and attempted murder after attacking four men and two women with an axe in 1917, Mackay tried to argue that he was not guilty because he was an 'epileptic subject' and committed the crimes in a fit of insanity. The jury disagreed and Bennier was sentenced to death. No further evidence of Bennier's epilepsy emerged, and he was executed on 19 January 1918. Mackay used a similar defence in 1915, when he defended Arthur Rottman, who attacked and killed a family with an axe. Mackay tried to argue that Rottman had a 'brain storm' — impulsive insanity linked with alcohol. The argument was rejected by the judge, who sentenced Rottman to death.

27   Little is known about the gun Mackay carried, which is variously described as a 'pistol', 'revolver' and 'automatic revolver'. He would easily have been able to obtain a gun but his use of it suggested he was not a skilled shooter, despite having served as an officer with the Auckland College Rifles Volunteers in his early twenties. Laws governing firearms were tightened shortly after the shooting, perhaps in response to this and other high-profile cases such as the murder of Augustus Edward Braithwaite by Dennis Gunn in March 1920. The first Arms Act was passed in October 1920 and came into force the following year. As a result, 'specific firearms were registered to specific owners. Persons wishing to purchase a gun had to obtain a permit to do so from the police and then register the weapon with the police once it had been procured. Pistols were subject to extraordinary restrictions from 1920, and ownership required a special licence.' Greg Newbold, 'The 1997 Review of Firearms Control: An appraisal', *Social Policy Journal of New Zealand*, Issue 11, 1999, pp. 115–29.

28   Quotes here from 'C. C. Mackay Sentenced', *Wanganui Chronicle*, 29 May 1920, p. 5; 'Mayor Mackay: Malefactor', *N.Z. Truth*, 5 June 1920, p. 5.

29   'C. E. Mackay Sentenced', *Wanganui Chronicle*, 29 May 1920, p. 5. Mercy was apparently less than life. See, for example, Alice Parkinson who was sentenced by Stout in 1915 to hard labour for the term of her natural life, for the manslaughter of Bert West. West was in a relationship with Parkinson, and initially agreed to marry her. West changed his mind after Parkinson lost a baby. The two cases were compared; see 'Mackay v Alice Parkinson,' *N.Z. Truth*, 12 June 1920, p. 3. Parkinson was released in mid-1921. See Carol Markwell, 'Parkinson, Alice May', *DNZB*, first published in 1996. Te Ara – the Encyclopedia of New Zealand, https://teara.govt.nz/en/biographies/3p9/parkinson-alice-may (accessed 25 September 2020).

30   Stout's comments are taken from reports of this hearing in *Wanganui Chronicle* and *Wanganui Herald*.

31   David Hamer, 'Stout, Robert', *DNZB*, first published in 1993. Te Ara – the Encyclopedia of New Zealand, https://teara.govt.nz/en/biographies/2s48/stout-robert (accessed 17 June 2021).

32   Emma M. Gattey, 'Sir Robert Stout as Freethinker and Eugenics Enthusiast', in Diane B. Paul, John Stenhouse and Hamish G. Spencer (eds), *Eugenics at the Edges of Empire: New Zealand, Australia, Canada and South Africa*, Switzerland: Palgrave Macmillan, 2017, p. 203.

33 Sir Francis Galton, 'Probability, the foundation of eugenics', Herbert Spencer Lecture, 5 June 1910, http://nzetc.victoria.ac.nz/tm/scholarly/tei-Stout80-t11-body-d1-d2.html (accessed 17 June 2021).

34 Stevan Eldred-Grigg, *Pleasures of the Flesh: Sex and Drugs in Colonial New Zealand, 1840–1915*, Wellington: Reed, 1984, p. 168.

35 'C. E. Mackay Sentenced', *Wanganui Chronicle*, 29 May 1920, p. 5: 'the attempt was not an impulsive act, as the placing of the revolver of the hand of young Cresswell showed'; 'The Ridgway Street Sensation', *Wanganui Herald*, 28 May 1920, p. 5: 'the attempt was an impulsive act, as was shown by Cresswell's statement'; 'Not an Impulsive Act', *Wanganui Herald*, 10 June 1920, p. 5: 'A telegram from Wanganui reporting the Chief Justice's remarks in sentencing Mackay made him say that it was an impulsive act, and he is so reported in one of the Wanganui papers, but not in the other. His honor wishes to say that what he really said was that it was not an impulsive act, basing his opinion on the fact that Mackay had placed the pistol in Cresswell's hands after he shot him.' This was later contradicted by the report written by the Prisons Board following the release of Mackay and two other prisoners in 1926. See Chapter 4.

4: MACKAY

1 Mackay's middle name was Ewing, but he later used Evan.

2 'All Sorts of People', *Free Lance*, 9 June 1906, p. 1.

3 Felicity Campbell, *Townhall: The Independent Years of Eastbrook, Gonville and Castlecliff*, Whanganui: Felicity Campbell, 2016, p. 9. See also the criticism from a member of the Wanganui Chamber of Commerce, who described Mackay as a malignant influence, who 'twisted the councillors around his fingers as he pleased', 'Wanganui's Parlous Plight', *Wanganui Chronicle*, 2 August 1921, p. 5.

4 Sir James Elliott, *Firth of Wellington*, Auckland: Whitcombe & Tombs, 1937, pp. 41, 42, 34.

5 Frank M. Leckie, *The Early History of Wellington College*, Auckland: Whitcombe & Tombs, 1934, p. 226.

6 Australasian autobiographies, *Sydney Bulletin*, qMS-0095, ATL.

7 V. H. Reid, 'A Short Historical Account of Wanganui, Wellington Province', MA thesis, University of Canterbury, 1940, p. 90.

8 'C. E. Mackay', in H. Collins, *Familiar Faces: A Short Historical Sketch of Wanganui Celebrities*, Whanganui: Hatherly & Johnson, 1907.

9 *Wanganui Chronicle*, 4 January 1902, p. 1.

10 *Wanganui Herald*, 20 January 1904, p. 7.

11 *Wanganui Herald*, 1 June 1905 p. 7, *Wanganui Chronicle*, 1 June 1905, p. 5.

12 'C. E. Mackay', in Collins, *Familiar Faces*.

13 Bruce Attwell, *The Wharves of Wanganui: How Maritime Commerce Built a City*, Whanganui: Hilltop Publishing, 2006, p. 81.

14 Whanganui Historical Society, *Historical Record: Journal of the Whanganui Historical Society Inc.*, Vol. 10, No. 2, November 1979, p. 6.

15 *Historical Record*, Vol. 3, No. 1, May 1972, pp. 24, 27.

16 'The Tramways', *Wanganui Herald*, 10 December 1908, p. 7.

17 Attwell, *The Wharves of Wanganui*, p. 82.

18 'All Sorts of People', *Free Lance*, 9 June 1906, p. 1.

19 'Throughout New Zealand, annual terms for mayors persisted until 1915, when they were aligned with the biennial councillor elections.' Graham Bush, 'Evolution of the Local Government Electoral Process', in Jean Drage (ed.), *Empowering Communities? Representation &*

Participation in New Zealand's Local Government, Wellington: Victoria University Press, 2002, p. 17. From 1900 to 1935 there were biennial elections for the whole council.

20 'Town Edition', *Poverty Bay Herald*, 5 September 1911, p. 6.

21 'The Mayoral Election', *Wanganui Chronicle*, 18 April 1912, p. 4.

22 See Brian S. E. Bellringer, 'Conservatism and the Farmers: A Study in the Political Development of Taranaki–Wanganui Between 1899 and 1925', MA thesis, University of Auckland, 1958, pp. 287, 288, 294. Mackay may have been disadvantaged by the second ballot system in place for the two elections he stood in. This meant that candidates had to win a first selection round among candidates before going forward to the national election.

23 'The Mayoralty: Mr Mackay Fires the First Shot' [April 1912]. From copy in Nicholas Meuli and Family papers at Whanganui Regional Museum, p. 6.

24 Josephine Duncan, oral history interview with Michelle Horwood, 14 May 1993, WRM OHA/WSCP 46, Whanganui Regional Museum.

25 'The Mayoral Election', *Wanganui Herald*, 17 April 1912, p. 2.

26 'Borough Doings', *Wanganui Herald*, 2 July 1912, p. 6. Reprinted in *Wanganui Chronicle*, 4 September 1912 and *Wanganui Herald*, 3 September 1912.

27 'Personal', *Wanganui Chronicle*, 10 June 1913, p. 4.

28 Andrew Francis, *'To Be Truly British We Must Be Anti-German': New Zealand, Enemy Aliens and the Great War Experience, 1914–1919*, Bern: Peter Lang, 2012, pp. 69–111.

29 'Mob Law', *Wanganui Chronicle*, 17 May 1915, p. 5.

30 'Anti German Riots', *Evening Post*, 17 May 1915, p. 2.

31 L. J. B. Chapple and H. C. Veitch, *Wanganui*, Hawera: Wanganui Historical Committee, 1939, p. 244.

32 'The Empire's Call', *Wanganui Chronicle*, 20 October 1915, p. 6.

33 For example, 'Married Men and Enlistment', *Wanganui Chronicle*, 22 October 1915, p. 3.

34 'Conscientious objection and dissent in the First World War', https://nzhistory.govt.nz/war/first-world-war/conscientious-objection (Ministry for Culture and Heritage) (accessed 17 June 2021); Paul Baker, *King and Country Call: New Zealanders, Conscription and the Great War*, Auckland: Auckland University Press, 1988, p. 93.

35 Mackay had served as a volunteer. In 1898 he was an officer with the Auckland College Rifles Volunteers, before leaving Auckland in November 1898 for Taranaki (*New Zealand Herald*, 3 November 1898, p. 3).

36 'Enlistment of a Mayor', *Evening Post*, 10 March 1916, p. 8.

37 In July 1916, Mackay was listed among the men called up for the Nineteenth Reinforcements (*Wanganui Chronicle*, 11 July 1916, p. 4).

38 'Statement by the Mayor', *Wanganui Chronicle*, 24 April 1917, p. 6.

39 'Williams to Rogers: Of the Mayors we have known', *Wanganui Chronicle*, 15 September 1962, p. 10.

40 'Mr Mackay and the Limelight', *Wanganui Chronicle*, 30 April 1919, p. 4.

41 'The Mayor in Reply', *Wanganui Chronicle*, 30 April 1919, p. 4.

42 For example, 'The Mayoral Battle', *Wanganui Herald*, 29 April 1919, p. 8. See also Steven Loveridge, *'Soldiers and Shirkers': An Analysis of the Dominant Ideas of Service and Conscientious Objection in New Zealand During the Great War*, Hamilton: University of Waikato, 2009, p. 74.

43 'As Others See Us', *Wanganui Chronicle*, 21 December 1918, p. 3.

44 'Wanganui Sensation', *Otago Daily Times*, 17 May 1920, p. 8. For example, the power plant, built originally to supply electricity for the town's trams, could not cope with the additional demand from other users. When the plant failed on 20 July 1920, Whanganui was without power

and electric trams for three months. Mackay was an advocate of hydro power, and from late 1919 had been pushing for an engineering investigation of the Whangaehu River as a source of electricity. There were strong advocates for other solutions. After the 1920 shooting, Mackay's Whangaehu River proposal was shelved. Instead an alternative to hydro, a new power station, opened in 1924.

45 'The Mayor and the Soldiers', *Wanganui Chronicle*, 23 April 1920, p. 5.
46 'The Mayor and the Soldiers', *Wanganui Chronicle*, 23 April 1920, p. 5; 'The Opera House Concert', *Wanganui Herald*, 23 April 1920, p. 5.
47 'R.S.A President and Secretary Reply to the Mayor', *Wanganui Chronicle*, 23 April 1920, p. 5.
48 Rupert Godfrey (ed.), *Letters From a Prince* (Little Brown: London, 1998), p. 290. In 2007 the Alexander Turnbull Library purchased letters sent by Edward Prince of Wales to his lover in London, Mrs Freda Dudley Ward. The letters revealed what the Prince really thought of New Zealand and the people he met, challenging his public image. https://www.scoop.co.nz/stories/CU0707/S00017/acquires-1920-nz-letters-of-edward-prince-of-wales.htm ; https://www.stuff.co.nz/dominion-post/news/local-papers/the-wellingtonian/3227486/Peeved-prince-revealed (accessed 17 February 2022).
49 'Prince of Wales Welcomed at Wanganui', *The West Australian*, 5 May 1920, p. 7.
50 Godfrey, *Letters From a Prince*, p. 295.
51 'Mayor Taken to Task', *Wanganui Chronicle*, 13 May 1920, p. 5; 'Mayor and R.S.A.', *Wanganui Herald*, 13 May 1920, p. 5.
52 'R.S.A. and Mayor', *Wanganui Herald*, 24 April 1920, p. 11.
53 'Municipal Affairs', *Wanganui Chronicle*, 16 April 1920, p. 5.
54 *Wanganui Chronicle*, 27 September 1919, p. 4; *Wanganui Herald*, 26 November 1919, p. 8.
55 *Wanganui Herald*, 28 November 1919, p. 8; *Wanganui Chronicle*, 2 December 1919, p. 4.
56 'Digger's Bomb', *Wanganui Chronicle*, 17 April 1920, p. 5.
57 'The Mayoralty', *Wanganui Herald*, 26 May 1920, p. 5.

5: MOTIVE

1   Jeanette Stace, 'Stace, Helen McRae', *DNZB*, first published in 1993, updated January, 2002. Te Ara — the Encyclopedia of New Zealand, https://teara.govt.nz/en/biographies/2s39/stace-helen-mcrae (accessed 4 May 2022).
2   D'Arcy Walter Cresswell, Military personnel file, AABK 18805 W5530 0030005, ANZ; 'On Service. Personal Notes About New Zealanders', *Press*, 27 July 1916, p. 3.
3   D'Arcy Walter Cresswell, Military personnel file.
4   'All Sorts of People', *Free Lance*, 2 June 1920, p. 4; 'Wanganui Sensation', *Sun* (Christchurch), 18 May 1920, p. 7; 'The Shooting Sensation', *Wanganui Chronicle*, 18 May 1920, p. 5.
5   See Donald Peter Brown Hosie, at Online Cenotaph, https://www.aucklandmuseum.com/war-memorial/online-cenotaph/record/C7206 (accessed 19 June 2021).
6   Eleanor Mary Cresswell and John C. M. Cresswell, *Grandma's Scrapbook: The Life and Times of Eleanor Mary Cresswell, Née Sleight, 1865–1946*, Whangarei: J. Gover, c. 1994, pp. 69, 103.
7   Ibid., p. 110.
8   In 1994 John Charles Marshall Cresswell (son of William Free and Ella Mary Clay) published his grandmother's scrapbook. The book includes John's own commentary about the Wanganui Affair: 'The D'Arcy Cresswell affair was never discussed and the second and third generations of the family were unaware of it until recently', Eleanor and John Cresswell, *Grandma's Scrapbook*, p. 15.
9   Phone conversation with John Cresswell, 11 June 2009. Note that this branch of the Cresswell family were known to each other by their second names.

10   Eleanor and John Cresswell, *Grandma's Scrapbook*, p. 66.

11   'Military Service Board', *Wanganui Chronicle*, 5 October 1918, p. 4.

12   Phone conversation with Keith Marshall Cresswell (son of Roland), 2 June 2011.

13   Letter, Charles Carrington to Helen Shaw, 10 December 1965, MS-Papers-88-252-1, Box 1, folder 26, ATL.

14   Note also the following references in the first volume of Cresswell's memoirs: 'I was already resolved on returning to England soon after [visit to New Zealand 1919–21], without being resolved to any profession, except perhaps authorship, and to this in the vaguest terms, when towards the end of this tour an event occurred which nearly ended my life, and drew so much attention at home to my wandering and idle ways, I judged it a suitable occasion soon after to say what I would do, and obtained my parents' consent, very anxiously given, that I should return to England at once, and on the very terms I have said.' Walter D'Arcy Cresswell, *The Poet's Progress; with a Portrait by William Rothenstein*, London: Faber & Faber, 1930, p. 12. 'My friend Ronald Cuthbert' was also mentioned three times in *Present Without Leave*, London: Cassell, 1939, pp. 33, 34, 35.

15   Letter, Ronald Cuthbert to Helen Shaw, 22 April 1966, 88-252-3, ATL.

16   Whanganui newspapers also mention criticism of Mackay's absences from the town. For example, letter from 'In Favour of a Change', *Wanganui Herald*, 23 April 1919, p. 6.

17   See Chris Brickell, *Mates & Lovers: A History of Gay New Zealand*, Auckland: Godwit, 2008, pp. 121–26.

18   See Morris B. Kaplan, *Sodom on the Thames: Sex, Love, and Scandal in Wilde Times*, Ithaca: Cornell University Press, 2005, pp. 166–223.

19   Prisons Board report, Criticisms of the Prisons Board, PD 1924/20/47; part of Prison Department Correspondence 1923/6/7 to 1933/21/4 (1923–1933), ANZ.

20   R v. Gordon William McNamara, BBAE A304 419, 1927, Vol. 1, ANZ. See also 'Serious Charge: Trial in Supreme Court', *New Zealand Herald*, 2 August 1927, p. 12; 'Serious Charge: Acquittal of Accused', *New Zealand Herald*, 3 August 1927, p. 15; 'Not Guilty: Serious Charge Fails', *Sun* (Auckland), 3 August 1927, p. 13.

21   Conversations with Derek Schulz, 17 March 2009; Margaret Vennell, 24 April 2010; and Colin Wright, 24 April 2010.

22   R v. Gordon William McNamara.

23   Chris Bourke, *Good-bye Maoriland: The Songs and Sounds of New Zealand's Great War*, Auckland: Auckland University Press, 2017, pp. 200–01.

24   Brickell, *Mates & Lovers*, p. 106.

25   Chris Brickell, '"Waiting for Uncle Ben": Age-Structured Homosexuality in New Zealand, 1920–1950', *Journal of the History of Sexuality*, 21(3), 2012, p. 468. As noted, there is no evidence Mackay was ever charged with offences relating to homosexuality. His work did, however, bring him into contact with youths, such as 15-year-old Percy Thompson, who in 1918 was reported by the police as having absconded from Mackay's 'licensed service'. Licensed service was when youths sent to training farms, industrial and reformatory schools (for children whose parents could not care for them) would be placed in the 'service' of residents. See *New Zealand Police Gazette*, 10 April 1918, p. 219, https://paperspast.natlib.govt.nz/periodicals/NZPG19180410.2.7. The case was apparently closed in 1921, with no further action to be taken, *Police Gazette*, 24 August 1921, p. 538 (https://paperspast.natlib.govt.nz/periodicals/NZPG19210824.2.5).

26   'Notes and Comments', *Patea Mail*, 2 June 1920, p. 2.

27   'The Wanganui Sensation: Cresswell Rapidly Recovering', *New Zealand Times*, 6 July 1920, p. 5.

28   Letter to Sir Graeme (Sir Graeme Sinclair-Lockhart) c. 4 December 1920. Full quote: 'By the

way, the art master, Hay Campbell, was just painting a big portrait of me, & had it half finished when I was pinched. Hard luck eh? However, my portrait—full face & profile, is now in the Rogue's Gallery.' C. Mackay Inmate file, ANZ.

29 Conversation with Peter Owens, 21 August 2010.
30 Conversation with Evelyn Cummins, 16 September 2009.
31 Prisons Board report, Criticisms of the Prisons Board.
32 Interview with Kevin Ireland, 20 May 2009.
33 Record of Letters sent and received, 1922 March to May, J, Acc W2636, 1920/31121, C. Mackay Inmate file, ANZ.
34 Letter to Margaret Jean Mackay (sister), c. 19 February 1922. Mackay Inmate file, ANZ.
35 Prisons Board report, Criticisms of the Prisons Board.
36 See Chapter 3, in particular note 35.
37 Hector Bolitho, *Older People*, London: Cobden-Sanderson, 1935. p. 34.

6: PRISON

1 Unless otherwise stated, all the letters, memos and reports quoted in this chapter come from Mackay's inmate file, J, Acc W2636, 1920/31121, C. Mackay Inmate file, ANZ.
2 Interview with B. L. Dallard. Papers of B. L. Dallard — Transcript of tapes, ACGS, 16247, J64, 2/2. ID: R3210472, ANZ.
3 Section 300, Regulations under the Prisons Act, 1908 (1913).
4 Section 222, Regulations under the Prisons Act, 1908 (1913).
5 Letter from Mackay to 'Sir Graeme', c. December 1920. Inmate file.
6 Ibid.
7 Ibid.
8 Letter, Mackay to Margaret Jean Mackay (sister), c. 19 December 1920 and c. 19 February 1922; Mackay to McBeth, c. 2 April 1922.
9 Letter, Mackay to Miss Mackay, c. 19 February 1922 (stamp).
10 Letter, Mackay to Margaret Jean Mackay, c. 29 January 1922.
11 Letter, Mackay to John Donald Welford McBeth, c. 2 April 1922. Henry Francis Cary (1772–1844) completed one of the first and most important English translations of Dante's *Divine Comedy*, first published in 1805–06.
12 Letter from Mackay to Margaret Jean Mackay, c. 12 February 1922.
13 'I respectfully report the above prisoner for assisting to secrete a newspaper today. Morrison stole the paper & passed to Mackie [sic] who in turn passed to Harrison. When Mackie heard me tell Wdr [Warder] McKenzie to search prisoner Morrison Mackay ran down the West Wing & when Morrison was locked up I heard him call to Prisoner Windsor to tell Mackie to dump the paper as quick as he could.' Report to Superintendent, 8 April 1921.
14 Berta Sinclair Burns, *Vedanta in Early New Zealand: A Tribute to Blanche Edith Baughan*, London: Ramakrishna Vedanta Centre, 1971, p. 5.
15 Memo, 23 February 1922, J40 Box 227, 1921/16/9, Re Appointment of Miss B Baughan as official visitor to Addington Reformatory, R 3 195 362, ANZ.
16 Letter, Mackay to Jean, c. 12 February 1922. It is unclear whether Baughan wrote to Mackay before this visit, or whether they had corresponded beforehand.
17 T.I.S. [B. E. Baughan and F. A. de la Mare], *People in Prison*, Auckland: Unicorn Press, 1936, pp. 111–12.
18 'C.E. Mackay Struck off the Rolls', *Evening Post*, 28 September 1920, p. 8.
19 'Local and General', *Evening Post*, 12 October 1920, p. 6.

20 Copy of letter [3] October 1920, from file: 'From: D. O. A. [Deputy Official Assignee], Wanganui Date: 13 October 1920 Subject: (1) That arrangements be made for Prisoner C. E. [Charles Evan] Mackay to be taken to Wanganui in connection with his bankrupt estate. (2) For directions in regard to the trust account of the bankrupt. (3) As to his remuneration in connection with dealing with the estate.' ACGS 16211 J1/984, 1920/1208, R 24 683 289, ANZ.

21 Letter from Silk to Department of Justice, 14 October 1920. From file 'From: D. O. A. [Deputy Official Assignee], Wanganui Date: 13 October 1920 Subject: (1) That arrangements be made for Prisoner C. E. [Charles Evan] Mackay to be taken to Wanganui in connection with his bankrupt estate. (2) For directions in regard to the trust account of the bankrupt. (3) As to his remuneration in connection with dealing with the estate.' ACGS 16211 J1/984, 1920/1208, R 24 683 289, ANZ.

22 From 'Tannhauser and Others,' in T.I.S., *People in Prison*, pp. 111–12.

23 Ibid.

24 Patricia Webb, *A History of Custodial and Related Penalties in New Zealand*, Wellington: Government Printer, 1982, p. 83; Greg Newbold, *The Problem of Prisons: Corrections Reform in New Zealand since 1840*, Wellington: Dunmore Publishing, 2007, p. 83.

25 Charles E. Matthews, *Evolution of the Prison System*, Wellington: Government Printer, 1923, p. 9.

26 Letter, Mackay to 'Sir Graeme', c. December 1920.

27 Patricia Mayhew, *The Penal System of New Zealand, 1840–1924*, Wellington: Department of Justice, 1959, p.108.

28 'Manchester Street Tragedy', *Press*, 19 November 1909, p. 6.

29 Letter, Mackay to 'Sir Graeme', c. December 1920.

30 Letter, Mackay to John Donald Welford McBeth, c. 2 April 1922.

31 Letter, Mackay to Margaret Jean Mackay (sister); c. 19 December 1920.

32 Memo, 27 June 1921.

33 Memo from Matthews, 27 June 1921.

34 Memo, 1 June 1921.

35 Memo, 6 July 1921.

36 Memo, 19 July 1921.

37 Report to Superintendent, 3 April 1921.

38 Discipline Report, 29 January 1921.

39 Report to Superintendent, 25 July 1921.

40 Letter from Mackay to Superintendent, 15 January 1922.

41 Letter, Mackay to Superintendent, 16 May 1922.

42 Transfer order from C-G [Controller-General] to Supt H.M. Prison Auckland, 12 May 1922.

43 Matthews, *Evolution of the Prison System*, p. 13.

44 Ibid., p. 6.

45 Letter, Mackay to George Crowther, 21 January 1923. 'Suppressed Hab Criminal' in pencil on envelope. Prison Regulations forbade contact with other prisoners, which may be why this letter was censored.

46 Letter, Mackay to George Crowther.

47 Memo, Matthews to Waikeria Superintendent, 23 June 1922.

48 Letter, Baughan to Waikeria Superintendent, 3 April 1923.

49 Memo, 17 August 1922.

50 Letter, Mackay to Ralph David Matthews, 24 June 1923. Suppressed because Matthews was an ex-prisoner.

51 Discharge granted 25 November 1922. Details in bankruptcy file, 'In the matter of "The Bankruptcy Act 1908" and of The estate of Charles Ewing Mackay, formerly of Wanganui now

of Auckland. A Bankrupt'. AAOG, Accession: W3559, Ref: 15/1920, ANZ. Letter, Mackay to Jean, c. 12 February 1922.

52   Discipline report, 19 March 1923.

53   Request in letter from Mackay, 16 September 1923; response on Prisoner's Interview sheet, 15 March 1923–October 1926 (Waikeria).

54   Mayhew, *The Penal System of New Zealand*, p. 100.

55   Peter Boston, 'A Caged Tiger: The Regulation of Male Sexuality in the New Zealand Penal System, 1917–1952', unpublished paper, p. 1; Chris Brickell, 'Psychiatry, psychology and homosexual prisoners in New Zealand, 1910–1960', *Medical History*, Vol. 65, 2021, pp. 1–17 (see especially note 15, p. 3); Matthews, *Evolution of the Prison System*, p. 13.

7: PUNISHMENT

1   'Mental Defectives and Sexual Offenders'. Report of the Committee of Inquiry, *Appendix to the Journals of the House of Representatives*, 1925, Session I, H-31A, https://paperspast.natlib. govt.nz/parliamentary/AJHR1925-I.2.3.4.39 (accessed 19 June 2021).

2   Bernadette M. G. Lavelle, 'Sexual Offences in the 1920s: Incidents and Attitudes', BA (Hons) thesis, University of Otago, 1986, p. 8.

3   'Mental Defectives and Sexual Offenders'. Report of the Committee of Inquiry, p. 25.

4   Evidence from inquiry, 5 June 1924, p. 329. See also 'Five Years For Sex Sin: Schoolmaster's Shocking Perversion', *N.Z. Truth,* 9 February 1924, p. 7.

5   Peter Boston, 'A Caged Tiger: The Regulation of Male Sexuality in the New Zealand Penal System, 1917–1952', unpublished paper, p. 1.

6   Ibid., p. 2.

7   Reference from Chris Brickell, from an inmate file from New Plymouth Prison from 1924. A 25-year-old prisoner, born in Auckland, was granted this request: 'Wishes to be given lessons in English by prisoner Mackay.'

8   Memo, 14 November 1924. Unless otherwise stated, all the letters, memos and reports quoted in this chapter come from Mackay's inmate file, J, Acc W2636, 1920/31121, ANZ.

9   Charles E. Matthews, *Evolution of the Prison System*, Wellington: Government Printer, 1923, p. 38.

10   Report from Prison Medical Officer, Mt Eden, 24 September 1925.

11   Memo, 24 September 1925.

12   Letter, Mackay to Baughan, c. 3 December 1925.

13   Memo from Superintendent, 5 December 1925.

14   Memo from Controller-General, 9 December 1925.

15   Memo from Superintendent, Auckland, 28 October 1925; Memo from Controller-General, 15 May 1926.

16   Memo from The Gaoler New Plymouth to C-G of Prisons, 21 April 1924.

17   Crimes Amendment Act 1920 (11 GEO V 1920 No 15), http://www.nzlii.org/nz/legis/ hist_act/caa192011gv1920n15234/

18   Controlling Officer's Report for Prisons Board Report, 15 October 1924.

19   T.I.S. [B. E. Baughan and F. A de la Mare], *People in Prison*, Auckland: Unicorn Press, 1936, pp. 111–12.

20   Controlling Officer's Report for Prisons Board Report, 26 September 1925.

21   The board met twice in 1926: in March and on 27 May. Stout only attended the May meeting. It would appear that the other members at the meeting were those appointed in March 1926: Hon. Mr Justice Thomas Walter Stringer (President), Sir George Fenwick, William Reece and Sir Donald McGavin. It is not clear whether Dallard, who was acting as controller-general from

February 1926 but was not formally appointed until October, was at the meeting. File, Prisons Board Appointments, AAAR, Series 500, Accession W3605, Box/Item 77, ANZ; Record No 21/5/2, Item ID R5174856, ANZ; Prisons Department. Prisons Board (annual report of) for 1926, *Appendix to the Journals of the House of Representatives*, 1927, Session I, H-20A.

22 Controlling Officer's Report for Prisons Board, 12 April 1926. The report is not signed but this may have been Jim Dickison, as Vincent retired during 1926. Mackay's petition is not in his inmate file.

23 Report to Justice Minister, p. 15, Prison Department, Prisons Board Correspondence 1923/6/7 to 1933/21/4, R21 387 824, ANZ.

24 Memo from C-G of Prisons to Supt H.M. Prison, Auckland, 22 July 1926.

25 Memo, 6 August 1926. Inmate file.

26 'Mackay, Ex-Mayor of Wanganui, Released from Mount Eden Gaol', *N.Z Truth*, 9 September 1926, p. 1.

27 Ibid.

28 Prisons Board report, p. 10 (Criticisms of the Prisons Board), ANZ. Ref: PD 1924/20/47; part of Prison Department Correspondence 1923/6/7 to 1933/21/4 (1923–1933), ANZ.

29 Christopher van der Krogt, 'Elliott, Howard Leslie', *DNZB*, first published in 1996. Te Ara – the Encyclopedia of New Zealand, https://teara.govt.nz/en/biographies/3e5/elliott-howard-leslie (accessed 17 February 2022).

30 '"They Do Exist"', *Evening Post*, 8 November 1926, p. 5.

31 'Baume's Release', *Evening Post*, 6 November 1926, p. 10.

32 'The Baume Case', *Evening Post*, 15 November 1926, p. 10.

33 'Prison Regulations: The Baume Case', *Evening Post*, 23 November 1926, p. 10.

34 'Policy of Prisons Board', *Evening Post*, 23 November 1926, p. 10.

35 From Controlling Officer's Report for Prisons Board: 'His conduct and industry in prison had been satisfactory. The controlling officers of the three prisons — New Plymouth, Hautu, and Auckland — where he was for various periods detained — each reported favourably, and stated that his conduct in prison was exemplary.' Note that Waikeria was not mentioned.

36 Prisons Board report (Criticisms of the Prisons Board), PD 1924/20/47; part of Prison Department Correspondence 1923/6/7 to 1933/21/4 (1923–1933), ANZ.

37 'Ex-Mayor Mackay Again', *N.Z. Truth*, 6 January 1927, p. 6.

8: LONDON

1 Hector Bolitho, *Older People*, London: Cobden-Sanderson, 1935, p. 34.

2 *N.Z. Truth*, 6 January 1927, p. 6.

3 Gerry Barton, *Abroad: The Travel Journals & Paintings of Cranleigh Harper Barton*, Wellington: Steele Roberts Aotearoa, 2018, p. 52. Given New Brighton's long-standing reputation as a meeting place for homosexual men, Barton may have been alluding to the pair visiting the beach in search of other like-minded men.

4 Cranleigh Barton Diary, Friday 17 December 1926, Vol. 30, 77-166-6/16, ATL.

5 The *Waitara Evening Mail* (1898–1938) was apparently the only Waitara paper published over the period Mackay worked as a freelance journalist.

6 Information from file Company No: 220592; Adelphi Publicity Company Ltd. Incorporated in 1927. Dissolved between 1927 and 1932. Ref BT 31/29791/220592, National Archives, Kew.

7 Mackay was listed as a director in February 1929, with his address in Berlin. The company was later wound up, but this process did not start until September 1929, four months after Mackay was shot. Information from file at Ref BT 31/29791/220592, National Archives, Kew.

8   Matt Houlbrook, *Queer London: Perils and Pleasures in the Sexual Metropolis, 1918–1957*, Chicago: University of Chicago Press, 2005, p. 123.

9   Ibid., p. 63.

10 Matt Houlbrook, 'For Whose Convenience? Gay Guides, Cognitive Maps and the Construction of Homosexual London 1917–1967', in Simon Gunn and Robert J. Morris (eds), *Identities in Space: Contested Terrains in the Western City since 1850*, Aldershot: Ashgate, 2001, p. 169.

11 Florence Tamagne, *A History of Homosexuality in Europe: Vols I & II*, New York: Algora Publishing, 2004, p. 49.

12 Houlbrook, *Queer London*, pp. 7, 169.

13 Bolitho, *Older People*, p. 35.

14 'In 1792 and 1808 there were calls for St James's Park to be locked up at night ("to prevent their being used as a resort for homosexuals"), but that this reason not be made public.' Matt Cook, *London and the Culture of Homosexuality, 1885–1914*, Cambridge, New York: Cambridge University Press, 2003, p. 10; A. D. Harvey, 'Prosecutions for Sodomy in England at the Beginning of the Nineteenth Century', *Historical Journal*, Vol. 21, No. 4, December 1978, p. 943.

15 Tamagne, *A History of Homosexuality in Europe*, p. 48.

16 Cook, *London and the Culture of Homosexuality*, p. 25.

17 Ackerley, quoted in Jeffrey Weeks, 'Inverts, Perverts, and Mary-Annes: Male Prostitution and the Regulation of Homosexuality in England in the Nineteenth and Early Twentieth Centuries', in Martin B. Duberman, Martha Vicinus and George Chauncey (eds), *Hidden from History: Reclaiming the Gay and Lesbian Past*, London: Penguin, 1989, p. 203.

18 Bolitho, *Older People*, p. 35.

19 'Shot Journalist', *Evening Standard*, 4 May 1929, p. 11.

20 'Cyril Connolly has spoken [in *The Evening Colonnade*, London, 1973] of the great homosexual trail-blazers in the arts in the early twentieth century who avenged on the bourgeoisie the latter's killing of Oscar Wilde . . . Diaghilev, Proust, Cocteau, and Gide . . . Diaghilev was the leader, or impresario of them all. This role of impresario was as important as that of homosexual in the model he provided to other men of sensibility.' Martin Green, *Children of the Sun: A Narrative of Decadence in England after 1918*. Pimlico, 1977, p. 52.

21 Christopher Moore, 'Camp in Francis Poulenc's Early Ballets', *The Musical Quarterly*, 95 (2/3), 2012, p. 319.

22 Sjeng Scheijen, *Diaghilev: A Life*, London: Profile Books, 2010, p. 391.

23 'Shot Journalist', *Evening Standard*, 4 May 1929, p. 11.

24 Herbert Farjeon, *Vogue*, July 1928.

25 Lynn Garafola, *Diaghilev's Ballets Russes*, New York: Oxford University Press, 1989, p. 374.

26 Bolitho, *Older People*, p. 35.

9: BERLIN

1   Sefton Delmer, *Trail Sinister: An Autobiography*, London: Secker & Warburg, 1961, p. 75.

2   Daniel Brandl-Beck, '"Berlin from Behind": A History of "Gay" Travel to Inter-War Berlin', PhD thesis, University of Queensland, 2014, p. 190.

3   Peter Gay, *Weimar Culture: The Outsider as Insider*, New York: Harper & Row, 1970, p. 128.

4   Colin Storer, *Britain and the Weimar Republic: The History of a Cultural Relationship*, London: I.B. Tauris, 2010, p. 104.

5   Wolfgang Kemp, *Foreign Affairs: Die Abenteuer einiger Engländer in Deutschland, 1900–1947*, München: Hanser Verlag, 2010, p. 190.

6   Harold Nicolson, 'The Charm of Berlin', in Anton Kaes and Martin Jay (eds), *The Weimar Republic Sourcebook*, Berkeley: University of California Press, 1994, pp. 425–26.

7   Delmer, *Trail Sinister*, p. 78.

8   'Shot Journalist', *Evening Standard*, 4 May 1929, p. 11.

9   Friedrich Hölderlin was a famous German Romantic poet.

10 Nicolson, 'The Charm of Berlin', pp. 425–26.

11 'Reds Renew Riots In Berlin Streets', *New York Times*, 5 May 1929, p. 6.

12 Registration Form in police investigation file. 219/55, 77, GStA.

13 Brandl-Beck, '"Berlin from Behind"', p. 120.

14 Ibid., p. 88. 'Whereas now it is most commonly used to designate a place of gambling, in the 1920s and 1930s a casino was a "pleasure house", a "public room used for social meetings", a "club house", or a "public meeting or dancing saloon"', *Oxford English Dictionary*, Oxford University Press, 2013, http://www.oed.com.ezproxy.library.uq.edu.au, s.v. 'casino' (accessed 3 February 2013).

15 https://www.greek-love.com/modern-europe/germany/michael-davidson-berlin-pederasty (accessed 17 May 2021).

16 Robert Beachy, *Gay Berlin: Birthplace of a Modern Identity*, New York: Knopf, 2014, pp. 189–90.

17 Ibid., p. 200. A 1917 article in *N.Z. Truth* about *Degenerate Germany* by Henry de Halsalle, which referred to 'sexual perversion' in Germany: 'Forty resorts patronizing sex-perverters are known to exist in Berlin, while 30,000 persons of homo-sexual inclinations reside in the German capital.' 'The Unspeakable 'Un', *N.Z. Truth*, 4 August 1917, p. 12.

18 Michael Davidson, *The World, The Flesh and Myself*, as quoted in Greek Love Through the Ages, https://www.greek-love.com/modern-europe/germany/michael-davidson-berlin-pederasty (accessed 17 May 2021).

19 See Beachy, *Gay Berlin*, p. 54, and rest of Chapter 2.

20 Ibid., p 81. Men cruising were also at risk of robbery.

21 https://www.greek-love.com/modern-europe/germany/michael-davidson-berlin-pederasty (accessed 17 May 2021).

22 Beachy, *Gay Berlin*, p. 56.

23 Ibid., p. 40.

24 https://josephjoachim.com/2014/09/26/villa-joachim-berlin/ (accessed 14 March 2022).

25 Page, *Auden and Isherwood*, p. 108.

26 Florence Tamagne, *A History of Homosexuality in Europe: Vols I & II*, New York: Algora Publishing, 2004, p. 168.

27 Brandl-Beck, '"Berlin from Behind"', p. 45.

28 'After having received at his club an insulting note from the Marquis de Queensberry, calling him a "somdomite", Oscar Wilde filed suit for slander. The trial opened on April 3, 1895, but quickly turned to his disadvantage, several young male prostitutes having been called to testify. The case was eventually dropped, but it set off two further lawsuits . . . in which Wilde was accused of offending morals and of sodomy. On May 25, he was sentenced to two years in prison, to the great joy of the public and the press.' Tamagne, *A History of Homosexuality in Europe*, pp. 16–17.

29 Yvonne Ivory, '"Aus Anlass eines Sensationsprozesses": The Oscar Wilde Scandal in the German Press', Seminar: *A Journal of Germanic Studies*, Vol. 48, No. 2, May 2012, p. 219.

30 'The journalist Maximilian Harden, in his newspaper *Die Zukunft*, accused two close friends of the Kaiser, Prince Philipp von Eulenburg and Count Kuno von Moltke, of being homosexuals. The motive was to discredit William II by casting suspicion on his entourage

and upsetting Germany's international relations.' Tamagne, *A History of Homosexuality in Europe*, pp. 17–18.

31 James D. Steakley, 'Iconography of a Scandal; Political Cartoons and the Eulenburg Affair in Wilhelmin Germany', in Martin B. Duberman, Martha Vicinus and George Chauncey (eds), *Hidden from History: Reclaiming the Gay and Lesbian Past*, New York: New American Library, 1989, p. 235.

32 A partial version was reconstructed using fragments found in an archive in Ukraine. See https://silentfilm.org/different-from-the-others/ (accessed 16 March 2022).

33 https://en.wikipedia.org/wiki/Different_from_the_Others (accessed 4 September 2021).

34 Intertitles from *Anders als die Andern* (*Different from the Others*), https://vimeo.com/503754569; https://archive.org/details/youtube-oEMeNthlvRQ (accessed 4 September 2021).

35 In 1989 a pink marble triangle plaque remembering homosexual victims of the Nazi regime was put on the wall of the Nollendorfplatz Underground Station. This was the first such memorial in any German city. It reads: 'Totgeschlagen, Totgeschwiegen – den Homosexuellen Opfern des Nationalsozialismus'; 'Beaten to death, silenced to death – to the homosexual victims of Nazism.' The plaque beneath explains that from January 1933 the Nazis closed almost all the gay venues around Nollendorfplatz and compiled 'pink lists' of homosexuals, who were imprisoned and sent to concentration camps. See Thomas Beckmann: Totgeschlagen – Totgeschwiegen. 30 Jahre Rosa Winkel am Nollendorfplatz in Berlin. In: HuK-Info 206 (2019), S. 23.

36 Brandl-Beck, '"Berlin from Behind"', p. 93.

37 See Andreas Pretzel, *Vom Dorian Gray zum Eldorado: Historische Orte und schillernde Persönlichkeiten im Schöneberger Regenbogenkiez*, trans. Nickolas Woods, Berlin: MANEO, 2012, pp. 47–55. See also Norman Page, *Auden and Isherwood: The Berlin Years*, New York: St Martin's Press, 1998, Chapters 1, 2 and particularly p. 18 for descriptons of queer venues in Bülowstraße and other parts of Berlin.

38 Brandl-Beck, '"Berlin from Behind"', p. 232.

39 Pretzel, *Vom Dorian Gray zum Eldorado*, p. 63.

40 Brandl-Beck, '"Berlin from Behind"', p. 196.

41 Christopher Isherwood, *Goodbye to Berlin*, St Albans: Triad/Panther, pp. 129–30. The Alexander Casino in Isherwood's book is thought to be modelled on the Adonis-Diele, in Alte Jokobstraße in the east of Berlin. See Beachy, *Gay Berlin*, p. 205.

42 Gauleiter was a term, drawn from old German, for the administrator of one of the areas, or Gau, into which the Nazis planned to divide Germany. At this stage, before they had seized power, Gauleiter referred to their own party administration: Goebbels was in charge of Berlin.

43 'Germany of To-Day', *New Zealand Herald*, 11 May 1929, p. 8; 'Germany of To-Day', *Wanganui Herald*, 14 May 1929, p. 9; 'Quo Vadis — Young Germany?', *Dominion*, 20 May 1929. Articles also included in Countries – Germany – General – Annual Reports, R17709050, ANZ.

44 Colin Storer, *Britain and the Weimar Republic: The History of a Cultural Relationship*, London: I. B. Tauris, p. 179.

45 Actually Lord Burghley, William Cecil, Elizabeth I's chief adviser.

46 'Shot Journalist', *Evening Standard*, 4 May 1929, p. 11.

47 Statement from Ruth Hethke in police investigation file, 219/55, 60 verso and 61, GStA.

48 John Chancellor, *How to be Happy in Berlin*, London: Arrowsmith, 1929, p. 162.

10: BLUTMAI

1   Peter Leßmann-Faust, '"Blood May": The Case of Berlin 1929', in Richard Bessel and Clive Emsley (eds), *Patterns of Provocation: Police and Public Disorder*, New York; Oxford: Berghahn, 2000, p. 14; Léon Schirmann, *Blutmai Berlin 1929: Dichtungen und Wahrheit*, Berlin: Dietz Verlag, 1991, p. 44.

2   Eve Rosenhaft, *Beating the Fascists? The German Communists and Political Violence 1929–1933*, Cambridge: Cambridge University Press, 1983, p. 5.

3   May Day was made a public holiday, *Der Tag der Nationalen Arbeit*, by the Nazi Party in 1933.

4   There was no national police force in Germany in 1929. Each Lande (state) had its own police force. Policing in Berlin was the responsibility of the Prussian police, made up of different branches. These included the security police (Schutzpolizei, or Schupo for short), the criminal police (Kriminalpolizei, or Kripo), the administrative police (Verwaltungspolizei) and the Political Police (Abteilung I).

5   Schirmann, *Blutmai Berlin 1929*, p. 77.

6   Sefton Delmer, *Trail Sinister: An Autobiography*, London: Secker & Warburg, 1961, pp. 89, 90.

7   Ibid., pp. 77, 72, 75.

8   Statement from Ruth Hethke in police investigation file, 219/55, 60 verso and 61, GStA.

9   Statement from Barber and Elmur Thomas in police investigation file, 219/55, 58 and 59 verso, GStA.

10 Delmer, *Trail Sinister*, p. 88.

11 Of the dead, 32 were killed by police firearms and one was struck by a speeding police van.

12 Delmer, *Trail Sinister*, p. 88.

13 Autopsy report in police investigation file, 219/55, 4-6, GStA.

14 Memo in police investigation file, Ref: 219/55, 76, 78, 79, GStA.

15 'A "Sunday Express" Correspondent Shot Dead In Berlin During The Communist Rioting', *Sunday Express*, 5 May 1929, p. 1.

16 Delmer, *Trail Sinister*, p. 91.

17 FO file ref K5714/5714/218, p. 141, 6 May 1929, National Archives, Kew.

18 Ibid., p. 142, 4 May 1929.

19 Ibid., p. 143, 6 May 1929.

20 'Journalist in a "Death Trap"', *Sunday Express*, 5 May 1920, p. 1.

21 'Vormittags in Neukölln', *Berliner Tageblatt*, afternoon edition, 4 May 1929.

22 Schirmann, *Blutmai Berlin 1929*, pp. 211–15.

23 'Berlin Riot Victims,' *Morning Post*, 9 May 1929, p. 14.

24 Tom Sullivan (1869–1947) won the Professional Sculling Championship of England in 1893 and went on to become one of the best coaches of his generation. He coached the German coxed four who won gold at the Los Angeles Olympics in 1932. See Michael Grace, *The Dolly Varden Legacy — The History of the Wellington Rowing Club*, Wellington: Wellington Rowing Club, 2010, pp. 43–48.

25 'Tom Sullivan Still Going Strong in Berlin', *Press*, 7 May 1929, p. 4. A different version of the article was also published in Australia. See 'Mr Mackay's last article for Register News-Pictorial', *Register News-Pictorial,* 10 May 1929, p. 4. Someone from the British colony — possibly Sullivan — offered to pay for Mackay's funeral. He was presumably able to afford it, working for such a well-heeled club.

26 'Die Kommunistische Partei solidarisiert sich völlig mit denjenigen, die auf den Barrikaden gestanden haben', from https://www.blutmai.de (accessed 4 September 2021).

27 Although Isherwood had visited Berlin briefly while Mackay was alive, he did not move

there until after Bloody May. His 1935 novel, *Mr Norris Changes Trains*, based on his own experiences in the city, depicted the political violence that increased in prevalence and severity after the May fighting: 'Berlin was in a state of civil war. Hate exploded suddenly, without warning, out of nowhere; at street corners, in restaurants, cinemas, dance halls, swimming-baths; at midnight, after breakfast, in the middle of the afternoon . . . In the middle of a crowded street a young man would be attacked, stripped, thrashed and left bleeding on the pavement; in fifteen seconds it was all over and the assailants had disappeared.' Christopher Isherwood, *Mr Norris Changes Trains*, New York: New Directions, 2013, p. 91.

28 Schirmann, *Blutmai Berlin 1929* p. 323. [In the original German: Nach Meinung des Verfassers markiert aber der Blutmai eine Station in der Geschichte, und zwar den Beginn des sichtbaren Aufstiegs der NS-Bewegung.]

29 See commentary about this part of the poem by Michael Kilby: 'There are also references to the civil strife in Berlin that spring, so prevalent apparently that Auden grew bored by it all and acted perversely — "I was angry, said I was pleased" — when he was told about police brutality. However, in manuscript it appears that Auden intended to communicate a different reaction, one that he possibly misinterpreted when he came to revise the entire poem for publication. "I was carried away, said I was pleased" suggests that Auden was excited by his friend's rhetoric and became an advocate of the impending civil unrest.' 'Some Thoughts on "1929"', *Auden Society Newsletter*, 15 November 1996.

30 The will was not finalised until 1932; court staff had trouble locating Campbell at the London address Mackay had listed in the will.

31 Statement from Ruth Hethke in police investigation file.

32 Will held by Amtsgericht Schöneberg, Berlin, AG. Schbg. 64/29 VI. 1574/30 S, and 64/29 IV 1185/30 S.

33 Mackay's story about the visit was published in Australian newspapers after his death, highlighted as one of his final reports. 'Touring Germany: Berlin's Interest in Australia', *Sydney Morning Herald*, 15 June 1929, p. 11.

34 The entry in burial register reads:
Running number: 217
Details of person buried/name and profession: Makay [sic] Charles Pressevertreter
Age: 45
Date of funeral: 8.5.29
Main register number: 56
Remarks (*Bemerkungen*): N[or V?] VI. 20 (section, row, and plot number?)

35 Email to the author from Rod Mackay, 3 November 2010.

36 'Tragic Life of Charles Mackay', *Daily Guardian*, 8 May 1929, R77555, AA.

37 'Chequered Career Ended', *N.Z. Truth*, 9 May 1929, p. 1.

11: CRESSWELL

1 J. E. Weir (ed.), *James K. Baxter Complete Prose*, Vol. 4, Wellington: Victoria University Press, 2015, pp. 439–40, http://nzetc.victoria.ac.nz/tm/scholarly/tei-Bax4Pros-t1-body-d8. html#t1-body-d8-x48-pb1

2 Walter D'Arcy Cresswell, *Present Without Leave*, London: Cassell, 1939, pp. 67–68.

3 This and following quotes: interview with David and Ruth Cresswell, 25 June 2010. Helen Shaw's explanation: Freda, a nurse in a London hospital, had probably fallen in love with Cresswell. He was lonely, attractive and in some ways childlike and so in need of the care of other people. He married Freda because he had given her a child. The marriage, which was of short duration,

may have turned him against women in general. Helen Shaw essay in Frank Simon Hofmann, Research papers and correspondence, MS-Papers-88-252-1, Box 1, ATL.

4   Interview with David and Ruth Cresswell.

5   Charles Carrington, letter to Helen Shaw, 10 December 1965, MS-Papers-88-252-1, Box 1, folder 26, ATL.

6   William Broughton, 'Curnow's Anthologies and the Strange Case of Walter D'Arcy Cresswell', *Journal of New Zealand Literature*, No. 15, 1997, p. 37.

7   Denis Glover, 'D'Arcy Cresswell, by his friends', *Landfall*, Vol. 14, No. 4, December 1960, p. 346.

8   Walter D'Arcy Cresswell, *The Poet's Progress; with a Portrait by William Rothenstein*, London: Faber & Faber, 1930, p. 71.

9   Queer History: New Zealand Gay, Lesbian, Bisexual and Transgender New Zealand History: Charles Mackay and D'Arcy Cresswell, http://www.gaynz.net.nz/history/Mackay-cress.html (accessed 19 June 2021).

10   Maev Kennedy, 'The real Lady Chatterley: Society hostess loved and parodied by Bloomsbury Group', *Guardian*, 10 October 2006, https://www.theguardian.com/uk/2006/oct/10/books.booksnews (accessed 19 June 2021).

11   Arnold Bennett letter to D'Arcy Cresswell, 12 November 1929, cited in Helen Shaw essay, pp. xxxvi–vii, Box 1, MS-Papers-88-252-1, ATL.

12   John Newton, 'Poetry and Other Marvels: D'Arcy Cresswell on His Own Terms', *Journal of New Zealand Literature*, No. 21, 2003, pp. 14–31.

13   Cranleigh Barton Diary, 1925, v. 28 77-166-6/14. ATL, 77-166-6/14.

14   Helen Shaw essay, p. xxxix.

15   'Wellington Seems a Nest of Robbers', *The Sun*, 27 January 1932.

16   Cresswell to Edward Marsh; 21 February 1932. Helen Shaw (ed.), *The Letters of D'Arcy Cresswell*, Christchurch: University of Canterbury, 1971, p. 64.

17   To Maurice Baring, Barnswood; 28 October 1932. Helen Shaw (ed.), 'A Stranger Here: The Letters of D'Arcy Cresswell', unpublished manuscript, MS-Papers-7809-15, ATL.

18   Instalments appeared in the *Press* on 13 and 27 February, 12 and 26 March, and 9 April 1932.

19   'The Art Gallery', *Press*, 27 January 1932, p. 8.

20   'The Poet's Progress', *Press*, 13 February 1932, p. 13.

21   Wystan Curnow, 'D'Arcy Cresswell in Castor Bay', http://www.jackbooks.com/Wystan/castorBay/dArcy.htm (accessed 19 June 2021). Works published between 1932 and 1938, when Cresswell was in New Zealand: *Poems, 1924–1931*, London: John Lane, The Bodley Head, 1932; *Modern Poetry and the Ideal*, Auckland: Griffin Press, 1934; *Eena Deena Dynamo*, Christchurch: Caxton Press, 1936; *Lyttelton Harbour: A Poem*, Auckland: Unicorn Press, 1936.

22   Charles Brasch, 'Notes', *Landfall*, Vol. 14, No. 2, June 1960, p. 117.

23   D'Arcy Cresswell, 'Ursula Bethell: Some Personal Memories', *Landfall*, Vol. 2, No. 4, December 1948, p. 282.

24   Bethell's first published collection was *From a Garden in the Antipodes*, published in London in 1929 by Sidgwick & Jackson under the pen name Evelyn Hayes. Bethell was the third New Zealand woman poet to be published.

25   Sargeson remembered walking past the hotel one night and seeing Cresswell in bed with another man. This seems unlikely. Interview with Kevin Ireland, 20 May 2009.

26   Allen Curnow (ed.), *The Penguin Book of New Zealand Verse*, Harmondsworth, Middlesex: Penguin Books, 1960; John Newton, 'D'Arcy Cresswell, 1896–1960', *Kōtare 7*, No. 3. 2008, p. 134; John Newton, *Hard Frost: Structures of Feeling in New Zealand Literature 1908–1945*, Wellington: Victoria University Press, 2017, p. 154.

27 Cresswell to Ormond Wilson, 16 July [1939], MS-Papers-7809-16, ATL. Original letter at MS-Papers-0170-107.

28 Alison Laurie, 'Lady-Husbands and Kamp Ladies: Pre-1970 Lesbian Life in Aotearoa/New Zealand', PhD thesis, Victoria University of Wellington, 2003, pp. 218, 270.

29 Ursula Bethell to Charles Brasch, 27 July 1938, in Peter Whiteford (ed.), *Vibrant with Words: The Letters of Ursula Bethell*, Wellington: Victoria University Press, 2005. p. 162.

30 Anna Cahill, *Colours of a Life: The Life and Times of Douglas MacDiarmid*, Auckland: Mary Egan Publishing, 2018, pp. 104–05.

31 Geoffrey Potocki De Montalk, *Recollections of My Fellow Poets*, Auckland: Prometheus, 1983, p. 29. In 1938, during a London pub crawl, Cresswell suggested to the expat New Zealand writer James Courage, who was also homosexual, that the pair pick up a guardsman or sailor 'and spend the night in mutual fornication à trois' (James Courage diary, 2 December 1938). Courage demurred on this occasion, though he had many fleeting encounters and affairs with sailors during his years in London. Another writer, Count Geoffrey Potocki De Montalk, recalled a story he was told by the painter George Hann, when Hann and Cresswell visited the Fitzroy Tavern ('the place Where You Meet the Real Bohemians'): 'He [Hann] said that Cresswell was taking absolutely no notice of him, though they had gone there together. In the end, he simply had to explain himself. So he said: "George, do you see that sailor over there? Don't you think he is a beautiful young man?" He indicated a sailor in the uniform of His Majesty's Battle Fleet. Hann replied: "Yes, certainly he is a beautiful young fellow. But what on earth would you say to him?" (Meaning, that you could tell from afar off that he was unintelligent and uneducated.) Cresswell replied, with his best stagey cynical effrontery: "I'd say – HOW MUCH?"' Geoffrey Potocki De Montalk, *Recollections of My Fellow Poets*, Auckland: Prometheus, 1983, p. 29.

32 Hannah Cresswell died in 1945 and Walter Joseph Cresswell on 18 March 1950. Copy of Cresswell family tree held by Laughton Pattrick.

33 D'Arcy Cresswell letter to Ormond Wilson, 9 June 1959, MS-Papers-0170, ATL.

34 Charles Carrington, 'D'Arcy Cresswell, by his friends', pp. 343–44.

35 Ormond Wilson, 'D'Arcy Cresswell, by his friends', p. 361.

36 Ormond Wilson, *An Outsider Looks Back: Reflections on Experience*, Wellington: Port Nicholson Press, 1982, p. 38.

12: NEMESIS

1 Tim Shoebridge, 'Stories in Books and Stories of Life: Helen Shaw, New Zealand Writer, c. 1937–1985', MA thesis, Victoria University of Wellington, 2004, p. 102.

2 Helen Shaw to Jean and John Bertram, 12 July 1949, MS-Papers-93-103-16 (1949–1968), ATL.

3 Ormond Wilson to Helen Shaw, 17 October 1965, MS-Papers-88-252, Box 2, Folder 34, ATL.

4 John A. Lee to Helen Shaw, 26 July [1968], MS-Papers-88-252, Box 3, ATL.

5 Helen Shaw essay p. xxx, Frank Simon Hofmann, Research papers and correspondence, MS-Papers-88-252-1, Box 1, ATL.

6 Helen Shaw essay, p. xxxi.

7 Helen Shaw Journal, 14 March 1983, MSX-6517, ATL; Helen Shaw (ed.), *The Letters of D'Arcy Cresswell*, University of Canterbury Publications No. 14, Christchurch: University of Canterbury, 1971, p. 11.

8 D'Arcy Cresswell to Ottoline Morrell, Thursday 'End of August 1933', in Helen Shaw (ed.), *Dear Lady Ginger: An Exchange of Letters between Lady Ottoline Morrell and D'Arcy Cresswell: Together with Ottoline Morrell's Essay on Katherine Mansfield*, Auckland: Auckland University Press; Oxford: Oxford University Press; in association with Alexander Turnbull Library

Endowment Trust, 1983, pp. 68–73; p. 72, n. 70.

9   William Stevenson Broughton, 'W. D'Arcy Cresswell, A.R.D Fairburn, R.A.K. Mason: An Examination of Certain Aspects of their Lives and Works', PhD thesis, University of Auckland, 1966, p. 21.

10 Mackay was nominated by Derek Schulz from the Sarjeant staff in 1984; Cresswell was nominated by Canterbury historian Geoffrey Rice in 1992 (forms in *DNZB* files held by MCH).

11 W. S. Broughton, 'Mackay, Charles Ewing', *DNZB*, first published in 1996. Te Ara – the Encyclopedia of New Zealand, https://teara.govt.nz/en/biographies/3m14/mackay-charles-ewing (accessed 28 August 2021). The quote from Cresswell's court statement was added by *DNZB* staff (*DNZB* file held by MCH).

12 Letter, W. S. Broughton to Jamie Mackay, 8 November 1994 (*DNZB* file held by MCH).

13 Copy-editor's queries, 30 January 1996 (Cresswell *DNZB* file held by MCH).

14 W. S. Broughton, 'Cresswell, Walter D'Arcy', *DNZB*, first published in 1998. Te Ara – the Encyclopedia of New Zealand, https://teara.govt.nz/en/biographies/4c42/cresswell-walter-darcy (accessed 28 August 2021).

15 Copy-editor's queries, 30 January 1996.

16 Michael King, *Frank Sargeson: A Life*, Auckland: Viking, 1995, p. 161.

17 King, *Frank Sargeson*, p. 391.

18 Letter to M. King, 24-Sep-[90], Bill Mitchell papers, MS-Papers-8752-154, ATL. Oddly, very little from Sargeson seems to have come through in Mitchell's three drafts of 'Resign or Else', apart from a reference to Cresswell telling Sargeson about his 'dark secret'. Mitchell's inconsistent referencing in his drafts makes it hard to be sure who said what. He does refer to Sargeson being in ill health when he started to research the story: 'Frank and I were engrossed in this strange, unsolved "Wanganui Affair" but unfortunately he became too ill to care about anything – even justice'. Letter to Eric McCormick, [1982], MS-Papers-5292-044, ATL.

19 W. Mitchell letter to Eric McCormick, 29 December 1982, MS-Papers-5292-044, ATL.

20 Ibid.

21 Annotations on draft article by Phil Parkinson, MS-Papers-548, Lesbian and Gay Archives of New Zealand, ATL.

22 Phil Parkinson, 'The Wanganui Affair of 1920', *Pink Triangle*, Issue 56, November/December 1985, p. 11.

23 W. Mitchell letter to Michael King, 24-Sep-[90].

24 C. K. Stead, *Book Self: The Reader as Writer and the Writer as Critic*, Auckland: Auckland University Press, 2008. p. 26.

25 For example, Michael King, 'Sargeson, Frank', *DNZB*, first published in 1998. Te Ara – the Encyclopedia of New Zealand, https://teara.govt.nz/en/biographies/4s5/sargeson-frank (accessed 19 June 2021).

26 Steve Braunias, 'Revealed: The truth about Frank Sargeson's imprisoned lover', https://www.newsroom.co.nz/@readingroom/2019/08/07/743158/revealed-the-truth-about-frank-sargesons-imprisoned-lover# (accessed 7 July 2020). See also Greg Dixon, 'Love in a Cold Climate', *New Zealand Herald*, 2 July 2008, http://www.nzherald.co.nz/entertainment/news/article.cfm?c_id=1501119&objectid=10519365 (accessed 27 October 2013); and Chris Brickell, *Mates & Lovers: A History of Gay New Zealand*, Auckland: Godwit, 2008, pp. 118–21; Chris Brickell, 'Story: Gay Men's Lives', Te Ara — the Encyclopedia of New Zealand, http://www.teara.govt.nz/en/gay-mens-lives/page-1 (accessed 3 November 2013).

27 King, *Frank Sargeson*, 1995, p. 161.

28 Peter Simpson (ed.), *Charles.Brasch: Journals, 1945–1957*, Dunedin: Otago University Press, Hocken Collections, and Hocken Library, 2017, 25 May 1951, p. 332.

29 *Landfall*, Vol. 14, No. 4, December 1960, p. 351.

30 John Newton, 'D'Arcy Cresswell, 1896–1960', in *Kotare*, 7, 3, 2008, p. 132.

31 Frank Sargeson, *More than Enough: A Memoir*, Wellington: A. H. & A. W. Reed, 1975, pp. 91, 92. A. R. D. Fairburn (1904–1957) was a New Zealand poet.

32 Sargeson, *More than Enough*, p. 79.

33 March 1955 to July 1956. Frame also came across the story when she was living in Whanganui. Derek Schulz remembers her 'being rather bemused by Cresswell's "Hollywood" response to being shot'. (Email from Derek Schulz, 26 May 2009).

34 Interview with Kevin Ireland, 20 May 2009. See also Sargeson's letter to John Macalister (8 May 1980), responding to a request for information about the 1920 shooting. Sargeson's reply contained many factual errors, and noted, 'Well, alas I can't at present persuade myself to tell you anything more', suggesting that he was unwilling, or too unwell, to help. Sarah Shieff (ed.), *Letters of Frank Sargeson*, Auckland: Vintage, 2012, pp. 594–95. By the time Mitchell began researching the story, Sargeson was too unwell to help. Mitchell letter to M. King, 24-Sep-[90]. See also Mitchell letter to McCormick, [1982]. ATL. Ref: MS-papers-5292-044.

35 Michael King, *The Penguin History of New Zealand*, Auckland: Penguin, 2003, p. 376.

36 'Charles Mackay and Walter D'Arcy Cresswell met in Wanganui in 1920. The circumstances of their meeting have been the subject of considerable interest, and the moment (known as "the Wanganui Affair") is well publicised in New Zealand's history. Charles Mackay was the borough's mayor, but the local Returned Services Association turned against him when he refused to host a joint civic reception for the Prince of Wales. Mackay's enemies knew about his interest in other men, and they hatched a plot: they would pay D'Arcy Cresswell, a handsome young returned solider, to entrap the mayor. Once Mackay made a move, the soldier would blackmail him into resigning from office.' Brickell, *Mates & Lovers*, p. 115.

37 Introduction to final draft of 'Resign or Else: The "Wanganui Affair"', dated 12 December 1986, MS-Papers-2298-7, ATL; W. Mitchell letter to Michael King, 16-Nov-[90].

38 W. Mitchell letter to Josephine Duncan, 15-Mar-1984, Duncan Papers, 2008.60.296, Whanganui Regional Museum 2008.60.296.

39 Parkinson's *Pink Triangle* article was the main source.

40 W. Mitchell letter to Derek Round, 8 December 1987. Copy provided by Derek Round.

41 W. Mitchell letter to Josephine Duncan, 15 March 1984. Mitchell was writing about himself and Sargeson, who told him about the 'Wanganui Affair'.

42 Works inspired by or featuring the Whanganui incident include the following published texts: Phil Parkinson, 'The Wanganui Affair of 1920', *Pink Triangle*, 56, 1985, pp. 10–11; Michael King, *Frank Sargeson: A Life*, Auckland: Viking, 1995; W. S. Broughton, 'Mackay, Charles Ewing', from the *DNZB* (1996), and Te Ara – The Encyclopedia of New Zealand, updated 30-Oct-2012, http://www.TeAra.govt.nz/en/biographies/3m14/mackay-charles-ewing; Peter Wells and Rex Pilgrim (eds), *Best Mates: Gay Writing in Aotearoa New Zealand*, Auckland: Reed, 1997; Michael King, *The Penguin History of New Zealand*, Auckland: Penguin, 2003; Maurice Gee, *The Scornful Moon: A Moralist's Tale*, Auckland: Penguin, 2003; Chris Brickell, *Mates & Lovers: A History of Gay New Zealand*, Auckland: Godwit, 2008, pp. 118–21; Stephanie Johnson, *Swimmers' Rope*, Auckland: Vintage, 2008. The following are unpublished: William (Bill) Mitchell, 1982–1986, 'Resign or Else, the Wanganui Affair', MS-Papers-2298, ATL; Helen Shaw's papers relating to D'Arcy Cresswell, undated (c. 1965–1968), Frank Simon Hofmann, Research and correspondence, 88-252-1, ATL; Ronald Trifero Nelson, 2009 and 2011, *Mates and Lovers* (play based on *Mates & Lovers* by Chris Brickell, performed in two versions in 2009 and 2011); David Charteris, *One of Those* (play performed in 2002, 2003, 2008, 2020).

43 *Infiltrations II*, 13 June 2015–31 March 2016, ex WRM Exhibition Archive, https://www.

wrm.org.nz/exhibitions/item/44/archive/ (accessed 21 February 2016). An F4 Project for *Infiltration II* at the Whanganui Museum, https://f4thehouseguest.wordpress.com (accessed 19 June 2021).

44 W. Mitchell letter to M. King, 24 September [1990].

45 David Charteris, *One of Those*, unpublished manuscript (version presented to Whanganui District Library, 2008), pp. 3–4.

46 Pat Lawlor circularised about 15 local writers to come together to write a joint detective novel, 'Murder by Twelve', in 1936. By 1939 it had become 'Murder by Eleven'. The contributors included Eric Bradwell, James Wilson Hogg, O. N. Gillespie, C. Stuart Perry, Victor Lloyd, Alan Mulgan, Leo Fanning, C. A. L. Treadwell, Pat Lawlor, C. G. Stewart and Charles Allan Marris. See Chris Hilliard, *The Bookmen's Dominion: Cultural Life in New Zealand 1920–1950*, Auckland: Auckland University Press, 2006, pp. 37–44.

47 Gee, *The Scornful Moon*, p. 146.

48 Email from Maurice Gee, 26 January 2010.

13: ERASURE

1 Whanganui District Council, *Pukenamu Queen's Park: Reserve Management Plan 2018*, https://www.whanganui.govt.nz/files/assets/public/plans/pukenamu-management-plan-2018.pdf (accessed 16 March 2022).

2 Pers. comm. (anonymous), 9 January 2011.

3 Barbara Brookes, 'Shame and Its Histories in the Twentieth Century', *Journal of New Zealand Studies*, No. 9, October 2010, p. 37.

4 Ibid., p. 41.

5 *Rangitikei Advocate and Manawatu Argus*, 11 June 1920, p. 8.

6 The citation prepared by Isobel's lawyers, served on Mackay in prison on 23 June 1920, was dated 19 May 1920. Divorce file, AAOM; Accession: W3265; Item Ref: D1924/1920, ANZ.

7 Petition for Dissolution of Marriage and Verifying Affidavit (dated 17 June 1920), AAOM; Accession: W3265; Item Ref: D1924/1920, ANZ.

8 One possibility is that the reference to sodomy relates to the suggestions that Mackay was part of a group of men having sex with younger men, as mentioned by the Prisons Board in its report (see Chapter 5).

9 Letter from Mackay, 6 August 1920, C. Mackay Inmate file, J, Acc W2636, 1920/31121, ANZ.

10 From Stout Notebook 26, page 40, Friday 4 September 1920, AAOM W3842, Box 204, Book 26, ANZ.

11 Notified in *New Zealand Gazette*, 9 September 1920, p. 2640. Isobel and Charles's son Duncan Charles Mackay, who died in 1912, was mentioned in the divorce file. He is apparently buried, with two of his siblings, his mother and other family members, in the Heads Road Cemetery in Whanganui (row RS12, 71 feet from the centre path, burial date 29-6-1912), but there is no reference to him on the family headstones. Information posted by Elwyn Goldsbury in reply to a query from Jo Mackay, February 2004.

12 Josephine Duncan's headstone says she died on 6 August 2008 aged 94. However, if the birth date recorded in her passport and newspaper reports, 4 October 1913, is correct, she would have been 95.

13 Josephine Duncan, oral history interview with Michelle Horwood, 14 May 1993, WRM OHA/WSCP 46, Whanganui Regional Museum.

14 Ibid.

15 Isobel Duncan advertised Totarapuka for sale in October 1920 but did not sell it. She and her sister Elizabeth Young liquidated the Duncan properties in Christchurch, which may have avoided the need to sell Totarapuka.

16 *Daily Guardian*, 8 May 1929. Other stones no longer extant may have been altered, but at least two — a brass plate at the Virginia Lake Band Rotunda and a marble stone at the entrance to the Durie Hill Elevator (replaced with a replica) — continue to show Mackay's name.

17 Athol Kirk, *Streets of Wanganui*, 2nd edn, Whanganui: A. L. Kirk, 1989, p. 26.

18 'Naming of Streets', *Wanganui Herald*, 3 June 1920, p. 6.

19 'Change of Streets', *Wanganui Herald*, 5 June 1920, p. 2.

20 Minutes of Ordinary Meeting of the Council, 21 December 1920, p. 108. WDC 00063:0:17, WDC.

21 *Wanganui Chronicle*, 22 December 1920, p. 4. Confusingly, the *Wanganui Herald*, on 21 December, reported a different decision: to refer the recommendation back to the Works Committee for further consideration.

22 John Paisley Belcher and Cornelius Burnett, *Wanganui from 1856 to 1929*, Wanganui: Evans, Cobb & Sharpe, 1930, Preface.

23 L. J. B. Chapple and H. C. Veitch, *Wanganui*, Hawera: Wanganui Historical Committee, 1939.

24 Letter, Wanganui Town Clerk to Helen Shaw, 20 August 1965, Frank Simon Hofmann, Research papers and correspondence, MS-Papers-88-252-1, Box 1, ATL.

25 Conversation with Jim McLees, 18 December 2009.

26 The name is spelt Sheila [Duncan] on Births, Deaths and Marriages online (Registration Number 1917/16703); Sheillah [Duncan] on the Duncan family headstone at Heads Road Cemetery and on her death certificate (Registration Number 1972/25737); and Sheelah [Mackay] in Divorce File: AAOM, Accession: W3265, Item Ref: D1924/1920, ANZ.

27 Josephine Duncan, oral history interview.

28 Births, Deaths and Marriage register and newspaper reports of her birth both say 1913. The birthdate is shown as 4 October 1915 in Divorce File: AAOM, Accession: W3265, Item Ref: D1924/1920, ANZ.

29 Prue Langbein notes following phone conversation with Josephine Duncan, 11 May 2005.

30 Text from exhibition at Whanganui Regional Museum, 17 March 2019.

31 Interview with Colin Whitlock, 25 May 2009.

32 'R.S.A Wants Gays Banned', *Pink Triangle*, No. 7, January 1980. See also Brent Coutts, *Crossing the Lines: The Story of Three Homosexual New Zealand Soldiers in World War II*, Dunedin: Otago University Press, 2020, pp. 253–55.

33 'Council Called To Reinstate Mayor's Name', *OUT!*, August–September 1978, p. 39.

34 'Wreath Takes A Walk', *OUT!*, August–September 1978, p. 39.

35 Interviews with Bill Milbank, 17 June 2008 and 21 October 2017.

36 Ibid.

37 After its completion, the Sarjeant Gallery was regarded as a council department run by committee until 1940, when the Advisory Committee was abolished (the Sarjeant Estate was by then fully the property of the council). Honorary curators had power over gallery acquisitions and exhibitions until 1974, when the first professional director, Gordon H. Brown, was appointed. See Chris Cochran, *Heritage Assessment for the Wanganui District Council*, pp. 8–14, https://sarjeant.org.nz/wp-content/uploads/2016/08/Heritage_Assessment_FINAL.pdf (accessed 17 June 2021).

38 3 April 1985, Memorandum To: Gallery Director, Foundation Stone Inscription, Wanganui District Council Archives File Collection: AAF 74 : 6/10/1 [Excerpt]. File Reference – Agency: AAF, Series: 74, Item No: 6/10/1, Title: Sarjeant Gallery – General, Date Range: 1982–1985.

39 Janet Paul speech at Sarjeant Gallery 75th anniversary function, 3 September 1994, pp. 4–5,

Sarjeant Gallery files, Box 1, Folder 9, WDC.

40 'Wanganui rocked by scandal of the Mayor and the poet', *Wanganui Chronicle*, 20 August 1994. Josephine Duncan's papers at the Whanganui Museum include a copy of Parkinson's article, indicating she was aware of the research into her father's story. Deference to Duncan was probably one reason why nothing more about the story appeared in local papers for around a decade, except for articles about David Charteris's play, *One of Those*, performed in Whanganui in 2002, 2003, 2008 and 2020. After Duncan's death in 2008, newspaper stories appeared about the shooting (e.g. 'Scandalous Crime the Ruin of Mayor', *Wanganui Chronicle*, 14 January 2012), but no new information emerged.

41 'Reopening big success', *Wanganui Chronicle*, 3 November 2014, p. 5.

42 This was when 'punk anarchist' Neil Roberts killed himself when he attempted to blow up the centre with a homemade gelignite bomb, https://www.annshelton.com/works/the-city-of-gold-and-lead (accessed 5 September 2021).

43 Wanganui District Council Archives File Collection: AAF 71 :1497 [Excerpt]. File Reference – Agency: AAF – (Wanganui Borough / City Council), Series: 71 – (Town Clerks Yearly Numbered File Series), Item No: 1917 / 1497, Title: Tenders Foundation Stone for Sarjeant Art Gallery, Date Range: 1917.

44 'Is it Serendipity or Coincidence?', *Wanganui Chronicle*, 15 August 2018; 'Artist Starts Own Horse Race', *Wanganui Chronicle*, 26 July 2018.

45 'Is it Serendipity or Coincidence?'

46 https://www.airbnb.co.nz/rooms/10144813 (accessed 5 September 2021).

47 'Interesting Facts about Whanganui', *Celebrating Whanganui*, Autumn/Winter, 2017, Whanganui: Whanganui Chronicle/NZME, 2017, p. 32.

48 See editorial 'Time to complete Charles Mackay's redemption', *Wanganui Chronicle*, 5 May 2018. Mayor Hamish Douall was interested but suggested renaming another street (Wakefield Street) Mackay Street ('Bid to change name', *Whanganui Chronicle*, 5 August 2020, p. 1).

49 'Whanganui aims to be the gay-friendly capital of NZ', *Whanganui Chronicle*, 19 March 2019.

EPILOGUE

1 T.I.S. [B. E. Baughan and F. A de la Mare], *People in Prison*, Auckland: Unicorn Press, 1936, pp. 111–12.

2 Justin McNab, 'A Social Historical Overview: Male Homosexuality in New Zealand', M. Phil. thesis, Auckland University, 1993, p. 53.

3 'Ex-Mayor Mackay Struck Off the Solicitor's Roll', *N.Z. Truth*, 2 October 1920, p. 6.

4 Gregory Woods, 'From gay conspiracy to queer chic: The artists and writers who changed the world', *Guardian*, 8 April 2016, https://www.theguardian.com/books/2016/apr/08/gay-conspiracy-homosexual-culture-liberated-arts (accessed 7 June 2022).

5 'Mayor Mackay: Malefactor', *N.Z. Truth*, 5 June 1920, p. 5. Coverage of Mackay's case was different to reporting of the Wilde case. New Zealand reporting of the Wilde trials did not mention homosexuality or sodomy. See Chris Brickell, *Mates & Lovers: A History of Gay New Zealand*, Auckland: Godwit, 2008, pp. 72–75.

6 Matt Cook, *London and the Culture of Homosexuality, 1885–1914*, Cambridge, New York: Cambridge University Press, 2003, p. 119.

7 Oscar Wilde, letter to Home Secretary, 2 July 1896, in Oscar Wilde (introduction by Colm Tóibín), *De Profundis and Other Prison Writings*, London: Penguin, 2013, pp. 16–20.

8 Letter, Mackay to 'Sir Graeme' (Sir Graeme Duncan Power Sinclair-Lockhart), c. December 1920. Inmate file.

9   Oscar Wilde, letter to Home Secretary, 10 November 1896, in Wilde, *De Profundis*, pp. 28–29.

10 W. H. Pearson to John Newton, 16 April 2000. Reproduced with permission of Donald Stenhouse, Paul Millar and John Newton.

11 Paul Millar, 'No Fretful Sleeper', 2 July 2010, https://publicaddress.net/great-new-zealand-argument/no-fretful-sleeper/ (accessed 7 July 2020).

12 Paul Millar, *No Fretful Sleeper: A Life of Bill Pearson*, Auckland: Auckland University Press, 2010, pp. 209–11.

13 Jeffrey Paparoa Holman, interview with Bill Pearson, 23 April 2001. Reproduced with permission of Donald Stenhouse, Paul Millar and Jeffrey Paparoa Holman.

14 Paul Millar, interview with Bill Pearson, 6 December 2001. Reproduced with permission of Donald Stenhouse and Paul Millar.

15 'Mayor Mackay: Malefactor', *N.Z. Truth*, 5 June 1920, p. 5.

16 John Newton, *Hard Frost: Structures of Feeling in New Zealand Literature 1908–1945*, Wellington: Victoria University Press, 2017, p. 266.

17 Pers. comm., Chris Brickell, 3 March 2021.

18 Eteocles — the name Baughan used for Mackay — was a son of Oedipus, the King of Thebes, who killed his father and unknowingly married his mother. After being insulted and neglected by Eteocles and his brother Polyneices, Oedipus cursed his sons, predicting they would argue over their inheritance and die at each other's hands. To escape the curse, his kingdom was meant to be shared by the two sons, who agreed to rule in alternate years. When Eteocles refused to stand aside, the brothers fought and killed each other.

19 'Late C. E. Mackay', *Wanganui Chronicle*, 11 May 1929, p. 8.

20 '"Go Slow" in Borough Matters', *Wanganui Herald*, 11 March 1920, p. 6.

21 'Late C.E. Mackay'.

22 Hector Bolitho and Wanganui Borough Council, *Wanganui: The River Town of New Zealand*, Wanganui: Wanganui Borough Council, 1920, p. 7.

23 'Reds Renew Riots In Berlin Streets', *New York Times*, 5 May 1929, p. 6.

24 Email from Ellen Jordan, 12 June 2020.

25 Chris Cochran, *Heritage Assessment for the Wanganui District Council*, pp. 39–40, https://sarjeant.org.nz/wp-content/uploads/2016/08/Heritage_Assessment_FINAL.pdf (accessed 17 June 2021).

26 Peter Ireland, *Frank Denton: Photographer in Time of Transition*, catalogue for Sarjeant Gallery exhibition, 8 February–27 April 2003.

27 'Mr C. E. Mackay's Fate', *Wanganui Chronicle*, 25 June 1929, p. 8.

28 'Rhinelanders' Ball', *Manawatu Standard*, 18 April 1929, p. 2.

29 'A "Sunday Express" Correspondent Shot Dead in Berlin During the Communist Rioting', *Sunday Express*, 5 May 1929, p. 1.

30 Sefton Delmer, *Trail Sinister: An Autobiography*, London: Secker & Warburg, 1961, pp. 87–88.

31 'Shot Journalist', *Evening Standard*, 4 May 1929, p. 11.

ACKNOWLEDGEMENTS

Peter Wells' essay, in *Best Mates*, the 1997 anthology of gay writing he edited with Rex Pilgrim, was the first place I read about the 'Whanganui Affair'. The path to this book about the affair has been a long one, starting in 2004. That year Prue Langbein, my colleague in the features department at Radio New Zealand, mentioned she had come across the story in Michael King's *Penguin History of New Zealand*. Prue suggested we write a radio feature proposal, which was approved, and we began researching. My first research trip to Whanganui was with Prue, who also spoke twice with Josephine Duncan, Charles Mackay's surviving daughter. We did not finish the feature before I left RNZ, but I will always be grateful to Prue for initiating the project which became this book, and for her ongoing support.

When I went to work at the Ministry for Culture and Heritage as an oral historian, the Chief Historian was Bronwyn Dalley, who was originally from Whanganui and had an interest in the history of crime and sexuality. Bronwyn encouraged me to keep working on the story to see where it led. Thank you, Bronwyn, for your encouragement, advice, for reading my drafts, and for being a referee for the Berlin Residency.

I am grateful for financial support which enabled me to complete this book. In 2011 I was the recipient of a New Zealand History Research Trust Fund Award from the Ministry for Culture and Heritage. I also received the Creative New Zealand Berlin Writer's Residency in 2017 and took this up in 2019-20. Thank you, Malcolm Burgess, for your support, especially when the Covid-19 pandemic meant I had to return from Berlin six months early. I was able to continue the residency in Wellington, thanks to Julie Williamson, David Strauss, and Gary Williamson-Strauss, who converted their spare room into a writer's studio.

I was also fortunate to receive two language scholarship from the Goethe Institut in Wellington. These enabled me to study German in Göttingen and Berlin, making it easier to research in Berlin. Thank you to institute staff, past and present, including Bettina Senff, Christian Kahnt, Anna Kalbhenn, Judith Geare, and Ulrike Rosenfeld. Thanks to Richard Hill and Lydia Wevers in 2011 I had a six-month residency at the Stout Research Centre, which gave me a place to write and connections with a supportive community of researchers, including Barbara Einhorn, who helped me with German language sources. In 2010 I was awarded a New Zealand Society of Authors mentorship and worked with Stephen Stratford, who helped me with a *Dominion Post* feature about my research.

For much of the time I have worked on this book my day job has been Curator, Māori at the Alexander Turnbull Library. I am hugely grateful to the Chief Librarian, Chris Szekely, for his constant support and allowing time away from the library to write and research.

I also owe a huge debt to the queer history nurturer and mentor Chris Brickell, who was an early supporter of my research. As well as being a great sounding board, Chris provided invaluable feedback on my drafts and generously shared his own research material. And he wrote the foreword to this book.

When Prue Langbein and I made our first research trip to Whanganui, we discovered Whanganui's good fortune to have many cultural institutions with wonderful collections and staff. These include the Whanganui District Council Archives, where I received help from Simon Bloor and his predecessors Penny Allen and Gerry O'Mahony. Other council staff and representatives who have helped me include James Barron, Helen Craig, Alice Fennessy, Scott Flutey, Pete Gray, Hamish McDouall, Annette Main and Colin Whitlock.

At the Whanganui Regional Museum, C. Wallis Barnicoat, Margie Beautrais, Sandi Black, Michelle Horwood, Bronwyn Labrum and Libby Sharpe are among the staff who helped me access collections and answer queries.

On my first visit to the Alexander Library, I met the late Wendy Pettigrew, who volunteered at the library to help with genealogical research. I discovered that Wendy was a heritage powerhouse, writing and researching reports on buildings and helping run a heritage festival at which I was honoured to speak. Wendy told me about her grandfather, Allan Robinson, one of the few borough councillors to speak out against Mackay. I am also grateful for help from library staff including Lynley Fowler, Jill Kosmala, Jasmin Ratana and Gillian Tasker.

Getting to know the staff and collections of the Sarjeant Gallery has been a highlight of writing this book. Thank you to the staff and governors, past and present, who continue the legacy of Henry Sarjeant, Ellen Neame and Charles Mackay: Greg Anderson, Jaki Arthur, Gordon H. Brown, Greg Donson, Raewyne Johnson, Sarah McClintock, Bill Milbank, Denis Rainforth, Paul Rayner, Jennifer Taylor-Moore, Celia Thompson and Sian Van Dyk.

Thanks to former Sarjeant Gallery staffers, Derek Schulz and Jill Studd, I got in touch with Des Bovey, who was in the process of moving back to Whanganui from France. I wanted to contact Des because he was part of the group which put a pink triangle wreath on the Sarjeant Gallery in the 1970s to draw attention to the removal of Mackay's name. Des became a great friend and supporter of my project. I am also grateful to Des and his partner Edvaldo Santos Santana for hosting me on many visits to Whanganui. Thanks also to Vivien

Lindsay, for your friendship and hospitality, including the chance to stay in a house in the street formerly known as Mackay Street. Thank you, Rosemary Norman, for your hospitality, Whanganui intel and company visiting soldiers' graves and other sites.

In Whanganui, the site of the shooting in 1920 still exists, remarkably intact, and I am very grateful to the owner Warren Ruscoe and his staff at Meteor Print for allowing me to visit and photograph the former office. Peter Johnston generously shared references to Mackay in his Great War database drawn from Whanganui newspapers. Kelvin Adam, Hinemoa Boyd-Ransom and Ed Boyd from H&A Print provided me with copies of images from their collection.

When I spoke about my research at the Meteor Print building, I met Alison Morrison, daughter of Bill Mitchell, whose research has been so important to the emergence of the story of the Whanganui Affair. Thank you, Alison, Bob and Fiona Murray for your support and help.

Others in or connected with Whanganui who helped me include Richard Austin, Diana Beaglehole, Felicity Campbell, David Charteris, Evelyn Cummins, J. Barry Ferguson, Mike Hartfield, Ian Hay-Campbell, Mary Laurenson, Alasdair McBeth, Paul McNamara, Gail Orgias, Peter Owens, Hugh Rennie, Derek Round, Lizzy Sommer, Mary Stevenson, Delphine Turney, and Marcus Williams.

My first research trip to Berlin was in 2007, with my then partner Bob Williams, who has been a constant supporter of this project. We stayed with Petra Hörig — the first person I met in Berlin — who has remained a friend. In Berlin, Hartmut Henicke and his daughter Kathleen Henicke spoke to me about the Blutmai exhibition that Hartmut curated. Film historian Anna Bohn spoke to me about the Blutmai film footage from 1929. I am also grateful for the help of historians who have written about Blutmai, including Conan Fischer and Eve Rosenhaft, who generously answered my queries. Prue Langbein's daughter, Sarah Silver, found Mackay's death certificate.

Andreas Kopfnagel, the manager of the cemetery where Mackay was buried (Ld. Friedhof Schöneberg IV [Priesterweg 17]) found the register containing the entry for Mackay's burial.

In July 2016, I met Matthias Brunner, who brought the city alive for me and taught me about German art and culture. Later that year he travelled across the world to visit this country and the Whanganui sites of significance. Thank you, Ma, for your great company, help and friendship.

Thank you to the staff who helped me at the archives and libraries I visited on my Berlin visits: Archiv zur Geschichte von Tempelhof und Schöneberg; Auswärtiges Amt; Bundesarchiv; Bundesarchiv-Filmarchiv; Deutsche Kinemathek — Museum für Film und Fernsehen (Ricardo Brunn, Anke Hahn, Diana Kluge); Deutsches Historisches Museum (Ariane Oppitz, Johannes Zechner); Geheimes Staatsarchiv Preussischer Kulturbesitz (Julian Schulenburg); Landesarchiv Berlin; Museum Neukölln; Schwules Museum (Jens Dobler, Karl-Heinz Steinle); Staatsbibliothek zu Berlin — Zeitungssammlung; Verein der Ausländischen Presse/VAP; and Zentral- und Landesbibliothek Berlin.

Many thanks to Peter Russell, who translated the German language newspapers and archival material I found in Berlin and read Léon Schirmann's book about the Blutmai riots to help me identify what was relevant for my project. Sascha Nolden and Margarete Ritzkowsky transcribed material in Sütterlinschrift, and Sascha translated documents from the file containing Mackay's will.

When Mackay died there was no New Zealand embassy in Berlin but, luckily for me, there is one now. I am grateful to staff, past and present, for their help, including James Andersen, Lisa Futschek, Rupert Holborow, Cornelia Löser and Alexandra Smithyman.

Others in Berlin and elsewhere in Germany for whose help I'm grateful include Hinemoana Baker, Catherine Gay, Arne Krasting, Loubna Messaoudi, Matthias Seidenstücker, Klaus Stanjek, Markus Stein, Boris von Brauchitsch and Tania Wehrs.

Through Jo Mackay (the granddaughter of Mackay's brother Philip and family genealogist), I met Alison Lafon, a Mackay relation and genealogist who was based in France. Alison came to London in 2010 and we researched together, finding the Foreign Office file about Mackay's death at the National Archives and newspaper coverage in the British Library.

Despite having amassed a lot of information about Mackay's death, I could not find his will, which had been made in London before he moved to Berlin. Knowing that I was going to study German in Göttingen, my friend Tanja Schubert-McArthur introduced me to Rolf and Gaby Husmann, her friends from that town, during their visit to New Zealand. In Germany, Rolf and Gaby suggested I try to find the will in the court in the Berlin district where Mackay died, the Amtsgericht Schöneberg. They also introduced me to their Berlin friend Barbara Kiefenheim, who lived in Neukölln, close to where Mackay was killed. Barbara told me about the 'Spurensuche' word which begins this book and helped me contact the court. We found out that the will was indeed at the court, but that I would need permission to see it. Rod Mackay, grandson of Mackay's brother Frank, wrote a letter of support so I could see the file containing the will. Matthias Brunner asked his friend Gumbert Salonek to help, and we finally saw the will at the court's Lichterfelde building on a snowy day in January 2017.

Mackay's will was the key to finding out more about what he did in London — where he spent a year and a half, compared with the six to seven months he was in Berlin. The will had an address, which was the key to finding out that Mackay was working in advertising and living in Bloomsbury, thanks to Ralph Sanderson, a family history expert from the National Library of Australia in Canberra. Bob Williams located the file for Mackay's company.

When Bronwyn Dalley encouraged me to follow this story, she advised not to try to solve it, but rather think about the effect it had on other homosexual men. This proved to be wise advice, particularly regarding Mackay's friend Hector Bolitho, who left New Zealand because of the shooting. The thinly disguised account of Mackay in Bolitho's book *Older People* was an important source, revealing more than I initially realised. Thank you to Joyce Fairgray, who shared her research for her book about Bolitho. Joyce also put me in touch with Michael Thornton, who knew Bolitho and who wrote his entry in the Oxford Dictionary of Biography. My Turnbull library colleague Anthony Tedeschi helped me access Bolitho's papers at the Dunedin Library. Anne McKinnon and Deb Jowitt put me in touch with their mother, who knew Bolitho.

Cranleigh Barton was another homosexual New Zealander who knew Mackay and Cresswell. I knew this because Philip Rainer and Gerry Barton got in touch to share their research about Barton, whose diaries give glimpses of both men featured in this book.

Thank you to Paul Millar, who gave me access to the research on Bill Pearson, which Bill's partner Donald Stenhouse and Jeffrey Paparoa Holman allowed me to reproduce.

I am indebted to members of the Cresswell, Duncan and Mackay families. Ian Cresswell got in touch and offered to help me. He shared his memories of his Uncle D'Arcy and introduced me to D'Arcy Cresswell's son, David Cresswell, who I met with his wife Ruth at their home in Eastbourne in 2010. Other Cresswell family members who have helped include Heather Burney, Brent Cresswell, John Cresswell, Keith Marshall Cresswell and Laughton Pattrick. I could not figure out much about D'Arcy Cresswell's relations in Whanganui until LAGANZ supporter John Webster sent me a copy of the scrapbook kept by D'Arcy Cresswell's aunt Eleanor. This was the key to finding out about this part of the family, who had moved away from Whanganui. I am grateful for help from Margaret Vennell and Colin Wright from the Duncan family. Thank you also to the family of Albert Mackay: Barbara Drinkall and James Moulder.

As my book started to take shape, I approached four readers, who read my drafts and gave invaluable feedback. Thank you to Lynn Jenner, Des Bovey, Bronwyn Dalley, and Ross Webb. Through Chris Brickell, I met Daniel Brandl-Beck, whose thesis about gay travellers to Weimar Berlin was a key resource. Daniel agreed to read drafts of my Berlin chapter and provided helpful feedback. Thank you also to members of my history-writing group who read several draft chapters: Ross Calman, Peter Clayworth, Elizabeth Cox, Mark Derby, Basil Keane, Emma Jean Kelly, Ewan Morris, Jock Philips, Ben Schrader, Tim Shoebridge, Jane Tolerton and Ross Webb.

My Library colleague Fiona Oliver provided valuable editing feedback when I was putting together my application for the Berlin Residency. In 2009 I wrote about Mackay for the CREW257 creative non-fiction course at the Institute of Modern Letters at Victoria University. Thanks to my fellow students and examiners Jane Westaway and Harry Ricketts. Thank you Harry for also being a referee for the Berlin Residency.

Having accumulated so much information, it was a challenge to shape this into a narrative. I want to acknowledge Rachel Scott and Sue Wootton from Otago University Press, and readers Chris Brickell and Redmer Yska for their feedback about my drafts. This led me to editor Anna Rogers, whose structural edit was a breakthrough, revealing Mackay's story and allowing his character to emerge. Thank you, Anna, for your deep read of my manuscript and pointing out aspects I had missed. Anna's edit was picked up by Nicola Legat from Massey University Press, a long-time supporter of this project. It has been a privilege for this book to have had the care and attention from Nicola and the team at Massey, including managing editor Anna Bowbyes and editorial assistant Anna Jackson-Scott. Thank you also to Megan van Staden for your stunning design, Gavin Hurley and Melanie Roger for the beautiful cover artwork, Susan Brookes for the index, and proofreader Gillian Tewsley.

I am indebted to libraries, museums and other organisations in places other than Whanganui and Berlin, and am grateful for help from my colleagues at the Alexander Turnbull Library; Heidi Kuglin, Donal Raethel and colleagues at Archives New Zealand; Keith Giles and Iain Sharp at Auckland Libraries Heritage Collections; Katherine Pawley at Auckland University Special Collections; Madison Pine at Auckland Museum; Bibliothèque nationale de France; Bob Baty, Jon Cumming, Paul Miller, Roger Mita, Charlie Post, Rebecca Reedy, Guy Reynolds from Corrections NZ; Tom Riley and his colleagues at the Hocken Collections; Linda Evans, Gavin Hamilton, Will Hansen, Kevin Haunui, Donal Raethal, Roger Smith and Roger Swanson, at the Lesbian and Gay Archives of New Zealand; Jeff Palmer from the McMillan Brown Library; Neill Atkinson, Imelda Bargas, Emma Dewson, Jamie Mackay, Ian McGibbon, Gavin McLean, Gareth Phipps and Nancy Swarbrick at the Ministry for Culture and Heritage; Dr John Crawshaw from the Ministry of Health; Munich Film Museum; Helen Pannett from the Nelson Provincial Museum; Richard Foster from NYPL Research Services at the New York Public Library; Matthew Buck, Carolyn Carr, Peter Connor, John Crawford from the New Zealand Defence Force; Ian Bradshaw and Sophie Giddens from New Zealand Police; Kerryn Pollock, Blyss Wagstaff and Marina Welch from Pouhere Taonga Heritage New Zealand; Jonet Moore from Stratford Library; Victoria Boyack from Te Papa; Ron Lambert from Pukeariki; Graeme Austin, Hayley Brown, Dianne Bardsley, Nigel Isaacs, John Macalister, Elisabeth McDonald, Geoff McLay, Sydney Shep, Robin Skinner, Marco Sonzogni, Margaret Sutherland, Tracey Thomas and Pamela Wood at Victoria University of Wellington; Stephanie Kane, Paddianne Neely and Mike Pallin at the Wellington College Archives; Richard Bourne at Whanganui Collegiate School Museum.

I have been lucky to have collaborated with three photographers, who documented sites associated with this story, in Berlin and New Zealand. Conor Clarke took photos of where the Blutmai fighting happened in Berlin. Leigh Mitchell-Anyon took photos in Whanganui. I met Ann Shelton during her residency at the Sarjeant Gallery, when the Whanganui Affair became part of her body of work, *city of gold and lead*. I wrote an essay for the book accompanying the exhibition. In 2013 Leigh, Ann and I travelled to New Plymouth to visit the prison, which had just closed. I am very grateful to all three photographers for allowing their work to be included in this book.

Others who provided assistance include Richard Arnold, Neil Bartlett, John Bean, Peter Boston, Barbara Brookes, William Broughton, Anna Cahill, Christine Cole-Catley, Kit Cuttle, Caroline Daley, Sharon Dell, Robert Dessaix, Harry Edgington, James Gardiner, Stevan Eldred-Grigg, Maurice Gee, Perrine Gilkison, Michael Grace, Jolisa Gracewood, Ariane Grimm, Jeremy Hansen, Lister Harrison, Emma Hart, Stephen Hofmann, Roger Horrocks, Megan Hutching, Kevin Ireland, Lloyd Jones, Ellen Jordan, Jane Kominik, Graeme Lay, Melanie Lovell-Smith, Norman Luck, Malcolm McKinnon, Anne Matheson, Geoff Mew, Noel Murphy, Phil Parkinson, Antony Paltridge, Bryan Patchett, Michael Pringle, Bruce Ralston, David Reeves, Mike Reid, Helen Reilly, Donald Riezebos, Sir Bruce Robertson, Juliet Rogers, Sarah Shieff, Tony Silke, Sally-Ann Spencer, C.K. Stead, Heather Toebes, Anne-Marie Wallace, Peter Wells, Caren Wilton, Diane Woods, Robert Young and Ben Zwartz.

Considerable time and effort was expended in tracing copyright holders, and I would like to offer my sincere apologies for any omissions.

Finally, huge thanks to my family and friends, in particular my partner, Richard King, for your support, encouragement and tolerance for my research and writing.

INDEX

S

Y

Z

MASSEY
UNIVERSITY
PRESS

First published in 2022 by Massey University Press
Private Bag 102904, North Shore Mail Centre
Auckland 0745, New Zealand
www.masseypress.ac.nz

Design by Megan van Staden
Jacket illustration: *Charles*, by Gavin Hurley,
courtesy of the artist and Melanie Roger
Gallery, photographed by Samuel Hartnett
Front cover: Cartographic Collection, Alexander
Turnbull Library, MapColl 832.4199gmbd 1922 29393
Back cover: Pharus

A catalogue record for this book is available
from the National Library of New Zealand

Printed and bound in China by Everbest Investment Ltd

ISBN: 978-1-99-101618-8
eISBN: 978-1-99-101620-1

The assistance of Creative New Zealand is
gratefully acknowledged by the publisher

creative nz
ARTS COUNCIL OF NEW ZEALAND TOI AOTEAROA